The Haitian Revolution in the Literary Imagination

NEW WORLD STUDIES

J. Michael Dash, *Editor*

Frank Moya Pons and
Sandra Pouchet Paquet,
Associate Editors

The Haitian Revolution in the Literary Imagination

Radical Horizons, Conservative Constraints

Philip Kaisary

University of Virginia Press
Charlottesville and London

mL the modern language initiative

THIS BOOK IS MADE POSSIBLE BY A COLLABORATIVE GRANT FROM THE ANDREW W. MELLON FOUNDATION.

University of Virginia Press

Printed in the United States of America on acid-free paper
First published 2014

9 8 7 6 5 4 3 2 1

Library of Congress Cataloging-in-Publication Data

Kaisary, Philip, 1978–
The Haitian revolution in the literary imagination : radical horizons, conservative constraints / Philip Kaisary.
pages cm — (New World studies)
Includes bibliographical references and index.
ISBN 978-0-8139-3546-1 (cloth : alk. paper)
ISBN 978-0-8139-3547-8 (pbk. : alk. paper)
ISBN 978-0-8139-3548-5 (e-book)
1. Caribbean literature—20th century—History and criticism. 2. Haiti—History—Revolution, 1791–1804—Influence. 3. Haiti—History—Revoution, 1791–1804—Literature and the revolution. 4. Haiti—In literature. 5. Literature and history. I. Title.
PN849.C3K35 2014
809'.933587294—dc23

2013023508

To Tara, Georgia, and Oscar

Contents

Illustrations

Acknowledgments

THE IDEAS BEHIND *The Haitian Revolution in the Literary Imagination* began to take shape while I was studying for an M.A. and then a Ph.D at the Universities of Sussex and Warwick, respectively. At Warwick, it was my privilege to enjoy the supervision of Benita Parry. I could not have wished for a more inspiring or committed mentor, and my life continues to be deeply enriched by her friendship, affection, and wisdom. At Sussex, I was fortunate enough to be taught by Marcus Wood. Marcus has also selflessly given time, energy, and inspiration to this project; his friendship and his deep understanding of slavery and its inheritance have had a profound influence on me and are, I hope, to some degree reflected in this manuscript.

The translating of mere ideas into a book was undertaken from 2010 to 2013, while I was a trainee solicitor at Darbys LLP (2010–12) and then teaching and researching at Warwick University School of Law (2012–). Again, I am especially grateful to Benita Parry, whose attentive readings of countless drafts of chapters during this period were invaluable in helping me to refine the book's ideas and arguments. The longstanding support and critique of Charles Forsdick and Neil Lazarus also helped me to strengthen the ideas I put forward in this book. Pablo Mukherjee provided comradely support and encouragement, helping me to shape my beliefs about life and work along the way. David Alderson offered encouragement, friendship, and advice that were vital to this project. Michael Largey generously provided me with an audio recording of the opera *Troubled Island*, and read and commented on chapter 2. Conversations and correspondence exchanged with Kimathi Donkor influenced my thought and writing in chapter 4. Nick Lawrence and Rashmi Varma offered encouragement and invaluable advice at various stages. Prithi Kanakamedala and Krista Kauffmann sustained me with humor and friendship from afar. And Jonathan Holyoak, Phil Marshall, and Charles de Segundo helped me to keep on at it.

At the University of Virginia Press, I thank J. Michael Dash and Cathie Brettschneider in particular. Cathie has been a knowledgeable, enthusiastic, and efficient collaborator from the outset and kept faith in this project through the long process of revisions. In addition, Ellen Satrom provided essential editorial support, and Raennah Mitchell always kept me in the loop. The staff of the Press have been a genuine pleasure to work with, and their hard work has improved this manuscript. I also thank the two anonymous readers whose incisive reports on earlier versions of this manuscript made important and illuminating suggestions which I have done my best to take on board. I also wish to thank Tim Roberts and Susan Murray at the Modern Language Initiative for their hard work.

Without the tireless assistance of the librarians and staff of the University Library, Warwick; the Bodleian Library, Oxford; and the British Library, London, this book could never have been researched and written. In addition, the staff at the Amistad Research Center, New Orleans; the National Portrait Gallery, London; the Châteaux de Malmaison, Rueil-Malmaison; the Châteaux de Versailles; the Louvre Museum; and the Berlin-Brandenburg Foundation were all helpful and efficient in responding to my requests for reproductions of artworks in their holdings. However, in particular, I must thank Christopher Harter, Director of Library and Reference Services at the Amistad Research Center, for his assistance and for making the Jacob Lawrence *Toussaint L'Ouverture* serigraphs available to me when I visited. I must also thank Maureen Bourne, Warwick University's Visual Resources Curator, for producing splendid reproductions of all the commemorative postage stamps featured in this book.

At Warwick, my new colleagues, without exception, have been nothing but supportive and encouraging. However, Paul Raffield and Andrew Williams both deserve special mention, as do Alan Norrie, Rebecca Probert, and Illan rua Wall, who have all offered valuable advice and support in the latter stages of this project. I thank Alexander Ffye and Andrea Selleri for their meticulous proofreading. The administrative help of Rosemary le Breton Bagley, Hannah Chappell, Emily West, and Jenny Wilson smoothed my encounters with scanners, photocopiers, and couriers.

I benefitted from excellent feedback at seminars and workshops too numerous to list. An earlier version of chapter 1 appeared in *Law and*

Humanities 6, no. 2 (Winter 2012): 197–216; I am grateful to the editors at Hart Publishing for granting me permission to reproduce that material here.

Finally, I am struck by the impossibility of finding the words with which to express my thanks for my family. My debt to them far exceeds anything that can be expressed in a formal acknowledgment. To my parents, Amir and Karen, for their love, friendship, and unshakeable faith in me, I will forever be deeply grateful. My brother, Peter, has long sustained me with his good humor, friendship, and love. And to Tara, I owe years of love, kindness, and friendship. This one is for you, and for our children, Georgia and Oscar.

The Haitian Revolution in the Literary Imagination

Introduction

> The plunge into the chasm of the past is the condition and the source of freedom.
>
> —Frantz Fanon, Address to the First Congress of Negro Writers and Artists (Paris, 1956)

The declaration of Haitian independence by Jean-Jacques Dessalines on January 1, 1804, was the culminating moment of the Haitian Revolution that had erupted some twelve years earlier in the French colony of Saint Domingue. The story of the birth of the world's first independent black republic has long held an iconic fascination for a diverse array of writers, artists, and intellectuals. The Haitian revolutionary war of independence overthrew slavery, white supremacy, and colonialism. As an entirely novel historical event that was, however, universal in its political aspirations and ideological implications, it was variously represented as a slave rebellion, an anticolonial war, and an atrocity, immediately spawning a remarkable series of culture wars. Initially it had shocked the Western world and its rising consumer culture, reshaped the debates about slavery, accelerated the abolitionist movement, precipitated rebellions in neighboring slaveholding territories, and intensified both repression and antislavery sentiment on both sides of the Atlantic. The Haitian Revolution must thus be accounted for as a world-historical event of paramount significance that galvanized people of African descent throughout the Americas and across the Atlantic world as no other event has done before or since. All these historical facts are reflected in the extraordinary and voluminous cultural archive the revolution generated.

This study is primarily concerned with the stories that have been told about the Haitian Revolution from the 1930s onward. It is my contention that these reveal the development of a radical restoration of Haitian history in the works of Aimé Césaire, C. L. R. James, Langston Hughes, René Depestre, Jacob Lawrence, and Kimathi Donkor. For these writers and artists, the recuperation and representation of the events of 1791–1804 offered the opportunity to articulate a narrative of emancipation in which black agency and universal intent were central. This corpus of radical works form a contrast with conservative retrievals undertaken by Edouard Glissant, Alejo Carpentier, Derek Walcott, and Madison Smartt Bell; these works, by way of comparison, convey visions of obscurity, tragic circularity, senseless violence, and history as eroticized fantasmics. Central to my endeavor, therefore, is the consideration of how certain aesthetic modes of recuperating the Haitian Revolution have enabled or hindered particular political visions. Dividing these texts along a single axis of distinction, the radical and the conservative, my object has been to draw out the *situation* and *ideological thrust* of each of the works considered.

A structural and thematic distinction of radical and conservative recuperations thus provides a framework in which to pose nuanced questions of forms and aesethetics, their political implications, and the politics of their metaphorics in the context of works representing or invoking the Haitian Revolution. Addressing the corpus of primary texts and artworks within this theoretical framework also enables certain commonalities and discrepancies to be discerned. For example, it will be seen that C. L. R. James's *Black Jacobins* reveals that an elitist narrative mode—narrating through great historical individuals—and radical politics need not be mutually exclusive, whereas Alejo Carpentier's *El reino de este mundo*, in denying the possibility of progressive political intervention, communicates a message of political conservatism in spite of an egalitarian strategy of narrating through a slave. Thus, both radical and conservative discourses might have elitist or populist forms, yet it will also be seen that in some cases formal innovation enabled the communication of radical political messages, as with the négritude poets Aimé Césaire and René Depestre. On the other hand, Madison Smartt Bell's efforts to revitalize the traditional historical novel as a vehicle to narrate the story of the Haitian Revolution succeeds only in communicating a conservative message which falls foul of stereotype and cliché. However, I also argue that the Haitian paintings of Kimathi Donkor succeed where Bell failed, communicating the Haitian Revolution's radicalism by revitalizing a traditional form—in Donkor's case, "grand history" painting. Donkor's method can, in turn, be contrasted with Jacob Lawrence's visual artworks, which plunge into the chasm of the past by a different methodology and instead share formal and political affinities with the négritude writing of Aimé Césaire, prompting us to consider the links between textual and visual representation.

Works of historiography, poetry, theater, novels, biography, and the visual arts are discussed, and these, together with the debate generated by the implicit dialogue between these radical and conservative "camps," form a corpus of material that impinges directly on the discourse surrounding the Haitian Revolution and its cultural legacies. Moreover and also more broadly, I argue that this discussion is relevant to mapping the cultural and intellectual history of the anticolonial, Black Nationalist, and Pan-African movements of the twentieth century.

The Haitian Revolution has always been an ideological battleground in which contenders have conjured with the inheritance of Atlantic slavery. Hence, part of the rationale for examining a series of major twentieth- and twenty-first-century literary and visual mediations of and imaginative responses to the revolution is explained by the primary material's shared engagement in the project of recuperating the revolution from its prior denigration as unregenerate and barbarous in swathes of proslavery propaganda[1]—although I argue that not every text is successful in this respect. Thus, the project's *fil conducteur* resides in the narrative of thinking through how, and to what effect, major Caribbean, American, European, and African artists and intellectuals have metamorphosed and appropriated this spectacular corner of black revolutionary history during the last century.

I argue that whereas each text generates its own special questions and each one requires its own formal solutions, there are recurrent key themes, including questions of temporality, progress, regression, and transformation. Thus, for the cohort of writers and artists that this study dubs as "radical," the Haitian Revolution is retrieved as a decisive and transformational historical moment. In Alejo Carpentier and Derek Walcott's versions, however, possibilities of progress and transformation are curtailed, and regression is ingrained in the theories of cyclical historical fatalism that their texts present. For Madison Smartt Bell and Edouard Glissant also, the possibility of transformation is diminished by, respectively, overwhelming presentations of eroticized violence and the obfuscation of emancipatory politics. Thus, the conservative recuperations can be characterized by a skeptical and pessimistic viewpoint on revolution per se, whereas the radical responses inscribe a readiness to acclaim revolution as a means by which egalitarian and ameliorative social transformation might successfully be actuated. Such reconfigurations conceive revolution dynamically, valorize its link to progress, and share a determination to perceive in the Haitian Revolution lessons for the possibilities of the liberation of the colonized subject; and because the event has been subject to repeated narrativization, the retellings are compelled to negotiate the "sedimentation" of a long-enacted dialogue in which the historical fact of black agency must be vindicated in the face of continuing denial of the interventionist capacities of enslaved blacks.

The comparative methodology that I have employed throughout this study is one in which a modernist belief in the value of the category of the aesthetic is paramount. However, my methodology strives to avoid the pitfalls of an exclusive literary approach by branching out from texts discussed in academic debate to consider popular and mass-produced forms, including the visual. Hence, for example, négritude poetry is discussed, but so too are the popular novels of Madison Smartt Bell, commemorative postage stamps, the elision of Haiti from the 2007 British state-led celebrations of the bicentenary of the abolition of the British slave trade, and the paintings of Jacob Lawrence and Kimathi Donkor, two painters embedded in their communities, Harlem, New York, and Brixton, London, respectively. My rationale for the critical construction of a diverse corpus of primary materials, from the 1930s through to the twenty-first century, and from the Caribbean, the United States, Africa, and Britain, is thus cognizant of the anti-elitism of cultural studies and the observations of critics who have noted that literary scholars working in the field of postcolonial studies "have tended to write with reference to a woefully restricted and attenuated corpus of works."[2]

The Haitian Revolution's Vast and Diverse Cultural Archive

The corpus of radical and conservative literary texts and artworks from the twentieth and twenty-first centuries with which this study is preoccupied constitutes just a fraction of what we might consider to be the Haitian Revolution's impact on representational forms. In the wake of the revolution, a vast range of literary and historical works, travelogues, memoirs, and artworks were produced by notable nineteenth-century writers seeking to celebrate, appropriate, or dramatize the event for their own social and political milieu. These included literary works by the English writers William Wordsworth and Harriet Martineau, the French writers Victor Hugo and Alphonse de Lamartine, the German writer Heinrich von Kleist, and the American poet and abolitionist John Greenleaf Whittier.[3]

Observing that as a literary subject, "the Haitian Revolution is contemporaneous with European Romanticism," A. James Arnold has noted that two of Romanticism's favored plot devices—the idealized noble savage, and dystopian depictions of gory violence—provided "two contrary modes of imagaining the Haitian Revolution" that endured throughout the nineteenth century and well into the twentieth.[4] Thus, it should not come as a surprise that early-nineteenth-century responses to the Haitian Revolution were frequently strongly inflected by the violence of the revolution. "Voodoo" also figured prominently in a long line of works that propelled a discourse in which Haiti and its fledgling history, revolution, and culture were all denigrated.[5] The power of these works that demeaned Haiti was such that it came to feature in the popular imagination as a den of evil, black magic, and savagery, or simply a cesspool. The revolution was also frequently cited in debates about the capabilities of Africans to live as free subjects. Among prominent figures disseminating this view was Thomas Carlyle, who, in his 1849 pamphlet *Occasional Discourse on the Nigger Question*, expressed his opinion that Haiti was a "tropical dog kennel and pestiferous jungle."[6]

Perhaps the most derogatory account of all, however, comes from Spencer Saint John's 1889 memoir, *Hayti; or, the Black Republic*, in which Saint John declared that "the black man" is "incapable of the art of government, and that to entrust him with framing and working the laws for our islands is to condemn them to inevitable ruin."[7] Spencer Saint John had been the British consul to Haiti for twenty years, and his other statements of opinion regarding Haiti and Haitians include, "As a rule, the abler a negro is, the more wicked and corrupt he appears," and that black people are "an inferior type of man."[8] Drawing on the scientific racism of Arthur Gobineau's 1853–55 text, *The Inequality of the Human Races*, which was a popular international success, Saint John's views go some way to illustrating how widely held opinions of black racial inferiority cited Haiti in support of their arguments.[9]

Even if these representations were challenged—Antenor Firmin, a remarkable black Haitian anthropologist, schoolteacher, journalist, and politician, published his 1885 text, *The Equality of the Human Races*, as a denunciation of Gobineau's earlier work—much of the damage was done.[10] By the time François Duvalier began his dictatorial reign in 1957, Haiti's status as uncivilized and dangerous was firmly fixed in the Western imagination. Consider, for example, Graham Greene's 1965 novel *The Comedians,* in which Haiti is simply a "nightmare republic," merely a bland and depraved backdrop.[11]

However, the twentieth and twenty-first centuries have also witnessed repeated attempts to contest what the nineteenth-century worldview had "enshrined in poetics, aesthetics, and historiography" when it came to the Haitian Revolution.[12] From the 1930s onward, the Haitian Revolution has repeatedly drawn international interest, particularly from the wider Caribbean, North and Latin America, Africa, and black communities in Europe. It has inspired imaginative and political writings, visual arts, music, and other art forms and cultural practices in all of those regions. Major figures within the négritude movement, notably Aimé Césaire and René Depestre, were particularly stimulated by the Haitian Revolution, and other acclaimed Caribbean writers who were inspired by the Haitian Revolution include C. L. R. James, Edouard Glissant, Alejo Carpentier, and Derek Walcott, all of whom are considered in this study. The list of African American writers, artists, and activists who were energized by it is also particularly distinguished, and includes Frederick Douglass, James Weldon Johnson, Langston Hughes, Arna Bontemps, Ralph Ellison, and Jacob Lawrence.[13] The Haitian Revolution has also long haunted and inspired the literary imagination of white writers of fiction in the American South. For example, a lingering and horrifying memory of the Haitian Revolution is evoked throughout William Faulkner's *Absalom Absalom*, particularly in its meditations on the themes of miscegenation, the fragility of white southern society, and the ever-present possibility of its destruction.[14] More directly and more recently, Madison Smartt Bell's trilogy of Haitian novels, which are considered in chapter 8, weave an epic and sensational fictional treatment around a narrative of the Haitian Revolution which further testify to the prominence of Haitian history in white writing of the American South.

This plethora of representations constitutes a unique field of cultural and political contestation that has always afforded space for both radical and conservative statements. One of its immediately noteworthy aspects is that it encompasses the francophone, anglophone, and hispanophone linguistic spheres of the Atlantic world. And looking beyond the realm of the literary, it becomes even more apparent that the Haitian Revolution's cultural archive both includes and transcends "high" art and reaches into popular culture. A cornucopia of evidence for this is to be found in music and film, where the Haitian Revolution has inspired a diverse range of tributes, representations, and evocations that span all manner of political, generic, and aesthetic divides. Consider, for example, Santana's 1971 largely instrumental Latin rock song "Toussaint L'Overture" (*sic*) and the Haitian American hip-hop artist Wyclef Jean's 2009 concept album *Toussaint St. Jean—From the Hut, to the Projects, to the Mansion,* which tells the story of the fictional title character, "Toussaint St. Jean," who is part eighteenth-century Haitian revolutionary and part twenty-first-century rapper.[15]

The presence of the revolution is also particularly strong in jazz. In 1938, Sidney Bechet formed the Haitian Orchestra, and this produced the first documented experimental fusion of jazz and African-Caribbean music.[16] Duke Ellington was also inspired to create music that commemorated the Haitian Revolution, but among the best-known jazz compositions to draw on Haiti's revolutionary tradition is bassist Charles Mingus's "Haitian Fight Song" that opens his 1957 album *The Clown.* More recently, the acclaimed black British jazz musician Courtney Pine has paid homage to Toussaint Louverture and Haiti on his 2009 album *Transition in Tradition (En hommage à Sidney Bechet)* in two tracks, "Toussaint L'Ouverture" and "Haiti."[17] Blending mournful bass clarinet tones with defiantly up-tempo rhythms inspired by the musical heritage of the Hispanic Caribbean in "Toussaint L'Ouverture," and virtuoso percussion and clarinet exchanges in "Haiti," Pine creates a musical language that proudly acclaims the Haitian Revolution, laments Toussaint's early death, and summons Haiti as a site of black achievement and cultural dynamism, but also as a site of as yet unfulfilled promise.

There have also been numerous feature films whose narratives have impinged on representations of the Haitian Revolution. The plot of the 1952 American film *Lydia Bailey*, directed by the Romanian filmmaker Jean Negulesco, centers on an idealistic American lawyer who travels to Haiti, whereupon he gets caught up in the revolution. He chooses to side with the rebel slaves, and falls in love with an American heiress, Lydia, the film's eponymous character, who after initially siding with the French, is persuaded by her romantic companion to recognize her error of judgment and support the rebel slaves.[18] However, the film's major character is the slave rebel and aide to Toussaint, King Dick, a principled and heroic black character who appears to have been loosely based on the historical figure of Henri Christophe. Adapted from Kenneth Roberts's 1947 novel of the same title, it is a swashbuckling period adventure yarn, which nevertheless remains notable in that it did not, as did many other Hollywood films of the period, render the revolution as diabolic. Thus, despite its colorful elements, including an excessively exotic take on "voodoo," *Lydia Bailey* can be seen as an unusual recuperation of the revolution.

Lydia Bailey's atypical characteristics are not difficult to discern when it is set alongside the vast number of Hollywood films of widely varying quality that have sought to demonstrate vodou as a sexual threat to white women, and have evoked fears of zombies, black revolt, and miscegenation as their dramatic themes. Invariably, Haiti and the wider Caribbean are depicted as infested with these threats and potent in black magic. Some prominent examples include *I Walked with a Zombie*, the James Bond film *Live and Let Die*, and, more recently, the popular *Pirates of the Caribbean* and its sequels.[19]

However, a project long in development entitled "Toussaint" has raised hopes that a serious and major film about the Haitian Revolution might be forthcoming. "Toussaint" is being produced by the American company Louverture Films, which is dedicated to making movies of historical relevance and social purpose.[20] The involvement of Danny Glover as director and a stellar cast, including Don Cheadle in the title role of Toussaint, demonstrates the considerable promise that the film may be both a commercial and an artistic success. The project has thus far been part financed by Venezuela, whose late president, Hugo Chavez, displayed an interest. If it is indeed made and achieves an international release, it could go some way toward promoting a proper knowledge of Haitian history to a wide audience. It is to be hoped that the proposed movie does not join promising projects about the Haitian Revolution that were never realized. Richard Wright, the African American writer famed for his classic existentialist tragic novel of social protest, *Native Son*, had hoped to make a film about the Haitian Revolution after his travels in Haiti in 1950.[21] His intention was to write a script focusing on Toussaint Louverture and himself play the leading role. Another frustrated venture was an adaptation based on Anatoli Vinogradov's novel about Toussaint Louverture, *The Black Consul*, for which Sergei Eisenstein had secured Paul Robeson in the title role.[22]

Thus, the cultural impact of the Haitian Revolution has been far-reaching and highly variable; that the revolution remains a fertile source for diverse imaginative and political interpretation indicates that its legacies and meaning are still the subject of intense ideological and historiographical debate.

Haiti as an Ideological Battleground: Politics and Historiography of Decolonization

Although postcolonial theory has largely—and as Doris Garaway has correctly observed, remarkably—erased the Haitian Revolution from its critical purview, it is my contention that this study also impinges on the current consideration within postcolonial studies on how the discipline might constructively relocate itself.[23] Therefore, I suggest that if certain explanatory categories—a capitalist world-system (and the fundamental importance of plantation slavery to its development), anticolonial agency, resistance, and struggle—are to play a more prominent and proper part in any reconstructed postcolonialism, then the historical and ideological analysis of the Haitian Revolution and its literary mediations must command more than a passing or selective attention.[24] Moreover, I contend that aesthetic constructions inspired by the Haitian Revolution should be considered as explorations and imaginative interventions into an unfinished anticolonial project and its obstruction by neocolonial imperialism. I thus draw on Nick Nesbitt's argument that "attention to the Haitian Revolution and its aftermath is of most pressing concern if we are to understand the origins and classic forms of these problems that continue to confront our twenty-first century."[25]

I suggest that radical and conservative recuperations of the Haitian Revolution form a special body of works because of their interaction with Haiti's unique and dual status as a nation founded on the "universal and unqualified human right to freedom"[26] and thus a beacon of hope for colonized and dispossessed people everywhere, but also as the exemplar sine qua non of a modern "broken nation" and failed state. This forms an implicit dialogue with David Scott's pessimistic argument in his recent important study of C. L. R. James's *Black Jacobins, Conscripts of Modernity: The Tragedy of Colonial Enlightenment*.[27] There, Scott argues that the political potential of decolonization has been long since dead and that all that remains for us today is the aestheticized delectation of "tragedy." However, Scott's pessimistic position can be constructively contrasted with Peter Hallward's defense of a "politics of prescription," which I suggest can guide us in our Fanonian "plunge into the chasm of the past" if it is to become a source of freedom in the present.

Scott's argument is founded on his conviction that, in our "dead-end present," revolutionary anticolonialism, nation, and socialism can no longer name or animate "visionary horizons of new beginnings any of us can look forward to as though they were fresh thresholds of aspiration to be fought for and progressively arrived at."[28] For Hallward, on the other hand, it is precisely in the moment of our present impasse that a "path of prescription and hope, of disruptive innovation and retrospective justification" is open to us and might be pursued.[29] Hallward thus argues that new forms of resistance and critique would do well to consider "the great anti-colonial movements of the 1940s and 1950s" not merely for their historical interest, but for the emancipatory potential of their unfulfilled project and the radicalism of their prescription of universal principles. The retrospective justification of anticolonial politics as a discourse of universalism thus becomes a means to politicize our intolerance of injustice in the present.

However, the notion that the Haitian Revolution's enduring political value might reside in its radically universalist vision of freedom remains a minority perspective. On this question of the event's radical universalism, J. Michael Dash has observed: "Unfortunately, despite the existence of C. L. R. James's *The Black Jacobins*, Haiti's symbolic presence in the Caribbean literary imagination has never been understood in terms of radical universalism. Rather it is the discourse of mysterious singularity and heroic uniqueness that has prevailed."[30] In fact, Dash finds that far more frequently the meaning of the Haitian Revolution has been co-opted by "those who fatalistically view Haiti in terms of the sigh of history and the fated failure of the antics of megalomaniac generals, or worse yet those who succumb to the Naipaulean nightmare of black savagery."[31]

This book in part seeks to develop and modify Dash's critique. While for Dash the works of Césaire and the négritude movement cannot be considered for their radical universalism, I argue to the contrary that these writings can and should be considered for their qualities of radical universalism and that if they have sought to represent figures or episodes of "mysterious" or "heroic uniqueness" that emerged in the unfolding of the Haitian Revolution, it was only in order to vindicate the actuality of black agency in colonial history.

It has been argued that the West's continuing failure to acknowledge the significance of the Haitian Revolution has been due to what Michel-Rolph Trouillot has described as the "unthinkable" nature of the most successful slave revolt in history.[32] Trouillot emphasizes that the widely shared late-eighteenth and early-nineteenth-century contention that "enslaved Africans and their descendants could not envision freedom—let alone formulate strategies for gaining and securing such freedom—was based not so much on empirical evidence as on an ontology, an implicit organization of the world and its inhabitants."[33]

Susan Buck-Morss has developed Trouillot's notion of "unthinkability" that results in a "silencing of the past" by drawing attention to the fact that it is necessary to distinguish between two silences when it comes to the Haitian Revolution—the past one and the present one.[34] Buck-Morss is of the same mind as Trouillot in noting the difficulties that eighteenth- and nineteenth-century men and women had in thinking about the Haitian Revolution in nonracial terms and as an expression of the fundamental equality of humanity, but she also argues that "today, when the Haitian slave revolution might be more thinkable, it is more invisible, due to the construction of disciplinary discourses through which knowledge of the past has been inherited."[35]

It is in this context identified by Buck-Morss that the continuing denial of the Haitian Revolution within mainstream Western political and cultural discussion must be placed. The 2007 bicentenary celebrations of the British abolition of the slave trade are a case in point. Amid the jubilation, the historical fact that a population of former slaves had risen up, fought an anticolonial war against the French, British, and Spanish, outlawed slavery, and successfully declared the independence of their black republic in the Caribbean well before any of the imperial nations had committed themselves to ending slavery was almost entirely silenced. All connections between British abolitionism and liberal imperialism were certainly overlooked, except for within a number of radical commentaries.[36] One of the ironic legacies of the 1807 Slave Trade Act was the encouraging of Britain's imperialist interventionism: the British navy was given the task of patrolling the Atlantic in order to prevent the continuing trade in slaves from Africa to Brazil, Cuba, and the United States, while Britain contemporaneously continued to profit from the trade in Asia.

Thus it remains the case that, despite a growing historiography, the ideological impact of the Haitian Revolution has not been absorbed into the mainstreams of public knowledge and consciousness in Europe and North America.[37] Whereas the American and French Revolutions are firmly fixed in establishment thinking as pivotal events shaping the Atlantic and modern world, the important advances made in the Haitian Revolution are erased. Certainly the American Revolution promoted the ideas of sovereignty and republicanism, thereby helping to bring down the French monarchy, and the French Revolution destabilized empire and slavery throughout the Americas. Yet only the Haitian Revolution marked a watershed in the history of the development of universal human rights. As Laurent Dubois explains, the Haitian Revolution was "the most concrete expression of the idea that the rights proclaimed in France's 1789 Declaration of the Rights of Man and Citizen were indeed universal. They could not be quarantined in Europe. . . . If we live in a world in which democracy is meant to exclude no one, it is no small part because of the actions of those slaves in Saint Domingue who insisted that human rights were theirs too."[38]

Furthermore, as Nesbitt reminds us, in universalizing the unfulfilled promise of the French Revolution, the Haitian Revolution led to the founding of a state in which "positive rights applied to all citizens, without exception,"[39] hence "the construction of a society without slavery, one of *universal* and *unqualified* human right to freedom, properly stands out as Haiti's unique contribution to humanity."[40]

Thus it follows that, for radical and progressive individuals and groups, one of the major attractions of recuperating the narrative of the Haitian Revolution has been the profound challenge that the event, properly understood, presents to the notion that the values of universal human rights are exclusively Western values. Another is that radical reconfigurations of the Haitian Revolution directly undermine the hegemony of the still massively influential cultural and historical body of works where the values of slave society have been romantically condoned or sanitized, and in which slavery itself has been represented as an essentially benign and paternalistic institution. This tradition was particularly strong in the American South and is exemplified by Ulrich Bonnell Phillips's historical works, particularly his recently republished 1929 work, *Life and Labor in the Old South*, and also the enduringly popular *Gone with the Wind*.[41] Yet there seems to be little appetite in the mainstream for debunking this potent fantasy. Could one then contend that for the northern nations to acknowledge the Haitian Revolution and its implications would require the dismantling of an entire canon of conservative mythologization on the history of Atlantic slavery, together with the abandoning of belief in the West's invention of the discourse of human rights?

The Protean Toussaint: His Enduring Appeal

The historical figure of Toussaint Louverture has been perceived by many as the embodiment of the revolution's values; he has proved over time to be a remarkably protean cultural icon, ripe for recuperation in radical and conservative dicourses alike.[42] In some aesthetic reconfigurations, Toussaint is a tragic hero, a beacon of antiracism, a standard-bearer for anticolonial struggle the world over, a symbol of anti-Napoleon sentiment, an embodiment of négritude and black power, and a precursor to a host of other anti-imperialists and black leaders including Fidel Castro, Martin Luther King, Malcolm X, and Patrice Lumumba.

The revolution also produced other heroic and captivating personalities, and while none have commanded the degree of fascination that Toussaint has, Jean-Jacques Dessalines and Henri Christophe, who were Toussaint's right-hand men, are center stage in numerous recuperations of the revolution. Dessalines, who became Haiti's first postindependence leader and declared himself emperor in 1804, has elicited the most extreme representations; in racist texts inspired by the revolution, he has been caricatured as a brutish black savage; in others, he is a sign of black racial pride, a vodou deity, and an icon of Haitian nationalism. Another key figure is Moïse, a popular and high-ranking black officer whose execution, ironically, was ordered by Toussaint himself, and who has on occasion been represented as the uncorrupted symbol and soul of the revolution.

Furthermore, the passing of time has not diminished Toussaint's political currency, and he remains as revolutionary an inspiration as at any moment in the two-hundred-year history of his evolving mythology. In 2007, a prison radio broadcast by Mumia Abu-Jamal, a former Black Panther activist and journalist who has been on death row in Pennsylvania since 1982, recalled Toussaint and the Haitian Revolution as an episode in an ongoing struggle for freedom and justice for all black people.[43] Again, Toussaint's symbolic presence on the world political stage was dramatically brought to attention in 2004 by the deposed Haitian president Jean-Bertrand Aristide. Giving his first speech in exile from the Central African Republic after falling victim to the U.S.–French–backed military coup that removed him from office, Aristide shadowed Toussaint's famous words on being captured by Napoleon:

> In bringing me down, all that has been cut in Saint Domingue is the trunk of the tree of black freedom; but it will grow again from its roots, for they are deep and numerous. (Toussaint Louverture, 1802)

> In the shadow of Toussaint Louverture, the genius of the race, I declare that in bringing me down all that has been cut is the trunk of the tree of peace; it will grow again from its roots because they are Louverturian. (Jean-Bertrand Aristide, 2004)[44]

In reiterating Toussaint's famous words, and presenting himself as a part of "the tree of black freedom" whose roots Toussaint had predicted would put forward new growth, Aristide's speech presented the struggle of Haitians for freedom and dignity in 2004 in concert with the values of the Haitian Revolution. In so doing, Aristide tempted critics and commentators to analyze contemporary Haiti and Haitian history negatively, as a story of a repeating tragic cycle of tyranny and resistance—a critical framework which, as I argue in my chapters on Alejo Carpentier and Derek Walcott, is flawed by omissions.

Interestingly, in an interview conducted by Peter Hallward in Pretoria, South Africa, on July 20, 2006 (and later published in the *London Review of Books*), Aristide again emphasized Toussaint's relevance to Haiti's ongoing struggle for freedom and self-determination, but on this occasion explicitly valorizing Toussaint's qualities, while rejecting those of Dessalines: "Toussaint L'Ouverture, as a man, had his limitations. But he did his best, and in reality he did not fail. He was captured, imprisoned and killed; but his example and his spirit still guides us now. . . . As for Dessalines, the struggle that he led was armed, and necessarily so, since he had to break the bonds of slavery once and for all. But our struggle is different. It is Toussaint, rather than Dessalines, who can accompany the popular movement today."[45] Here Aristide mistakenly suggested that Toussaint did not lead an armed struggle, which can be read as a desire to recuperate Toussaint as an icon of peace and diplomatic resistance relevant to the struggles of his own Lavalas political movement.

The many varying political applications of the figure of Toussaint Louverture highlight Toussaint's and the revolution's iconic flexibility. Even France, on the two-hundredth anniversary of Toussaint's death, has sought to canonize him as a French national hero, lighting a flame in the memory of both Toussaint and the martyring of millions of slaves, in ceremonies attended by the then French president Jacques Chirac.[46] Although the revolution was uniquely successful as a slave-led revolution that within the century triggered the abolition of slavery everywhere in the Atlantic world, its limitations must be recognized. Independence was achieved, but not the liberation of the people. In its wake came the new obstacle of neocolonial interference, a domestic culture of political authoritarianism buttressed by militarism, the reemergence of color prejudice, and the destabilizing consequences of periods of foreign occupation.

These failures and setbacks have at times been erased in imaginative rewritings and visual imagery: as Paul Breslin has observed in his essay on literary representations of the revolution, "events do not write themselves, and those who write them inevitably intervene by selecting and arranging incidents, framing events in available narrative patterns."[47]

Further, when it comes to the subject of Toussaint, imaginative reconstruction may, according to Percy Waxman, writing in 1931, be considered mandatory: "So much that is purely legendary has been written about Toussaint Louverture and so little trustworthy 'source material' exists that it is extremely difficult for one with no gift for fiction to attempt a complete story of his life."[48]

I have endeavored in this introduction to trace the evolution of the contested cultural space that has arisen as part of the fallout accumulated in perceptions of the Haitian Revolution. This study is an attempt to elucidate the inheritance of the revolution for a body of writers and artists whose recuperations mediate the politics of revolution, black agency, and questions of universalism or heroic singularity. From 1930s anticolonialism and négritude to 1960s radicalism; from the "marvelous real" to the contemporary historical novel of slavery; and from African American and black British paintings to Caribbean, African, and British stamps, I argue that these aesthetic-historical objects should be divided along a single axis of distinction: the radical and the conservative.

I take as my starting point for the book's first part, Aimé Césaire's *Cahier d'un retour au pays natal* (*Notebook of a Return to My Native Land*) (1938) and C. L. R. James's *The Black Jacobins* (1939) as two groundbreaking radical texts which forever transformed Toussaint Louverture into an iconic, international model of black power, fundamentally changed the standing of the Haitian Revolution in black history and cultural memory, and renewed the relevance of the Haitian Revolution to the anticolonial struggles of the twentieth century. Their impact on all the subsequent interpretations of the revolution cannot be overestimated. Alongside Césaire's *Cahier* and James's historical text, I also address two works written for the theater by these writers. I discuss James's play *Toussaint L'Ouverture* (1936), and Césaire's 1963 play *La tragédie du roi Christophe* (*The Tragedy of King Christophe*) in order to examine the different possibilities that the genre of drama offered, and in the case of Césaire's play, to contrast the representation of a black hero figure of the Haitian Revolution very different from Toussaint, Henri Christophe.

I then consider Langston Hughes's imaginary version of the Haitian Revolution. Among all of the cultural locations in which positive recuperations of the Haitian Revolution have developed, the Harlem Renaissance was one of the most fertile, attested to in an astonishing variety of texts, theater projects, and artworks inspired by the Haitian Revolution. Any number of these could have merited substantial consideration, including the 1936 Federal Theatre Project's production of Orson Welles's *Voodoo Macbeth*, and the subversive 1938 production of the play *Haiti* that was loosely based on a play script written in 1917 by a white southern newspaper reporter named William DuBois. There are also Arna Bontemps's accomplished melodramatic novels *Black Thunder* (1936) and *Drums at Dusk* (1939), as well as Jacob Lawrence's 1938 series of paintings entitled *The Life of Toussaint Louverture*. Also, Eugene O'Neill's play *The Emperor Jones* (1920) had a massive impact on the Harlem Renaissance, drawing high praise from W. E. B. Du Bois. *The Emperor Jones* is notable for its complex and contradictory representation of Haiti that communicated a radical critique of imperial exploitation even while it falls foul of many of the traps of the easy portrayal of Haiti as a primitive nation.

However, I have elected to discuss Langston Hughes's play and opera based on the Haitian Revolution, *The Emperor of Haiti* (1936) and *Troubled Island* (1936), as evidence that Hughes, a writer often referred to as the African American poet laureate, was more closely associated with the international contexts of the radical Left and Pan-Africanism than has previously been thought. The discussion will thus suggest that the figuration of Hughes entirely as a gay icon, as is the case in Isaac Julien's 1987 film *Looking for Langston*, overlooks other aspects of his work that are brought to the fore in his writings about Haiti.

I then examine René Depestre's 1967 poem *Un arc-en-ciel pour l'occident chrétien* (*A Rainbow for the Christian West*) before considering the radical paintings of Jacob Lawrence and Kimathi Dinkor, ending the discussion of the "radical" recuperations of the Haitian Revolution.

The book's second part, which examines conservative visions of the revolution, opens by considering Edouard Glissant's perplexing play *Monsieur Toussaint*. Alejo Carpentier's 1949 novel *El reino de este mundo* (*The Kingdom of This World*) is then examined for the particular aesthetic model that emerged from Carpentier's writing on Haiti, the "marvelous real." This is followed by a discussion of Derek Walcott's three plays on the Haitian Revolution, written between 1949 and 1984. Finally, the popular Haitian novels and biography of Toussaint written by Madison Smartt Bell will be considered.

These representations form a corpus of primary material in which canonical texts are complemented by works to which less critical attention has been devoted. This selection, formed predominantly by Caribbean and African American writers and artists, also privileges what might be classed as "hemispheric" representations of the Haitian Revolution. This thereby emphasizes the revolution's internationalization and highlights connections within and between the varied cultural and linguistic spheres of the Caribbean, the United States, and Latin America. Radical and conservative alike, each text or artwork reconfigures the raw materials of history, mapping the political and social reality of the Haitian Revolution via differing aesthetic strategies and innovations, directing this study's inquiry into those twentieth- and twenty-first-century narratives from across the Atlantic world that counter the marginalization of the Haitian Revolution, and seek to overturn the derogatory representations of a people's inherent depravity.

Part One

Radical Recuperations

Universalism and Transformation

1 Radical Universalism

The Haitian Revolution, Aimé Césaire, and C. L. R. James

Haiti is the country where Negro people stood up for the first time, affirming their determination to shape a world, a free world.
—Aimé Césaire, interview by René Depestre (1967)

Toussaint L'Ouverture and the Haitian slaves brought into the world more than the abolition of slavery.
—C. L. R. James, *The Black Jacobins*

AIMÉ CÉSAIRE'S AND C. L. R. JAMES'S Haitian texts articulate a case for the recuperation of the story of the Haitian Revolution within the context of twentieth-century anti-imperialist struggle in Africa and the Caribbean. C. L. R. James made clear that this was one of his objectives when he gave a lecture series in Atlanta, Georgia, in 1971 on his historical masterpiece *The Black Jacobins*: "Now, what did I have in mind when I wrote this book? I had in mind writing about the San Domingo Revolution as the preparation for the revolution that George Padmore and all of us were interested in, that is, the revolution in Africa."[1]

This chapter suggests that both James's *Black Jacobins* and Césaire's *Cahier d'un retour au pays natal* (*Notebook of a Return to My Native Land*), the founding poetic text of the négritude movement, spoke to the singular imperative of African and Caribbean decolonization via recuperations of the Haitian Revolution that articulate a radical project of universal freedom.[2] Therefore, the anticolonial discourse that these texts present, framed and founded in a discourse of radically enlightened universalism, must not be consigned to the waste bin of history as a result of the perceived failings of the decolonization movement, as has been suggested by some critics.[3] James's and Césaire's determined revalorizations of Haitian history, I argue, share similar preoccupations with the representation of black agency and the pioneering of a collective black memory that could challenge the seemingly infinite number of narratives in black history that emphasize the status of the black subject as victim;

yet at the same time, their celebrations of the Haitian Revolution were always premised on universal ethical and political values.

In the foreword to the 1980 edition of his seminal historical text on the Haitian Revolution, *The Black Jacobins*, James retrospectively wrote the following in order to underscore his intentions: "I was tired of reading and hearing about Africans being persecuted and oppressed in Africa, in the Middle Passage, in the USA and all over the Caribbean. I made up my mind that I would write a book in which Africans or people of African descent instead of constantly being the object of other peoples' exploitation and ferocity would themselves be taking action on a grand scale and shaping other people to their own needs."[4]

If James, at one stroke, repudiates the white archive of Atlantic slavery by refusing a history predicated upon assumptions of black passivity, exploitation, and powerlessness, Césairean négritude too can be interpreted as a means of confronting this same problem. In the midst of a plethora of narratives that emphasized black victimhood, négritude signified, among other things, not only a political and aesthetic theory, but also "a textually invented history, an identity effected through figurative operations, and a tropological construction of blackness as a sign of the colonized condition and its refusal."[5] Furthermore, for Césaire's historical/cultural négritude, as opposed to Senghor's essentialist version,[6] Haiti was fundamental as the site of original and powerful refusal, the place "où la négritude se mit debout pour la première fois et dit qu'elle croyait à son humanité" (where negritude stood up for the first time and said it believed in its humanity).[7]

Thus, despite their different forms and languages, it is instructive to consider James's history, *The Black Jacobins*, first published in 1938, alongside Césaire's négritude poem, *Cahier d'un retour au pays natal*, first published in 1939. In the appendix essay to the second edition of *The Black Jacobins* published in 1963, James quotes from Césaire's *Cahier* at length in order to make some of the connections between their projects explicit. This he did by praising Césaire's *Cahier*, "the finest and most famous poem ever written about Africa,"[8] for making "a union of the African sphere of existence with existence in the Western world," for linking historically and logically mankind's past to mankind's future, and for offering a vision of independent African being and an integrated humanity.[9] By these means, Césaire and James offer emancipatory visions of decolonization, inextricably linked to the liberation of the subject, as a principle of a universal freedom to be shared among all races and peoples.

The discussion that follows extends the frame of analysis to take into account the works for the theater which both James and Césaire wrote on the Haitian Revolution, Césaire's *La tragédie du roi Christophe* (*The Tragedy of King Christophe*), and James's play script *Toussaint L'Ouverture* (later retitled *The Black Jacobins*), which can be seen as the predecessor to his widely acclaimed history.[10] The analysis also pays attention to the means by which the character of Toussaint or other heroic figures, sometimes historical and sometimes archetypal, were starting points for Césaire's and James's efforts to communicate the historical fact of black agency, its contemporary and future possibility, and the achievement of the renewal of communal black memory.

Aimé Césaire: Négritude and Haiti's Revolutionary History as a Universal Myth

An examination of the recuperation of the Haitian Revolution in Césaire's *Cahier d'un retour au pays natal*, and in his 1963 play *La tragédie du roi Christophe*, together with the radical discourse of liberation that they instantiate, enables a reexamination of the productive capacities and the limitations of the much-maligned and frequently misunderstood concept of négritude and its attitude to history and the past. In his article "Marvelous Realism: The Way out of Négritude," J. Michael Dash sketches what he perceives to be "the essential difference between 'Marvelous Realism' and 'Négritude.'"[11] For Dash, the limitation of négritude lies in its inability to "see beyond the tragedy of circumstance" and hence its alleged inability to celebrate the cultural inheritance of slavery.[12] Thus, while conceding that négritude correctly recognized the double alienation of the black man, on a politicoeconomic level as well as on a psychological and cultural level, he maintains that a "totally un-creative" attitude to the past renders it incapable of addressing the problem of psychological regeneration.[13] But whereas négritude, it is alleged, could not move beyond the negativity of committed protest, marvelous realism allows for the flowering of the Third World personality. This negative view of négritude has now been reinforced by the Créoliste group—Martinican writers Patrick Chamoiseau, Raphaël Confiant, and Jean Bernabé—whose writings have propelled a devaluation of both négritude and Césaire.[14] However in the context of an ongoing debate, I argue that in its dialogue with history, négritude cannot be so comprehensively dismissed.[15] By rereading Césaire's highly imaginative representations of Haitian history, I attempt to show how historical/cultural négritude, in opposition to a Senghorian essentialist version, enabled the installation of black achievement. My interpretation thus ascribes to négritude a universalism that distinguishes it from mere identity politics.[16]

The *Cahier* and *La tragédie du roi Christophe* are not simple rewritings of history from the perspective of the colonized "other"; nor do they fall foul of that other accusation that has been leveled at négritude: the retrograde desire to recover an idealized but now vanquished identity. Rather, they constitute textual interventions that lay claim to a reenergized subjectivity and promote critical participation in the process of decolonization, refusing to ignore or to be held prisoner by the traumas of colonial history. Césaire's works politicize history and boldly demand that we rethink received narratives. Hence in the *Cahier*, Césaire's transformative aesthetics enable a once debilitating past to emerge as rich with regenerative potential for the present, as a source of renewal and radicalism. Consider the triumphant and closing lines of the *Cahier*:

> . . . le grand trou noir où je voulais me noyer l'autre lune
> c'est là que je veux pêcher maintenant la langue maléfique de la
> nuit en son immobile verrition!
>
> (. . . the great black hole where I wanted to drown a moon ago
> this is where I now want to fish the night's malevolent tongue in
> its immobile revolvolution!)[17]

These enigmatic lines indicate the formal radicalism of Césaire's text; and although their metaphor-laden poetics lend themselves to multiple interpretations, they speak of the omission of black agency in the white archive, and the way in which the Haitian Revolution transports the speaking subject from death-desiring despair ("grand trou noir où je voulais me noyer") to a resolve for recovering black achievement ("je veux pêcher").

Césaire's *Cahier* has been the subject of many readings over the years, and its status as a classic francophone text of decolonization has long been established.[18] Christopher L. Miller has gone so far as to argue that the *Cahier* has done more than any other text, before or since, "to rethink the French Atlantic," inhabit its "oppressive logic," and suggest "a way out of it."[19] Indeed, escape from the legacies of Atlantic slavery accounts for the many readings of the poem that have stressed its powerfully affirmative narrative, in which the black diasporic poetic subject experiences an awakening of consciousness.[20]

However, to read the *Cahier* as a text that primarily charts a unilnear movement from submission to freedom is to overlook the text's "inherent ambiguity or double character."[21] Edouard Glissant argued that the *Cahier* cannot be read as "a text of triumphalist exaltation, while conceding that "it was to become a source of inspiration for the African diaspora." In noting the poem's use of the fundamental concept of "return," Glissant pointed out that the *Cahier*'s relationship with Africa does not consist of a poetic replication of Marcus Garvey's position, and hence does not sound a clarion call for "another *return* that could have resembled an occupation," but rather "a profound poetics of the historical sufferings of the Africas and of the shared knowledge of the world."[22]

Various misreadings of Césaire's work have been highlighted by Christopher L. Miller, who maintains that critics who conflate Senghor's and Césaire's conceptions of négritude have incorrectly catalogued the *Cahier* as an inflexibly doctrinaire manifesto.[23] While it is true that Senghor's essentialist interpretation of négritude argued for "an unchanging core or essence to black existence," Césaire regarded the "specificity and unity of black existence as a historically developing phenomenon that arose through the highly contingent events of the African slave trade and the New World plantation system."[24] This distinction has not always been appreciated by critics who denounce both as essentialists and applaud hybridity as the appropriate theoretical perspective. Others have deplored Césairienne négritude for its alleged blindness to the Caribbean itself, Afrocentrism, and hyperromanticization of Africa.

A response to these allegations, and especially to suggestions of the poem's alleged militant Afrocentrism, is, I suggest, to be found in a close reading of the poem's ambiguous nature and drawing attention to the importance it attaches to the Haitian Revolution as a foundational *world* revolution, rather than a regional event of significance only for Africa and Africans. Therefore my own reading of the *Cahier* seeks to emphasize the recuperation of the Haitian Revolution the poem offers via the symbolic presentation of Toussaint, the view of négritude as a concept positing the negation of subjugation—not through the celebration of racial or strategic essentialism—but via a radical spiritual and political project of black, as well as universal, liberation.

For Césaire, the Haitian Revolution was a confirmation of what he later termed "négritude in action." Speaking with René Depestre in 1967, Césaire explained: "Haiti represented for me the heroic Antilles, the African Antilles. I began to make connections between the Antilles and Africa, and Haiti is the most African of the Antilles. It is at the same time a country with a marvellous history: the first Negro epic of the New World was written by Haitians, people like Toussaint Louverture, Henri Christophe, Jean-Jacques Dessalines."[25]

In the *Cahier,* Césaire puts Haiti's "marvellous history" to work toward the construction of a coherent and empowering subjectivity. Césaire's route to this goal is via an imaginative recuperation of the heroic persona of Toussaint Louverture and his climactic moment of great ironic tragedy: his death while imprisoned in the French Jura Mountains at Napoleon Bonaparte's command. The circumstances of Toussaint's death have proven to be particularly ripe for artistic and literary reinvention, although a great number of these reinventions have blandly represented the event in the tenor of mournful melodrama—Wordsworth's sonnet "To Toussaint L'Ouverture," in which Toussaint is represented as a whitewashed generic martyr to freedom, is a good example of this approach.[26] However, the recalling of Toussaint's death to present memory in the *Cahier* departs from these many prior descriptions by imaginatively possessing the inheritance of Toussaint's death in a poetic recasting of history as a politically enabling myth. The poem's narrator, who here adopts an inclusive revolutionary rhetoric that encompasses disenfranchised and alienated blacks throughout the Atlantic diaspora, is thus empowered to initiate his own movement towards dis-alienation:

> Ce qui est à moi aussi: une petite cellule dans le Jura,
> une petite cellule, la neige la double de barreaux blancs
> la neige est un geôlier blanc qui monte la garde devant une prison
>
> Ce qui est à moi
> c'est un homme seul emprisonné de blanc
> c'est un homme seul qui défie les cris blancs de la mort blanche
> (TOUSSAINT, TOUSSAINT LOUVERTURE)

> (What is mine too: a small cell in the Jura,
> the snow lines it with white bars
> the snow is a white gaoler who mounts guard in front of a prison
>
> What is mine

a man alone, imprisoned by whiteness
a man alone who defies the white screams of a white death
(TOUSSAINT, TOUSSAINT LOUVERTURE)[27]

The repeated refrain "Ce qui est à moi" ("What is mine") emphasizes the act of individual imaginative possession; the canto is also remarkable for the repetition—twelve times in all—of "la mort" ("death"). But in the context of myth, death is not terminal. Instead, death is connected to a circular chain of birth, death, and resurrection: "La mort décrit un cercle brillant au-dessus de cet homme" ("Death describes a brilliant circle above this man").[28]

The *Cahier* thereby pays homage to the regenerative possibilities of the spirit of Toussaint as a black revolutionary leader who became a heroic martyr to liberty. The imprisoned and dying Toussaint epitomizes struggle and suffering, but rather than portraying him as a black Christ, Césaire re-creates Toussaint in the mold of a Nietzschean tragic hero, a technique on which Césaire would later draw for the representation of the archetypal anti-Promethean, Nietzschean "Rebel" in his play *Et les chiens se taisaient* (*And the Dogs Were Silent*).[29] Although there is a religious quality to the symbolism of Toussaint's fate, "death stars gently above his head" (la mort étoile doucement au-dessus de sa tete), it is a poetic mysticism worlds away from Christianity.[30] Here, death is not redemptive, but rather it acquires its own volition. It dominates the prison, and it is equated with symbols of evil: the gaoler, the snow, and whiteness itself. Death represents a "*destin tenace*" (tenacious destiny) that is both romanticized, "la mort est un oiseau blessé" (death is a wounded bird), and stripped of false beauty, "soubresauts de mort figée" (spasms of clotted death).[31]

Césaire's treatment of the death of Toussaint reverberates with Freud's concept of the death wish and Nietzsche's self-sacrificing tragic hero, as well as the mythology of Haitian vodou. As a complex, composite, and symbolic representation, Toussaint may thus also be seen as a site for the exploration of the connections between Hellenic and Haitian cultures.[32] By extrapolating from Wole Soyinka's claim that the West African Yoruba and Haitian vodou deity "Ogun is best understood in Hellenic values as the totality of Dionysian, Apollonian and Promethean virtues,"[33] the critic Keith L. Walker reads Césaire's Toussaint as exemplifying the characteristics of Ogun.[34] This reading of Césaire's representation of Toussaint, with its emphasis on his cultural syncretism, helps to unveil a figure who embodies the gravitas of a universal tragic hero charged with the responsibility for awakening the subjectivity of the narrator of the *Cahier*. As such, the mythic paradigm that Césaire ascribes to Toussaint is that of the fertility myth following the pattern of the dying and reviving god, adapted for Césaire's project of négritude by the substitution of the reviving god in lieu of the revived narrator and a revived people.[35]

The depiction of the historical black revolutionary leader in the role of the tragic hero and as a godlike figure was a theme to which Césaire was to return in two of his plays, *La tragédie du roi Christophe* and *Une saison au Congo*.[36] Here Césaire portrayed Henri Christophe, Haiti's first postindependence king, and Patrice Lumumba, the first and only democratically elected prime minister of the Congo, who was assassinated in 1961, as tragic heroes and models of black agency.[37] Notably, whereas in the genre of drama Césaire was able to grant both Christophe and Lumumba their own voices and personas, in the *Cahier* Toussaint does not utter a word, being cast as a mythical presence and not a real figure, whose blood invests the land with a metaphysical and revolutionary pregnancy: "de terre muette / la splendeur de ce sang n'éclatera-t-elle point?" (from the mute land / won't the splendour of this blood burst out?).[38] Césaire would return to the challenge of how to synchronize the historical and the mythic in the representation of black agency when he imaginatively revisited Haitian history in the historical drama *La tragédie du roi Christophe*.

La tragédie du roi Christophe (*The Tragedy of King Christophe*)

In *Caribbean Discourse*, Edouard Glissant writes: "Myth disguises while conferring meaning, obscures and brings to light, mystifies as well as clarifies and intensifies *that* which emerges, fixed in time and space, between men and their world. It explores the known-unknown. Myth is the first state of a still-naive historical consciousness, and the raw material for the project of a literature."[39]

Glissant's analysis of myth as a means of exploration, a stage of historical consciousness, and the raw material for the project of a literature is a useful way into Césaire's *La tragédie du roi Christophe*. Although ostensibly a historical drama, Césaire's play occupies a liminal space where history, myth, and the occult converge. From the powerful symbolism of the supernatural in the prologue, to the play's vodou and

Roman Catholic rituals, the play is clearly no straightforward dramatic reenactment of history. Rather, Césaire regarded his task as a dramatist to transcend historical particularity in order to reveal the universal values of black anticolonial and postindependence struggle through myth: "The truth is that I have departed from history, sometimes from chronology, but I wanted to give to this story *the dimension of myth, to broaden it out to myth, to deepen it into myth*."[40]

Thus, although *La tragédie du roi Christophe* is rooted in Haitian history, its dramaturgy is indebted to a mythic structure which is evoked by the play's multiple generic forms and aesthetic registers. *La tragédie du roi Christophe* contains elements of high tragedy as well as burlesque and occasionally downright vulgarity. Throughout, the play also fluctuates between myth and history, emphasizing the distinctions between mythical time and historical time. We might thus be tempted to consider Césaire's plays in the light of T. S. Eliot's article "*Ulysses*, Order and Myth," which offers productive insights into Césaire's mythic apparatus, notwithstanding the two writers' incompatible politics.[41] By converting history into drama and taking myth as its principal ordering structure, *La tragédie du roi Christophe* reveals an affinity with that which Eliot praised in Joyce, making us aware of "not only the pastness of the past, but of its presence."[42]

On a formal level, the language of the play lurches from poetry to prose and back again, frequently within the space of just a few lines of a speech or dialogue. At its center resides the eponymous tragic hero, Henri Christophe, around whom the narrative swirls. The play tells the tale of Christophe's conquest of power in Haiti and the subsequent dilemmas that confront him at the level of state building and policy making. We are then shown the descent of Christophe's rule into tyranny, and the Haitian people's resistance to his cruel authority. However, Christophe becomes politically isolated, and even his closest and most trusted political and military friends and allies betray him and defect to Haiti's Republican South. Finally, Christophe, by now physically debilitated by a stroke, commits suicide, his vision of a just and truly emancipated society in tatters.

In telling Christophe's story, Césaire uses some well-known Brechtian dramatic devices.[43] The historical aspect of the play never masquerades as naturalism, and there are direct addresses to the audience from the play's Commentator. More accessible than much of his poetry, Césaire's theater makes good on his own claim that "it must incite the public to think critically," and reminds us of the way in which drama functions as a social and public event that is inclined to foster debate in a way that poetry does not.[44] Thus *La tragédie du roi Christophe* prompts its public to relate the dramatic investigation of the nature of political power in the nineteenth-century postcolonial state of Haiti across a temporal divide to the twentieth-century independence struggles in Africa and the Caribbean. This engagement with matters of politics, anticolonialism, and the postcolonial situation is more transparent than in his poetry. It has led some critics to perceive that Césaire's theater is "less inclined to have recourse to mythical or idealized images of Africa" than is his poetry.[45] However, this should not be mistaken for the supplanting of an interest in the mythic by the political. On the contrary, not only is the political quality of *La tragédie du roi Christophe* extrapolated to universality through myth, but the mythic structure of the play evokes an alternate worldview that rouses the modern world to an awareness of its blindness to human exploitation. It is Césaire's achievement that he made an artistic language not in order to aestheticize the past or only to protest against the injustices of the past, but rather to celebrate a past that has been denied for too long but without idealizing it, and to make the past an avenue for pursuing universal emancipation in the present.

C. L. R. James: *The Black Jacobins*

The representation of the history of the Haitian Revolution in order to promote the anticolonial struggles of the twentieth century in Africa and the Caribbean is also prominent in C. L. R. James's *The Black Jacobins*, which remains the seminal biographical construction of Toussaint as a historic black hero and a remarkable account of the Haitian Revolution. The significance of *The Black Jacobins* as a dissenting text is made clear by James himself, who in the foreword to the 1980 edition of the text recounts how he had learned that mimeographed copies of sections of the text had been in circulation in apartheid South Africa during the 1950s.[46] The text is also widely known as a classic of Marxist historiography, a precursor to E. P. Thomson's thesis of "history from below," as well as a touchstone for thinking about decolonization. Under consideration here will be the productive capacities and limitations of James's emphasis on recuperating Toussaint as a "great man" who dominated the world-historical stage. It is suggested that although this was to prove a majesterial means by which to vindicate black agency in history, it is a technique that stands in contradiction to the text's celebrated values. In this regard, the text's little-known predecessor, the play *Toussaint Louverture*, which James wrote in 1936 and was performed on the

London stage to mixed reviews with Paul Robeson and C. L. R. James himself in the lead roles, indicates some of the difficulties of representing Toussaint.[47]

Perhaps the most striking feature of *The Black Jacobins* relates to its imposing narrative style, which was directly inspired by a novel, not a historical work, Tolstoy's *War and Peace*. As the critic Robert Hill has argued, "Like Tolstoy's *War and Peace*, which describes the epic story of Russia's struggle during the Napoleonic wars, James' account of the Haitian Revolution expresses a parallel national vision for the West Indies."[48]

The book is also reminiscent in tone of Trotsky's history of the Russian Revolution, and indeed Cedric Robinson has noted that James's history "framed the Haitian Revolution against the Bolshevik model."[49] Finally, that stylistically it recalls Michelet's history of the French Revolution should not surprise the reader, given James's enthusiastic self-immersion in the writers of the French historical school of the French Revolution, of whom, for James, the "greatest of them all is Michelet."[50] Each of these influences reveals something of the aesthetic taste and ideological direction favored by James. Furthermore, James's casting of Toussaint Louverture as a tragic figure, and James's insistence on reading the revolution through the prism of tragedy, in its literary generic sense, prompts urgent questions about the tensions between the employment of an elite European historiographic mode that at times occludes the Haitian masses in the interests of a "great man" history, and the writing of a suppressed non-European history.[51] Even though James does provide a class analysis of slave society in prerevolutionary Saint-Domingue, it is fascinating to examine *The Black Jacobins* as a classic text of Marxist historiography whose approach at times appears akin to the traditions of a Victorian-style biographical history.

This fraught ideological relation first makes itself known to the reader in James's preface to the first edition of *The Black Jacobins*. This remarkable, and contradictory, two-and-a-half-page preface contains an unforgettable statement of the purpose and methodology of the project. James indicates that the work will necessarily be biographical since, he argues, the Haitian Revolution was "almost entirely" Toussaint's individual work, and, other than Napoleon, Toussaint was the most "greatly gifted" world-historical figure of his time.[52]

But although James characterizes Toussaint as a "great man," he will not allow that he is also a tragic hero in the greatest sense of the term. In the climactic chapter, "The War of Independence," James writes that

Toussaint was "in a lesser category" than his literary comparators, Prometheus, Hamlet, Lear, and Ahab.[53] James's construction of a fictitious Toussaint to sit alongside his favorite tragic heroes stands out as a peculiar moment in the text. What James achieves by his deliberation on the degree of Toussaint's "greatness" is far from clear, although it should be recognized that by imagining Toussaint in conjunction with classical Greek tragedy, Shakespeare, and Melville at the very forefront of his mind, James was making a radical statement for the time, even if we may read this today as symptomatic of James's troubling traditionalism.

James's representation of Toussaint is nothing if not contradictory. For Wilson Harris, Toussaint is just too slippery for James to be able to pin him down with real authority, in the end escaping James's authorial "self-determination."[54] Toussaint also appears ultimately to escape James's control as he resides at the center of two irreconcilable historical methodologies. While attempting to stay loyal to his developing adherence to Marxism, James was also reluctant to relinquish his affection for the notion of the great individual who single-handedly makes history. Thus, in the preface, James evokes and then refigures Marx's famous phrase from "The Eighteenth Brumaire of Louis Bonaparte": "Men make their own history, but they do not make it just as they please; they do not make it under circumstances chosen by themselves, but under circumstances directly encountered, given, and transmitted from the past."[55] James's rewording makes explicit his intention to write a "great man" history: "Great men make history, but only such history as it is possible for them to make."[56]

This tension between a Marxist and a tragic approach to writing the history of the Haitian Revolution flares up intermittently throughout the text. It becomes particularly apparent in the analysis of Toussaint's ultimate failure, which James attributes to Toussaint's lack of communication with the masses and his generals ("His error was the neglect of his own people. They did not understand what he was doing or where he was going"),[57] as well as to his calamitous decision to order the execution of his radical nephew and fellow revolutionary Moise: "It was almost as if Lenin had had Trotsky shot for taking the side of the proletariat against the bourgeoisie."[58]

Thus, James's Marxist analysis of Toussaint's failure sits in uneasy contrast with the many accounts of his successes: Toussaint's astonishing accomplishments as an administrator were not achieved through cooperation with the people but rather because "Toussaint made himself into a whole cabinet like a fascist dictator, except that he actually did the work."[59] At other times, James's desire to represent Toussaint as an individual bestowed with extraordinary abilities appears to reveal lapses of judgment when dealing with historical sources: "[Toussaint] was as completely master of his body as of his mind. He slept but two hours every night, and for days would be satisfied with two bananas and a glass of water."[60] This implausible account of Toussaint's endurance is more revealing of James's humor than of any insight into the historical being—the man with his two bananas and a glass of water being parodies of "jungle blacks" and prior racist representations of Toussaint.

Ultimately, however, James's figuring of Toussaint as a mythopoetic hero and an extraordinary individual must be recognized as serving to intensify the inherent tension between the revolutionary politics of the work and its elitist occlusion of the masses.[61]

In order to clarify my own reading of James, it is necessary at this juncture to specify my dissent from David Scott's analysis in *Conscripts of Modernity*, his book-length study of *The Black Jacobins*. According to Scott's thesis, one that is repeatedly stressed, the political potential of anticolonial theory and praxis has for many years now been an anachronism, out of date and out of tune with our radically changed circumstances—a fact, he claims, not sufficiently acknowledged by postcolonial critics. Scott offers detailed and nuanced close readings of James's book, paying careful attention to the first edition of 1938 and the extensive revisions made to the 1963 second edition. What he discerns is the shift from the mode of anticolonial Romanticism in the 1938 edition, to an anticolonialism circumscribed by a tragic sensibility in the 1963 edition, from which he concludes that by the time of the 1963 second edition, James foresaw the political limitations of anticolonial narrative. In Chris Bongie's attentive critique of Scott's thesis, he notes that Scott's antiteleogical "appeals to the future" tend "to come across as purely rhetorical gestures,"[62] due in large part to Scott's denial of the emancipatory potential of proleptic alternatives to anticolonial Romanticism on account of our age of politically "impossible options."[63]

Whether Scott writing in 2004 truly speaks for the James writing in 1963 is doubtful. The 1963 second edition of *The Black Jacobins* contains a powerful affirmation of the politics of revolution, resistance, and struggle in its appendix, "From Toussaint L'Ouverture to Fidel Castro." Here James states that he does not link Toussaint Louverture to Fidel Castro simply because both led Caribbean revolutions, and "nor is the link a convenient or journalistic demaracation of historical time."[64] Instead, James insists that "what took place in French San Domingo in 1792–1804 reappeared in Cuba in 1958,"[65] and while conceding that "what will happen to what Fidel Castro has brought new to the world no one can say,"[66] he asserts that the project of anti-imperialist struggle in the Caribbean has decisively brought "something new"[67] into the world, signifying that "the work of man is not finished."[68] James's 1963 appendix essay speaks to an unfinished political project of freedom, nationhood, and self-determination animated by a claim of universal equality. Its politics, I maintain, cannot be reconciled with Scott's proclamation that there no longer exist foundations for political commitment of any kind.

James's interest in Toussaint Louverture had been long-standing. One of his earliest essays, "The Intelligence of the Negro," published in the *Beacon* in August 1931, invoked the greatness of Toussaint Louverture, and it foreshadows the kernel of what would become Toussaint's heroic characterization in *The Black Jacobins*.[69] Also, in *Beyond a Boundary,* James explained that the project of writing a biography of Toussaint had been "stuck away in the back of [his] head for years" and that shortly after his arrival from Trinidad in 1932 in the Lancastrian English town of Nelson, the project of writing about Toussaint became a new priority: "I had not been long in Nelson before I began to import from France the books that I would need to prepare a biography of Toussaint."[70]

Instead of a biography, however, James's first literary engagement with the Haitian Revolution was a stage play in which he revealed an awareness of the role of the ordinary slaves and slave culture in the revolution, as well as the preeminence of Toussaint.[71] And although it could not be said that James's stage play reads the history of the Haitian Revolution from below, the script does initially pay considerable attention to "the masses," and attempts to ascribe to them a vital political function. One of the first stage directions states that crowds "say little but their presence is felt powerfully" and that the presence of crowds is "essential to action in the downstage areas."[72]

James's use of an anonymous crowd, labeled as either "The Slaves" or "The People," assists in the evocation of a sense of catastrophic drama, and recalls Césaire's installing of a chorus drawn from myths ancient and modern in *Et les chiens se taisant*. However, the play does not achieve the tragic register that we find in Césaire's drama. Moreover, James does not sustain the represention of the people throughout the play; instead

James opts to use individual characters to represent ideological and diplomatic positions.[73] However, the play opens with an interplay of voices and montage through which James evokes the dehumanizing capacity of slavery in a ritualistic representation of a slave work gang—the revolutionary songs alleged by some historians to derive from the Bois Caiman vodou ceremony which sparked the initial revolutionary uprising of 1791:

> Eh! Eh! Bomba! Heu! Heu!
> Canga bafio te!
> Canga moune de le
> Canga, do ki la
> Canga, li[74]

These famous words are accompanied by drums, recalling the subversive power of vodou. Later the status of a number of slaves is contrasted with the privileged position of an unnamed white lady at a hairdresser's. The climactic moment of the barbershop scene, "the lady's small cry of disappointment" as one of her curls is accidentally undone by an attending slave,[75] recalls the horrified face of the white woman who finds a "Hottentot's" skull in her soup tureen in Césaire's *Cahier.* Although both scenes resonate with uncomfortable gender stereotyping, they do illustrate the presence of resistance within the hollow decorum of slaveholding and colonial society.[76]

In both the history and the play, the impact of the French Revolution is represented as having been of paramount importance to the events in Saint Domnigue, at the expense of the revolution's indebtedness to earlier leaders of slave and maroon insurrections in the colony. An anonymous speaker in the play, to whom James attributes a consciousness of international solidarity, announces to the masses at the Bois Caiman forest vodou ceremony which is already teeming with insurrectionary potential: "The white slaves in France are fighting their masters. . . . You must join your brothers in revolt, we must fight."[77]

Significantly it is Dessalines, not Toussaint, who is ready to rise to this call to arms:

> Dessalines: (He looks up with determination and hate on his face. He raises a fist to the sky and shouts.) We will kill them all. Every one.[78]

Dessalines's rage is contrasted immediately with Toussaint's cautious and intellectual approach. Whereas Dessalines is represented as emerging from the thick of the insurrection from its earliest stages, Toussaint is absent, his knowledge of revolution reaching him through his reading of the antislavery priest Abbé Raynal. In a sense, Toussaint and Dessalines function as dramatic foils: although portrayed as a supreme military tactician and soldier, Dessalines is also brutish and uneducated, animalistic and threatening, his speech semi-broken. By contrast, Tousaint is characterized as intelligent and learned, his eloquence and Dessalines's inarticulacy raising questions relating to the problems of authenticity of language and dialogue in a fictional reconstruction of history. This problem is compounded by the limited lexicon and range of tone and expression that James grants Dessalines, as for example in his response to the uprising of October 1791: "Revolution in France. Revolution in San Domingo. Freedom for slaves. Kill master. Burn down plantation."[79] Dessalines's speech, which re-creates the staccato diction associated with racist constructions of faux black idiot characters, fails to stage the breakdown of language in a moment of extreme drama. Nor does James find a convincing dramatic voice for Toussaint. Thus, the frequently lengthy stage directions and information about protagonists are not integrated as articulations of character and dialogue expressive of interactions between characters. I have already argued that the play fails as a historical reconstruction; and because the characters labor under the weight of conveying ideological position taking and diplomatic maneuvering—consider the scenes in which Toussaint protects his former master and orders the execution of his radical nephew Moïse—it fails also as a drama.

Aimé Césaire and C. L. R. James can be situated as writing—and inventing—Haiti's revolutionary history at particular moments when the colonial world was beginning to mobilize anticolonial struggles and black intellectuals were engaged as theoreticians, and often as activists, participating in liberation movements. Hence, their recuperations of the Haitian Revolution were necessarily informed by a political ethic of universalism and anticolonial sentiment, and were motivated by the desire to demonstrate and celebrate black agency. The political urgency of their texts has not diminished with time, and they remain potent sources with which to critique the material and political realities of our present, and to imagine a different future.

2 Langston Hughes

Harlem and Haiti

> I had read of Toussaint L'Ouverture, Dessalines, King Christophe, proud black names, symbols of a dream—freedom—building a citadel to guard that freedom.
>
> —Langston Hughes, *I Wonder as I Wander*

THE INFLUENCE OF THE HARLEM RENAISSANCE on both Aimé Césaire and C. L. R. James was fundamental. Langston Hughes and other poets and writers of the Harlem Renaissance, including Claude McKay, Jean Toomer, and Countee Cullen, "enjoyed a heroic status among black intellectuals when Césaire arrived in Paris in 1931."[1] Hughes was dubbed "the father of negritude,"[2] his work known to and admired by writers adhering to its agenda as well as C. L. R James.[3]

It is thus instructive to turn to Langston Hughes's recuperations of the Haitian Revolution and to trace their commonalities with Césaire's and James's radical anticolonial projects. Langston Hughes has long commanded an iconic status in the history of African American letters, and viewing him in the company of Aimé Césaire and C. L. R. James, as one part of a global triptych of radical black anticolonial intellectuals, is a productive critical perspective, and one that departs from the discourse of celebration now surrounding Hughes's legacy. Here there has emerged a cult of personality that has made it possible to discuss and portray Hughes and his work in highly decontextualized terms, divorcing Hughes's work from its original political and historical location.

Isaac Julien's 1987 film *Looking for Langston* is an eminent example of this approach.[4] This presents us with a reduced portrait of Hughes which foregrounds his sexuality and occludes his politics. In stunning visual monochrome, complemented by an emotive sound track that ranges from impressionistic jazz to early house music, *Looking for Langston* constructs Hughes as a black gay icon, playing associations and stereotypes of blackness and homosexuality off against each other. But by essentializing Hughes as black and gay, and by giving a very limited space to Hughes's writings, the film offers only an impoverished representation of Hughes's life and significance, obfuscating many of the reasons for his status as the most creative and original writer of the Harlem Renaissance.[5]

An understanding of the radical political path that Hughes pursued from 1930 onward remains fundamental to any critical appreciation of his life and work. This happened after his sudden break with his domineering early patron Charlotte Osgood Mason, who had yearned for his art to be "primitive," "more African than Harlem."[6] Hughes's political radicalism took him first to the American South and West, to Cuba, and then on to Haiti for six months in 1931. Hughes also traveled to the USSR in 1932, where he spent a year having been invited to make a film about American race relations with a group of other young African Americans; to China and Japan in 1932; and to Barcelona in 1937, where he worked as a newspaper correspondent during the Spanish Civil War. Although Hughes—unlike C. L. R. James—has not been primarily associated with the international contexts of the radical Left, Pan-Africanism, and the struggles of the 1930s against colonialism, capitalism, racism, and fascism, his art from early on in his career was wedded to his understanding of the need for a global and radical political struggle.

Hughes's self-presentation, as well as his critics, may have something to do with this misconception. For example, it is difficult to get a sense of the depth of Hughes's political convictions from his autobiography, *I Wonder as I Wander*. In that text, the critic Arnold Rampersad has observed:

> Hughes is by no mean completely candid or detailed about his politics. He makes no mention of hard-hitting essays dispatched from Cuba and Haiti to the radical magazine *New Masses* in 1931. He cites not a line of the powerful, almost incendiary poems he wrote in the Soviet Union. Much of his time in the fall of 1933 . . . was devoted . . . to the activities of the local branch of the John Reed Club, the arts and literary organization founded by the Communist Party [but] virtually nothing of this appears in *I Wonder as I Wander*.[7]

This chapter, however, through reading Hughes's Haitian works, the play *Emperor of Haiti* and the opera *Troubled Island*, asserts that there is a need to relocate Hughes in a more politically and historically contextualized space, in which Hughes's undoubted cosmopolitan tastes do not impinge on his sympathies for Pan-Africanism. An analysis of Hughes's writings on Haiti, following on from the analysis of Césaire and James in the previous chapter, thus enables us to deepen our understanding of the relationship between 1930s political radicalism and the event of the Haitian Revolution.

The Context of Hughes's Engagement with Haiti

Critical opinion has, broadly speaking, agreed that one of the weaker areas of the Harlem Renaissance's artistic and cultural achievement was in the genre of drama.[8] Langston Hughes's works, however, break with this general pattern. His lifelong commitment to writing for the theater and other performance arts yielded more than forty dramas: folk comedies, melodramas, historical plays, works of radical didacticism, satirical sketches, gospel song-plays, and operas among them. The Haitian Revolution provided Hughes with the material for two of these projects: the 1936 play published and performed as both *Emperor of Haiti* and *Troubled Island*, sketches for which were written during Hughes's six-month stay in Haiti in 1931, and the libretto for the opera *Troubled Island,* which was based on the earlier play and was nearly ready for performance by 1938. Hughes's works for the stage reflect his long-term commitment to represent African Americans, as well as Afro-Caribbeans and Afro-Latinos, in a public forum with complexity and self-knowledge. Furthermore, Hughes's Haitian works in particular reveal a desire to communicate an important message of the possibility of black liberation to an African American audience, precisely as James was doing at the same time, and as Césaire would do somewhat later. Hughes's Haitian works reveal Hughes to be a Pan-Africanist in the sense that they are notable expressions of the interconnectedness of transnational contemporary and historical black experience.

Hughes's interest in Haiti had been long-standing: from childhood he read everything he could find on Haiti.[9] But Hughes's firsthand experiences of Haiti begin in 1931, which he recorded in his second autobiography, *I Wonder as I Wander.* There, Hughes explained that his journey to Haiti was the result of his desire to begin a career as a serious writer on the subjects of black culture and history.[10] Hughes's early sense of the interconnectedness of Haitian and African American history, and his determination to communicate this, appear to have been affirmed by his knowledge of his own family history in Haiti, which Hughes gained from his grandmother. The voyage to Haiti was thus for Hughes "a dream fulfilled," since from his childhood he had listened to stories of Haiti's legendary history.[11] The black Haitian generals of the revolution "remained Hughes's heroes even as an adult," and Hughes was "especially proud that his own great-uncle, John Mercer Langston, had twice served in an independent Haiti as American consul general during the nineteenth century."[12]

However, once in Haiti, Hughes found himself appalled at both the material realities that black Haitians faced and the actions of the occupying U.S. Marines. All the same, he was proud of the dignity with which everyday Haitians composed themselves in the face of poverty and occupation. Hughes found himself in a nation, "poor and black," that was "quietly recharging his political and racial zeal."[13] Of paramount importance to the sharpening of Hughes's critical understanding of contemporary Haitian culture and society was his meeting with Jacques Roumain, the prominent Haitian writer and communist in Cap Haitien. It was a significant meeting from a creative and intellectual point of view, and particularly for its role in intensifying Hughes's rage at the treatment of Haiti's black peasantry at the hands of a mulatto elite. This opinion is strongly reflected in the articles that he wrote on Haiti for the radical African American journals *New Masses*, the *Crisis*, and the *Messenger*, as well as in the representation of mulattoes in both *Emperor of Haiti* and *Troubled Island*.

It was thus with an uncanny similarity to Césaire's representations of Haitians standing upright and tall, and to their status as the forebears of négritude, that Hughes's first published writings about Haiti emphasized the dignity and the blackness of the Haitian peasantry: "People strong, midnight black. Proud women whose heads bear burdens, whose backs are very straight."[14] Hughes's sharp perceptions also yielded stinging condemnation of the manner in which Haiti's black peasantry was exploited by the urban elite of Port-au-Prince.[15] And in a later report, Hughes wrote that it was in Haiti that he first came to understand how "class lines may cut across color lines within a race, and how dark people of the same nationality may scorn those below them."[16]

Hughes's politics were maturing rapidly in the course of his trip to Haiti, but the development of Hughes's identification with Haiti and Haitian history must be placed in a wider context than his personal travels. Hughes's writings on Haiti serve as a case study through which to examine the significance of Haiti and the Haitian Revolution to the Pan-African movement and the international Left in the 1930s.

The rehabilition of the cultural and political currency of Haiti and the Haitian Revolution among African Americans played a key role in the formation of a radical black Atlantic discourse in the 1930s. The Harlem Renaissance writer and early civil rights activist James Weldon Johnson provides an early example of this development: Johnson, who had been in Haiti investigating conditions under the U.S. occupation, brought Henri Christophe to the attention of African Americans in 1920, when, at a meeting of the NAACP, he called on African Americans to reflect on their own negative views of Haiti and Christophe: "We, too, have been snobs—laughing at Haiti because we knew no better—simply taking as true the lies that have been told about her. . . . How many of us have not laughed at Christophe's court?"[17] As Césaire would do later in his 1963 play *La tragédie du roi Christophe*, Johnson countered ridicule with an alternative view of Christophe as a powerful black leader. The example of Haiti enabled a revalorization of black history and an assertation of race pride, and these were to become defining features of the radical black Atlantic dialogue of the 1930s that was formed by négritude and the Harlem Renaissance.

However, although Hughes's Haitian works in the 1930s can be seen as following on the path initiated by Johnson in 1920, the U.S. and international contexts in which African American writers such as Hughes turned to Haiti had changed dramatically by the time Hughes sent his reports for the *Crisis* from Haiti in 1931 and the publication of *Emperor of Haiti* in 1936. The way in which African Americans perceived Haiti in the 1930s was marked not only by the development of the Pan-African and radical Left movements and the U.S. Marines' occupation of Haiti, but also by their rising political and economic expectations, which had been fostered by the New Deal. These factors combined to prompt African Americans to see in Haitian history not just an iconic expression of racial pride, but also the real possibility of revolutionary change.[18]

Thus, Hughes's trip to Haiti provided him with a firsthand appreciation of the diversity of black history and culture in the Americas and served as a catalyst for his growing appreciation of Haiti's historical and ideological significance to Pan-Africanism and the movements of the radical Left in the United States and internationally. Much of his writing about Haiti reveals a desire to dissolve linguistic and cultural barriers, to speak of Haitians as brothers and sisters, and to substantiate a radical racial and political solidarity with Haiti's black peasantry. This political desire underpins both *Emperor of Haiti* and *Troubled Island* as efforts to communicate the heritage of the Haitian Revolution to African Americans, and in telling the story of the Haitian Revolution, to make it stand as a metonym for black agency in the context of a black Atlantic modernity.

Once in Haiti, Hughes's first objective was to see Christophe's Citadel at Cap Haitien, which he had described in advance of his visit as a "great relic of Negro pride."[19] Hughes visited the Citadel three times in all and wrote with wondrous appreciation of its beauty, noting that it stands as a defiant landmark of black achievement, although he was all too well aware of the human sacrifices involved in its building. These sacrifices are the other, darker aspects of the Citadel's story. The widespread conscription and the high mortality rate of workers during the construction of the Citadel are the difficult historical facts that prevent any blind celebration of the Citadel as a monument to black freedom in Haiti.

In *Popo and Fifina*, a short story for children about a Haitian family written by Hughes in collaboration with Arna Bontemps, this problem is carefully negotiated. The human suffering that the building of the Citadel required is not hidden away, yet the building is still recalled as a great achievement. The eponymous characters Popo and Fifina are young Haitian children, a brother and sister whose family leaves their home in the hills to live in the town of Cap Haitien. While the young Popo is working with his cousin as an apprentice carpenter and wood carver for his uncle, the great stories of the Haitian Revolution, and the construction of the Citadel, are relayed to him.[20] With an eloquent simplicity reminiscent of a fairy tale or a fable, *Popo and Fifina* recuperates aspects of Haiti's heroic history in a style that is particularly appropriate for children. Popo's growing consciousness of Haitian history and his own relationship to it serves as a guide for the reader, mirroring the development of the reader's own awareness of Haitian history. Thus in reading *Popo and Fifina* as a didactic text, the ruined Citadel functions as a tangible relic through which to imaginatively access the achievements of the Haitian Revolution, as well as the sacrifices the revolution demanded.

The ruins at Sans Souci also figure prominently in Hughes's journalistic articles about Haiti: in his article "People without Shoes," originally published in the *Crisis*, Hughes described the ruined Citadel as "one of the lustiest ruins in the world."[21] And in another article, the ruins provide a dramatic means through which to compare the Haiti Hughes visited in 1931 with the land that he had heard so much about as a child. Finding the mythical first black republic suffering under the illegal occupation of U.S. Marines and American gunboat imperialism, Hughes was at pains to emphasize that the black people of Haiti had "freed their land from slavery and began to work out their own national destinies a full half-century before American Negroes were freed by the Civil War."[22] Hughes drew attention not only to the glorious achievement of the winning of independence, but also to the building of a new country complete with the infrastructure required by a modern nation-state—roads, schools, factories, mills, and a system of law. Thus for Hughes, Christophe's Citadel was far from a vanity project, but an audacious monument in stone to these achievements of which Haitians should be proud: "That Citadel today, standing in lonely majesty against the clouds twenty miles from the city of Cap Haitien, is still one of the wonders of the New World, and one of the most amazing structures ever built by man."[23] No matter for which audience Hughes was writing, the Citadel at Sans Soucci figured prominently. For Hughes they recalled the success of the revolution, signaled the importance of the reign of Christophe, and made clear to the reader that the paternalism of the U.S. occupation of Haiti was an affront to the independence, dignity, and achievements of Haitians, and indeed to Africans throughout the diaspora. The Haitian Revolutionary period also immediately appeared to Hughes to hold tremendous potential as the material for a stage play. In the life of Dessalines, Hughes perceived all the elements of a tragic drama, and in the summer of 1931 Hughes begain writing about Dessalines.

The Haitian Revolution as Drama: *Emperor of Haiti*

Emperor of Haiti premiered at the Karamu Theatre in New York on November 18, 1936, although the play was not published in Hughes's lifetime and was only professionally performed eight times. When, in 1936, Hughes was approached by the African American composer William Grant Still with the offer of collaborating on an opera based on the events of the Haitian Revolution, Hughes, who was eager for his play to reach a wider audience, accepted, and the play would become the framework for the libretto to the opera *Troubled Island*. However, commercially the opera fared little better in terms of its performance history, and it received only three performances.

Despite their commercial failures, both the play and the opera are noteworthy as original recuperations of the Haitian Revolution that reveal a politically radical Hughes. The bloody events of the revolution itself are absent from both scripts: as act 1 draws to a close, the colony is on the eve of insurrection, and at the opening of act 2 we enter the new independent Haiti; the war of independence is banished to an interim. Both the play and opera depart from the historical record in order to provide a single hero who leads the slaves of Saint Domingue from the beginning of the revolution through to independence, whereupon he assumes the title and position of "Emperor." Hughes chose Dessalines for this role, cutting Toussaint out of the narrative, and almost completely excising the early revolutionary leaders Makandal, Boukman, and Biassou from his play's version of events. The other major players in the revolution's leadership, notably Henri Christophe and Moïse, are also erased. Thus, in both the play and the opera, Dessalines is used not so much as a representation of a historical individual, but rather as a composite character. The Dessalines of the play's first act invokes Makandal and later resembles the rebel slave Boukman, who at the infamous Bois Caiman vodou ceremony commanded a crowd of gathered slaves ready for rebellion to rise up and attack their masters. Certain aspects of the Dessalines character in the second act, however, seem to be based on Toussaint Louverture, especially the scenes in which Dessalines is engaged in thoughtful discussion with his chief counsellor, the elderly Martel, on matters of postindependence rule, the enduring frictions of race and class in independent Haiti, as well as matters of administration and government.

In making Dessalines a composite, symbolic character,who represents a greater breadth of opinions and positions than the real-life Dessalines ever could have done, Hughes both gains and loses certain dramatic possibilities. Hughes forgoes the possibility of creating dramatic tension through the representation of the conflicting positions and opinions of the various players at the command of the revolution. By replacing Makandal, Biassou, Boukman, Toussaint, Moïse, and Christophe with an amalgamated representative character, the play erases the divisions and infighting that was present in the revolution's vanguard. Whether this erasure of internal conflict signifies a romanticized simplification of black liberation in Haiti or a necessary artistic culling of historical events is a moot point. But it should be noted that the play does gain a single tragic hero, a tragic protagonist who lends the complexly twisting and turning narrative of the Haitian Revolution and its many factions greater coherence as a working piece of drama.

The play is also made accessible for its intended audience by Hughes's use of an African American vernacular in order to represent the language of the majority of Saint Domingue's slaves, thereby emphasizing the sense of solidarity that the play intended to inspire.[24] However, one of the play's key characters, the African-born slave Martel, who becomes Dessalines's most important advisor and counsel, is notable for his affected speech. His lines are accorded grandeur, wisdom, and knowledge that Dessalines, in the first act at least, conspicuously lacks. Martel is frequently addressed as "Father Martel" and calls others "Son" throughout the play, indicating his position of moral and political superiority. However, although the elevated style of Martel's speech is intended to indicate a deep wisdom associated with Africa, often expressed through sensitivity to nature, the language is only rarely adequate to the theme:

> Africa! So long, so far away! But tonight the moon weeps tears of joy, son, for Africa. And when in its next passage across the sea, it shines on our sweet motherland, it'll smile and say, "Thy black children in Haiti have thrown off the yoke of bondage, and are men again!" Josef, my children grew up slaves. My grandchildren, too . . . but yours will be free![25]

Despite the clichéd language, which recalls James's failed attempt at the theatrical recuperation of 1804, Martel's melancholy recollection of Africa highlights the significance of memory and the impossibility of making of the slave populations of the Americas a tabula rasa. Africa is evoked as a painfully distant memory, an emotive myth, and as an exemplar of freedom and happiness, contrary to the notion of Africa as a savage or barbarous land.

From the start, the play gives prominence to vodou in its representation of the outbreak of the revolution, making it clear that as an organizational tool and as a means of communicating a spirit of insurrection, vodou was indispensable to the revolution's success. The first scene represents a clandestine meeting of slaves in an abandoned sugar mill, and Dessalines's absence is explained by his attendance at a nearby vodou meeting. The play begins *in medias res* with the plans for the insurrection already laid, weapons being smuggled, and spies and revolutionaries giving each other coded signals that indicate the highly organized and meticulously planned nature of the resistance.

The theme of civilization versus barbarism reverberates throughout the play—especially through the representation of the opposition of vodou and court life in Haiti under Dessalines. The powers of vodou, and especially vodou drums, are intimately linked to insurrection and to freedom, and Martel speaks with great anticipation of "the great drum" that the rebel slave Boukman will play to initiate the thunderous call "to rise and seek freedom."[26] However, Hughes demonstrates that Haiti's revolutionary leadership was dependent on vodou yet hesitated to embrace it unreservedly for fear of seeming uncivilized. As the play progresses, Dessalines's court, under the influence of his treacherous mulatto consort, Claire, becomes more and more resistant to vodou, regarding it as barbarous. In its stead, the court begins to ape French culture, customs, and politics, and this is paralleled by Dessalines's rejection of his African wife in favor of the mulatto Claire. Thus perceived, the play contains a critique of the black/mulatto class divide about which Hughes had so powerfully written previously in his journalism. However, it is a problematic critique since Dessalines's wife, Azelia, and Claire are depicted in such stereotypical terms. Azelia is presented as saintly, loving, and wholly good, although she is fearful of what the revolution may mean for her relationship with her husband. In the first act, we see Azelia emotionally and intellectually setting up what she sees as her husband's revolutionary determination and her valuation of the importance of their marriage as opposing forces, thus foreshadowing the fate of their relationship.

Claire's characterization, on the other hand, conforms to the stereotype of the exotic female mulatto: she is frivolous, deceitful, and enamored with Parisian culture. Moreover, her duplicity is presented as being a characteristically mulatto trait. Although a lack of emotional depth is apparent in all of the play's characters, in the case of Claire it is particularly pointed. Alone with her lover and fellow conspirator, the mulatto Vuval, who is Dessalines's secretary, Claire reveals her true feelings as the two discuss their plans to overthrow Dessalines and flee to Paris: "That fool, my husband? Vuval, darling, often I can't bear to look at him. He's so common and so—so boorish! And his back! *(With a little cry)* I cannot bear to touch his back! It's all covered with welts! Ugh! Marks of a rebellious slave! And yet he thinks I love him! Bah!"[27] Dessalines's rejection of Azelia and his lust for Claire is used as a device to illustrate how he would ultimately lose contact with the culture and values of his own people. Dessalines's relationship with Claire also becomes a source of comic drama as it becomes the subject of street gossip: Claire is referred to as the emperor's "hussy of a new wife," described as being bejeweled with diamonds, and having charmed Dessalines to the point of blindness: "Baron Congo's crazy about her."[28]

Although Hughes's play generally attends quite carefully to the historical record, the play fails to convey the complex conflicts present in revolutionary Saint Domingue and Haiti. This is evident in its simplification of the unstable class and race tensions that existed between the *grands* and *petits blancs*, between the mulatto class and the blacks—represented in the stories of Azelia and Claire—as well as within the black slave population divided between the Creole black slaves and the African-born black slave population. However, some critics, recognizing the daunting task facing the artist attempting to represent such a complex sociopolitical history on the stage, have suggested that the play is deserving of qualified praise for its attempt to convey, even in a simplified form, the sociopolitical divisions that threatened to tear the fledgling state apart. Thus, for example, while recognizing that the play is clearly not epic enough in scope or range to treat the issue fully, the critic Errol Hill has noted that Dessalines's relationships with Azeila and Claire do serve to offer a window onto Haiti's social and racial fractures, giving us glimpses of the Haiti that Dessalines was to inherit, "one deeply rent with psychological, racial, and social scars." [29]

Ultimately, the play attributes Dessalines's fall to his failure to overcome these divisions and to unite Haiti. The play shows, with affecting tragic irony, that the more Dessalines adopts the customs and culture of the mulatto elite in his court, the more he becomes the subject of mockery, though Dessalines remains blind to this as well as to the consequences of his dismissal of popular black culture to the last. The play also communicates a great deal of historical information in narrating Dessalines's demise. As it becomes clear that Dessalines is neither an administrator nor a statesman, the play recalls Toussaint Louverture's abilities in contrast to Dessalines's limitations, as one of Dessalines's court counselors, Popo, remarks: "I wish Toussaint was here. It looks like Jean Jacques don't know how to run things very well. I wish I could help him."[30]

The play also communicates Dessalines's increasing political isolation, demonstrating that his failed attempts to woo the mulatto elite served only to alienate him from the black peasantry, hastening the loss of the bedrock of his political support, and provoking vodou priests to stir up the peasants against him.[31] Attributing Dessalines's betrayal of the black peasantry to his belief that his nation's black and "savage" culture was an impediment to progress, *Emperor of Haiti* presents a tragic hero estranged from his people, as James's *Black Jacobins* also does. But whereas James attributes Toussaint's estrangement to his respect for Enlightenment thinking, Hughes's Dessalines is estranged from the Haitian people as a consequence of his eschewal of Haitian peasant and folk culture. Whereas James's Toussaint was drawn to the culture of European Enlightenment as in it he saw the highest stage of civilization he could imagine, Dessalines failed to distinguish between the frivolities of a decadent culture and the values of a truly enlightened civilization. In Hughes's hands as a dramatist, this accentuates his tragic potential: Dessalines's failings and his poor decision making as a political leader become the noble failures of a man striving to do good, but, having been deprived by his upbringing as a slave of the requisite capacities and skills, finding himself unequal to the task. Thus, Hughes's play shows us how, under Dessalines's leadership, the revolution was arrested at the bourgeois stage as it began to repress the peasantry. With vodou outlawed, one character laments that independence did not bring liberation to the people: "Well, if we can't be Duchesses, we at least ought to be let alone to dance obeah if we wants to, and have our voodoo here in the Court."[32]

Although in *vodou* Hughes saw great theatrical potential, and the play contains one instance of *vodou* being put to dynamic dramatic purpose, the representation of vodou dance is the catalyst to a crisis. Claire, referred to now as "The Empress," is appalled and terrified by the vodou drums, and on her appealing to Dessalines, he orders that they be silenced. His ensuing rage signifies a crisis of national identity symbolized in their rejection: "Drums in the Court! The idea! Suppose we had guests from abroad, what would they think of us? They'd think we were all savages, that's what. Savages! Here I am, trying to build a civilization in Haiti good as any the whites have in their lands. Trying to set up a Court equal to any Court in Europe. And what do I find—voodoo drums in the banquet hall!"[33]

Dessalines's rage signifies that not only has he internalized colonial prejudices, but also that he has reached the limit of his capabilities as a political leader. His crack-up, like Henri Christophe's breakdown and suicide as represented in Aimé Césaire's *La tragédie du roi Christophe*, is indicative of a postrebellion society in the midst of a crisis of identity and direction. Dessalines's recourse to martial law in order to put the population to work against their will amounts to the failure of Haiti's first postindependence government. Furthermore, Dessalines's limited self-knowledge is not enough to rescue the situation, as his words to Claire reveal he does not see the inevitable rising tide of opposition to his increasingly despotic governance or the limits to his style of governance: "Oh, I know I'm nothing much but a fighter. . . . But if fighting's the only way to get things done—then I'll get 'em done!"[34] Nor does Dessalines foresee that the mulatto elite will not tolerate the leadership of someone whom they regard as "a black monster" for much longer. The play shows us the inevitability of Dessalines's fate, to be murdered by a mulatto elite fearful for their own prospects in a "Black Republic." As such, Dessalines's demise as a tragic-heroic black leader is both a compelling drama and a significant rehabilitation of Dessalines that does not conform to what were the widely held contemporary negative views among the international and African American communities.[35] Outside Haiti, Dessalines has mostly been regarded as beyond the pale of celebration, being either reviled or ignored, and it is telling that not a single English-language biography of Dessalines has been published. However, Deborah Jenson's recent work *Beyond the Slave Narrative: Politics, Sex, and Manuscripts in the Haitian Revolution* completely revises the way in which Dessalines must now be seen and helps us to discern the radicalism of Hughes's presentation of his subject. Convincingly making the case that Dessalines must be regarded as one of a chain of radical black Atlantic figures that includes Frederick Douglass, Aimé Césaire, Frantz Fanon, and Malcolm X, and that together these figures form a specific ensemble of radical African diasporic thinkers, Jenson argues that Jean-Jacques Dessalines's independence proclamations are "manifestoes of postcolonial freedom" and that his letters constitute "an overlooked dialogic foundation in a longer chain of radical African diasporan thinkers."[36] It is highly significant to this project that positioning Dessalines within a constellation of radical black Atlantic thinkers and actors is precisely the approach that René Depestre adopted in his presentation of Dessalines in his epic poem *Un-arc-en-ciel pour l'occident chrétien*, which is discussed in the next chapter.

Thus, Hughes's choice of Dessalines rather than Toussaint as tragic protagonist is revealing of the play's rehabilitation of the Haitian Revolution as a popular uprising and an important recuperation of Dessalines's character against the grain of a long history of denigration. However, inside Haiti the rehabilitation of Dessalines can be traced to early in the nineteenth century, where it took on two distinct forms. Haiti's black peasantry had begun to mythologize Dessalines by incorporating him into the pantheon of vodou *lwas,* where he became "Ogou Desalin." This process, discussed in detail by Joan Dayan and Michael Largey, was also highly significant to René Depestre's representation of Dessalines as a black liberator in his epic vodou mystery poem *Un-arc-en-ciel pour l'occident chrétien.*[37] For Haiti's peasantry, the two most important aspects of Dessalines's biography were his greatness as a soldier and his gruesome death at the hands of the mulatto elite, a contradictory memorialization that, as Largey explains, "fused two compelling and contradictory images:

the powerful general who protected the Haitian state from invasion and the dismembered corpse torn asunder by his enemies."[38] Haiti's intellectual and political classes, however, took a little longer to recall Dessalines as heroic, and when they eventually did so, they chose to remember a rather different Dessalines, one with whose qualities of bravery, courage, and ambition they associated themselves.[39]

Internationally, examining the evolution of representations of Dessalines tells a rather different story and reveals a very different set of perspectives and prejudices. White historiography of the Haitian Revolution throughout the nineteenth and even into the twentieth century traditionally favored the more diplomatic, literate Toussaint, and frequently emphasized his mercy in contrast to the more "barbarous" Dessalines, who, outside Haiti, remained most infamous for having ordered the extermination of all the whites who remained in Haiti early in 1805. C. L. R. James was one of the first non-Haitians to confront what had become a powerful, and sordidly racist, misrepresentation of Dessalines by examining this most notorious episode in the Haitian Revolution in full and with characteristic aplomb: "Early in the new year, 1805, the whites in Haiti were massacred by the orders of Dessalines. All histories are full of this. A representative of the British Government once threw it in the face of the Haitian delegate at a meeting of the League of Nations. He would have been more cautious if he had known the part his own highly civilized country played in this supposedly typical example of black savagery."[40] In a typically committed, but suave, narrative style, James rebuked the racist myth of Dessalines "the black butcher" by carefully analyzing the background to Haiti's race war and Dessalines's orders to the black population to massacre the whites. James persuasively concluded that the fate of Haiti's white population had been sealed "due not so much to the justified hate of the blacks but the calculated savagery of imperialism."[41] James's analysis on this matter illustrates that, first, General Leclerc had already resolved on a war of extermination that began with the deliberate drowning of more than one thousand blacks in Le Cap harbor as a means of ending the Saint Domingue crisis. Second, James pointed out that Leclerc's successor, General Rochambeau, attempted to finish the job by attempting to exterminate not just all the blacks but the mulattoes as well. And third, James argued that Dessalines's attitude to Saint Domingue's whites remained moderate. James noted that Dessalines even invited the white émigrés, who could see Rochambeau's mission to bring the colony back under French control failing, to return to their former properties. Finally, and crucially,

James highlighted the presence of three Englishmen at the meeting of the Haitian Congress of December 1804. At that meeting, the Englishmen—dubbed "these civilized cannibals" by James—offered Dessalines the promise of British diplomatic recognition, military protection of Haiti's independence, and trade in return for the extermination of all the remaining whites still living in Haiti in order "to drive a wedge between Haiti and France."[42] That the massacres only took place months after the issuing of the proclamation, when Dessalines felt that Haiti's independence was threatened once more by the French military, has also been swept under the carpet.[43]

Thus although James explicitly condemned the 1805 massacre as unnecessary "vengeance," though without the racist denigration of previous authors, he defended Dessalines's total war as justified by its conceptual grounding in the fight for radical antislavery. For James, Dessalines's massacre formed a strict corollary with the senseless, unthinking, and reflexive vengeance of the slaves in his description of the initial uprising of 1791. Hughes's play and libretto should be considered remarkable for the creation of a Dessalines who is really an amalgam of Toussaint, Dessalines, and Christophe, a figure of uncompromised black national identity and his literary elevation as a tragic protagonist. Writing on *Troubled Island* in conjunction with another African American opera about Haiti entitled *Ouanga* by the composer Clarence Cameron White and the librettist John Frederick Matheus, Michael Largey contends:

> By choosing a dramatic subject [Dessalines] whose reputation as a fierce defender of black sovereignty pitted him against the white oppressor, Matheus and Hughes positioned their respective libretti as alternatives to the narrative of Louverture's tragic legacy. Dessalines, whose revolutionary battle cry was "koupe tèt, boule kay" (cut heads and burn houses), invoked the idea of black national identity without assuaging white audiences.[44]

Thus, in *Emperor of Haiti*, when Dessalines is questioned on the necessity of the brutality of the revolution, he justifies it with a frank assessment of the Manichaean reality of the situation for Saint Domnigue's slaves on the eve of the outbreak of the revolution by recalling to memory the fate of the heroic maroon Makandal: "They burned Mackandal for trying to be free, didn't they? They had no mercy on him. We'll show no mercy on them now."[45] The memory of Makandal's burning at the stake affirms for Dessalines the brutal reality of the situation in Haiti and the impossibility of bloodless revolution:

MARTEL: I'd let them live, if they'd leave us free.

DESSALINES: They won't, so there's no *if* about it. We have no choice but to kill . . . wipe out the whites in all this island . . . for if the French are left alive to force us back to slavery, we'll never get a chance to rise again. And for us, you and me . . . there'd be only the rack, the wheel, or burning at the stake like Mackandal.[46]

No mention of Makandal's mythical "escape" is made by Dessalines, although Martel invokes his spirit. Hughes's recuperation of Dessalines's political judgment is thus very different from James's critique of Dessalines: Hughes's Dessalines offers a principled statement of the necessity of defensive violence which is quite convincing given the very real and compelling threat of the reconquest of Haiti and the reimposition of slavery at various moments up through 1848.

Dessalines's political vision is thus rooted in the brutal realities of Saint Domingue's slave society, and not in its mythologies or the mysteries of vodou.[47] Nor does the play hide that, unlike Toussaint and Christophe, Dessalines could not read or write. In its representation of the fall of a brave and committed but tragically flawed black liberator and leader, *Emperor of Haiti* should be considered a prescient and significant attempt to secure and rehabilitate Dessalines's place in black history, making it clear to an African American audience that accepting the prevailing opinion of Dessalines as a butcher and an embarrassment could no longer be accepted. Thus the play rehabilitates Dessalines's identity as a black liberator in tragic terms, while avoiding hagiographic treatment.

The Haitian Revolution as Opera: *Troubled Island*

The critics have not been kind to *Troubled Island*; one contemporary review concluded that the opera was a "turgid, confused mishap."[48] Certainly the opera's turbulent genesis cannot have helped matters: with Hughes spending so much time outside the United States at critical moments during the opera's making, William Grant Still and Hughes had insurmountable problems of communication that, along with artistic differences, would cause them to break off their partnership before the opera was completed.[49] Furthermore, critics have found that Hughes and Grant Still's artistic differences are visible in the disparities between the opera's libretto and the opera's music. Michael Largey has observed that whereas Hughes's libretto clearly reflects his "antipathy for the upper-classes of Haitian society, the opera's music was less concerned with reinforcing the message of class conflict."[50] The opera's music is reminiscent of symphonic Hollywood mood music of the period, and it does not consistently find a suitable idiom to complement Hughes's highly charged libretto.[51] Furthermore, Grant Still, being unable to discover any authentically Haitian musical material in the United States, resorted to using two Haitian musical themes that he obtained from a former U.S. Marine officer who had served in Haiti during the occupation. The first of these, a vodou theme, was greatly altered and used in the opera's first act, and the second, a merengue, was used in the last act. For the rest of the opera's musical score, Grant Still attempted to create his own musical language through which to represent Haiti. And as if all this were not problematic enough, the U.S. Marine who provided Grant Still with musical material, John Houston Craige, went on to write two crude and sensationalist books, *Black Baghdad* and *Cannibal Cousins,* that "cast Haiti as a place where tropical heat, isolation, and sexually loose women posed a threat to American troops."[52] Thus, equipped with only one highly dubious source of Haitian music and musicological advice and having never visited Haiti himself, Grant Still found himself in a situation wherein he needed to invent rather than represent but with no grounding in the real.

Troubled Island begins at the same moment in time as the play but with a slightly different thematic emphasis. The opera's stage directions are far more emotive than the play's and reveal a more ambitious project. The opera, like the play, opens under the cover of nightfall, a night which is "ominous, throbbing with a power long suppressed, full of strange portent" as a mother's voice sings "calm and clear" of how the bond between mother and child is broken by slavery and of how a flame "will sweep / Our slavery away!"[53] Thus the beginning of the opera with its representation of how slavery undermined the strength of family bonds, strikes a deeply personal and not a high political note.

As in the play, the character Martel is used to articulate the memory of Africa with deep melancholy and as a lost utopia "far, far away," although the opera's music lacks much in the way of African elements, and indeed sounds very European. Martel's words, however, do convey a sense of Africa as a grand and civilized land, although the clichés that marred his speech in the play were not excised from the libretto:

Africa!
I remember Africa!

A black man's land where,
Tall and proud,
Black kings and chiefs held sway!
Well do I remember Africa!
Well do I remember, too,
That most unlucky day
The slavers came,
Stole me away.[54]

The opera does, however, strive to represent Haitian vodou as a cultural repository of Dionysian power, and in the first act a vodou dance signifies the imminence of the uprising, although in performance the dance can have hardly been any more authentic than Grant Still's "voodoo" music. It is here that the opera misses Hughes's influence: Hughes had observed vodou ceremonies during his trip to Haiti, whereas Grant Still had no firsthand knowledge of the physical, visual, and oral elements of vodou. But, with Hughes and Grant Still estranged by the time of production, Hughes was not at hand to provide Grant Still with his local knowledge. Nonetheless, drums are used in an attempt to portray the ferocious power of vodou as a band of slaves chant the names of various vodou gods before Dessalines makes a dramatic entrance into the scene and plays the role that was historically fulfilled by Boukman, inciting the slaves to revolt:

Our time has come!
Over all Haiti now the time has come
To give the signal, sound the great drum–
. . . .
Give out the weapons!
Men, away!
Slaves to the hills!
Arise! Follow me!
Strike to be free![55]

Following the play's script very closely, the opera narrates the story of Dessalines's betrayal and demise, although there is a tension in the opera that does not exist in the play, due to a collision of form and content. In the elevated artistic form of opera, *Troubled Island* can be read even more clearly as a product of an African American perception of Haiti than the play *Emperor of Haiti* can be, although both texts must be seen in the context of the changing perception of Haiti in the African

American diaspora. Lacking authentic materials and local knowledge, the libretto also cannot attempt to convey the language of the Haitian slaves and peasantry through the use of an African American vernacular as Hughes did with the play. Yet the opera can still be regarded as what Largey has termed "diasporic cosmopolitanism," primarily valuable as a text now for its ability to tell us about the cultural currency of Haiti's history of anticolonialism within radical African American circles.[56] Both texts can be seen as attempts to rethink and to renegotiate diasporic relationships to Haiti, and to rehabilitate Dessalines's reputation and standing as a great black political and military figure, worthy of a place on the international stage alongside Toussaint Louverture. As such, both *Troubled Island* and *The Emperor of Haiti* are important fictional reinterpretations of the achievement of Haitian independence, and through their representation of Dessalines's tragic fall, they carry a powerful message of an unfinished revolution, and the ongoing need to remain unreconciled to the many and varied debilitating legacies of slavery, while also celebrating black historical achievement in the Americas, and throughout the diaspora.

3 Return to Négritude

The Haitian Revolution and René Depestre's *Un arc-en-ciel pour l'occident chrétien*

> This victorious revolution of slaves . . . was in itself an act of civilization which showed the entire world that human liberty and human dignity also has a black face. It released into universal history the personality of the black man, and permitted him to travel through a liberating social experience, to achieve a new perception of himself.
>
> —René Depestre, "Les métamorphoses de la négritude en Amerique"

René Depestre, one of Haiti's most renowned men of letters, belonged to a second generation of négritude poets, and although he was also a novelist and essayist, it is on his poetry that his international literary reputation rests. This chapter is concerned with his book-length radical poem *Un arc-en-ciel pour l'occident chrétien* (*A Rainbow for the Christian West*) in order to analyze the means by which its recuperation of the Haitian Revolution articulates a poetics of radical liberation. At the outset it is necessary to note that Despestre's radical political position as set out in *Un arc-en-ciel* has not endured: his renunciation of négritude was confirmed in 1980 with the publication of *Bonjour et adieu à la négritude*.[1] At that moment, Depestre also dispensed with the "worn out," "outmoded" concepts of the Third World, revolution, nationalism, and the oppressed, justifying his move by claiming that, "when a concept dies, when a concept goes mad, you must mistrust it and look for other kinds of explication."[2] However, when he was asked in 1990 which of all of his books of poetry he believed to be his most accomplished, Depestre stated that the one book that he would hold onto would be *Un arc-en-ciel pour l'occident chrétien*, a poem written when he was still one of négritude's most original exponents.[3]

Given Depestre's politics at the time of the interview, it is a remarkable choice for him to have made. *Un arc-en-ciel* was first published by Présence Africaine in 1967 at the zenith of Depestre's belief in revolution and at the midpoint of his residency in Cuba. It is a poem that displays a bold commitment to those same concepts that Depestre would later so publicly renounce. It is remarkable on many grounds: it is an ingenious work, lyrical, bold, comic, sexual, and its aesthetic radicalism is inseparable from its political radicalism, thus enabling us to examine closely the relationship between form and content, poetry and revolution. *Un arc-en-ciel* is also Depestre's poetic work that best evokes his native and African heritage, and its poetic voice is articulated in a language that marries surrealism to social commitment. It thus marked a new beginning for Depestre, who had earlier been committed to the aesthetics of Louis Aragon, spokesperson for the orthodox communist writers of the 1950s, who championed socialist realism and a return to nationalist literary traditions in order to unite poetry and the people. Depestre's earlier decision to align himself with Aragon and his followers had prompted the following gentle, but ironic, rebuke from Césaire in his 1955 poem "Le verbe Marronner / à René Depestre, poète haïtien" ("The Verb 'Marronner' / for René Depestre, Haitian Poet"):

Camarade Depestre
C'est un problème assurément trés grave
des rapports de la poésie et de la Révolution
le fond conditionne la forme

(Comrade Depestre
It is undoubtedly a very serious problem
the relation between poetry and Revolution
the content determines the form)[4]

Un arc-en-ciel demonstrates that not only had Depestre withdrawn his commitment to socialist realism by 1967, but also that he had found his own way to reconcile the problem of "forme et fond"—form and content—and in this, vodou and the inheritence of the Haitian Revolution were to play critical roles.

In *Un arc-en-ciel*, the vodou gods descend upon the American South in the form of the black militant poet who arrives to take his vengeance upon the "Christian West" and to expose its dark underbelly. The poem hinges upon the union of the spiritual and the material, and its evocation of the revolutionary in both is mediated through vodou. The power of this duality can perhaps be best explained by Depestre himself: "The beliefs of my youth, especially vodoun, coincided with my experiences as a revolutionary in Cuba. [In *Un arc-en-ciel*] I tried again to find the meaning of vodoun, which was revolutionary in origin."[5]

In making vodou the vehicle of the poem's revolutionary message, it also becomes a link between the Haitian and Cuban Revolutions, both of which are invoked in *Un arc-en-ciel* in order to revitalize the reader's consciousness of these two revolutionary events. As C. L. R. James wrote in his appendix essay to the second edition of *The Black Jacobins*: "From Toussaint L'Ouverture to Fidel Castro," Depestre also saw that "what took place in French San Domingo in 1792–1804 reappeared in Cuba in 1958."[6] *Un arc-en-ciel*, then, is a work that, when placed in the historical context of its production, offers the opportunity to consider Depestre's project of political and aesthetic radicalism and its relation to history, and specifically the event of the Haitian Revolution. This discussion, therefore, focuses on an analysis of the poetic recuperation of the Haitian Revolution that Depestre's radical political and aesthetic project enabled.

Poetics of Commitment: Exile, Revolution, Négritude, and Vodou

Like many of Haiti's most prominent writers, Depestre has long lived in exile from his native land, although he has denied the applicability of the term "a writer of exile" to his situation.[7] After being forced to leave Paris in 1951 because of his political activism, Depestre journeyed to Prague, Havana, Vienna, Chile, Argentina, and Brazil before he returned to Haiti, via Paris once more, in 1957. However, 1957 was also the year that François Duvalier became president of Haiti via a rigged election, and Depestre immediately became one of Duvalier's most outspoken critics. His situation in Haiti rapidly became too dangerous to remain tenable, and when Che Guevara invited Depestre to continue his literary and political work in Cuba, he accepted, remaining there until 1978.[8] In Cuba, Depestre held a variety of official cultural and political positions: he became involved in the Pan-African and Tri-Continental movements, directed a library in Havana, and produced regular radio broadcasts to Haiti. While in Cuba, Depestre also penned some of his most powerful revolutionary and surreal prose-poems, essays, and criticism, including *Un arc-en-ciel*, which, much influenced by Césaire, were insistent on the hypocrisy and contradictions inherent in capitalism and bourgeois liberalism. He aligned himself with the concepts of the Third World and anticolonialism, and, like Fanon, he adopted the Trotskyist theory of permanent revolution, seeing in its theorizing of how the proletarian revolution for national liberation could surpass the bourgeois democratic revolution, a manifesto for Third World liberation.[9] Never forgetting his heritage as a Haitian, it is one of the great achievements of Depestre's poetics in *Un arc-en-ciel* that he found an aesthetic language that articulated not just his politics, but also one that evoked the history and culture of his native land. In discovering this language, Depestre also discovered the surreal and the revolutionary in Haitian history, culture, and reality.[10] In arriving at a perception of Haiti's inherent surrealism, Depestre saw that in the Americas, where there was a unique fusion of indigenous pre-Colombian, African, and European cultures and epistemologies, surrealism was not just an aesthetic doctrine as it was in Europe.[11] This vision recalls Jacques Stephen Alexis's argument that the explanation for the seemingly surreal marvelous realism of the dominant aesthetic forms of the black and creole Americas is to be found in historical and material factors:

> The under-developed populations of the world . . . know a blend of mechanical civilization and "natural" life. . . . [S]ince reality is not intelligible in all its aspects to the members of under-developed communities, he naturally transposes his conceptions of relativity and of the marvellous into his vision of everyday reality. A bird in rapid flight is, above all, a pair of wings, a woman giving suck impresses by her round and heavy breasts, a wild beast is essentially a footfall and a roar. . . . The Marvellous Realism of the Haitians is thus an integral part of Social Realism.[12]

As will be seen later in this study, these visions of the surreal and the marvelous were shared by Carpentier, but the contrasting ideologies revealed in their imaginative works that this shared vision produced is striking. Whereas Depestre's vision of the material-surreal fostered a radical and optimistic recuperation of the Haitian Revolution, Carpentier's produced a recuperation in *El reino de este mundo* that must be noted for its conservatism, notwithstanding the brilliance of the novel's aesthetic achievements.

Depestre embraced Césairean négritude, and it quickly became the working tool that enabled his development as a young artist and an intellectual. For Depestre, it was a functional aesthetic theory, a declaration of coming to consciousness, an expression of being unreconciled to the status quo, and a movement that enabled him to locate himself within a Pan-African and transnational black history without losing sight of the local specificities of his own formation as a Haitian. Like Césaire, Depestre also recognized an aesthetic kinship in Wilfredo Lam's visual expressions of the marvelous in the black cultures of the Americas. These influences enabled Depestre to conceive of his poetic writing as a revolutionary weapon, and a profound connection between aesthetics and material realities came to underline all of Depestre's most radical works. According to Joan Dayan: "For Depestre, the truth of poetic imagination emerges as the demand for political action; poetry becomes productive as it becomes practical—a living force in the transformation of society. As Depestre himself urges, 'Rise up also my verse, your place is in the street.'"[13]

I will return to Depestre's renunciation of this position; meanwhile I am concerned with his radical poetry, which was, and remains to this day, deeply committed to communicating the material realities of contemporary injustice, to opening our eyes to black revolutionary history, and to promoting the realization of socialism. The poetry of this period was also deeply Haitian: Depestre took up the mantles of the preeminent Haitian writers and communists Jean Price-Mars and Jacques Roumain, whose work had also engaged with the task of dispelling derogatory myths about the Haitian peasantry, their culture, folklore, and history.

Drawing on the heritage of Price-Mars's work, Depestre allowed his knowledge of Haitian vodou and its special status within Haitian folk culture to infuse his poetry with the rhythms and rites of Haitian life. He married this to his understanding of vodou's vital revolutionary role in the achievement of Haitian independence and thereby confronted vodou's misrepresentation and manipulation as a tool of repression during the years of the Duvalier dictatorships. Depestre's revolutionary poetics identified the heritage of Haiti's revolutionary history and vodou as, in Césaire's phrase, "miraculous weapons" that held the potential to empower Haiti's peasantry. *Un arc-en-ciel* is very much a product of that perception; the poem unites the spheres of poetics and revolutionary politics. It accentuates the contemporary circumstances of anticolonial and anti-imperial struggle, and poetically manipulates the rites and *loas* of vodou to express the inherently surreal and revolutionary in Haitian culture, politics, and history.

Un arc-en-ciel pour l'occident chrétien

Un arc-en-ciel's poetics of history and vodou, politics and surrealism, determine its canny and politically infused recuperation of the Haitian Revolution that focuses on the vodou spirits of some of the revolution's leaders and heroic influences. The maroon Makandal and the revolutionary leaders Toussaint Louverture and Jean-Jacques Dessalines are invoked as part of the poem's lyrical expression of blackness as a political concept. As heroes and martyrs of black liberation, Makandal,

Toussaint, and Dessalines form a critical part of the poem's assault on Western racism, colonialism, and the institutional and casual racist hypocrisy of white American middle-class values. The poem, like much of Depestre's writing, expresses the utopian feeling of the infinite perfectibility of mankind, and Makandal, Toussaint, and Dessalines are taken as historical examples that substantiate the poem's utopian bent. But the invocations of Makandal, Toussaint, and Dessalines serve a purpose beyond inspirational memorialization; they function as a demand for political action to be conscious of the heights of humanistic possibility, and advance the poem beyond its call for violent revolt.

The title, which demonstrates the poem's sympathetic and volatile character, provides the first hint that *Un arc-en-ciel* is much more than just an angry polemic: in the context of Depestre's powerful color symbolism, which draws heavily on Césaire, the beautiful image of the rainbow signifies plurality, and the possibility of a democratic and socialist multicultural society.[14] The rainbow is also the antithesis of the dogmatic, singular "Christian West" to which the poem's title also refers. Yet, while the poem presents this as an unequivocal obstacle to the antiracist, socialist ideal, it does not enact its destruction, but instead, despite its explosive, revolutionary call to arms, offers itself as an edifying gift for the Christian West: a nobler example that contains a spiritual dimension. This quality derives from Depestre's deep knowledge of Haitian vodou, which he uses to meld the supernatural to an aesthetic poetic form in order to represent an unfinished story of more than two hundred years of anti-imperial resistance, from Makandal, Toussaint, and Dessalines, to Patrice Lumumba and Malcolm X, to Depestre's speaker, and his audience.

Part I. "The Prelude"

Un arc-en-ciel opens with a statement of militant self-affirmation that situates a politically charged notion of blackness within the multicolored milieu of the rainbow:

> Oui je suis un nègre-tempête
> Un nègre racine-d'arc-en-ciel
>
> (Yes I am a tempest nigger
> A nigger rooted in the rainbow) (108–9)

The rainbow symbolically reinforces the structure of the poem, which is divided into seven sections. The poem's fifth section is entitled "Seven

Pillars of Innocence," and further emphasizes the structural, metaphorical, and spiritual power of the number seven. The "Seven Pillars" of the fifth section are the Haitian revolutionaries Makandal, Toussaint, and Dessalines, as well as four other celebrated heroes from black history: the nineteenth-century black Cuban revolutionary Antonio Maceo, who died in 1896 while fighting against the Spanish for Cuban independence; Charlemagne Péralte, the Haitian nationalist who became a guerrilla leader and died in 1919 leading the resistance to the U.S. invasion and occupation of Haiti; Patrice Lumumba, the African leader and revolutionary who was murdered in the Congo in 1961; and Malcolm X, the black nationalist leader murdered in 1965. Thus, the poem's historical sweep is enormous: more than two centuries of anticolonial and anti-imperial resistance across two different continents are all invoked within the poem's arc.

Whereas the poem is rooted in historical responsibility and its own material reality, it is also rich in spiritual qualities. The rainbow, which functions as much more than just an organizational tool, symbolically reveals the poem's central drama and purpose, as Dayan has argued: "The symbol of the rainbow, connecting heaven to earth, dramatically embodies the interdependence of the earthly and eternal. . . . [I]t combines the Black militancy of [two of Depestre's other major poetic works] *Minerai noir* and the lyricism of *Journal d'un animal marin*."[15]

From the outset, the poem draws on this dualism, combining religious and revolutionary images, subverting many sacred Christian images as it does so. For example, Depestre places the crown of thorns of which the Christian West is "so proud" (109) on the head of his trained bear before claiming that he has also drowned in alcohol "The little Christ who was smiling in me" (111). The vanquishing of a Christian worldview is an intrinsic part of celebrating an alternative and truly compassionate spirituality and a liberating, progressive social order. In *Un arc-en-ciel*, conservative Christianity is identified with two contemporary principal enemies of racial equality and social progress: apartheid South Africa and the American South—these two are the "Monsters of Birmingham monsters of Pretoria" (111), and it is thoroughly tainted by its instrumental role in devaluing indigenous cultures. The dramatic poetic narrative is propelled forward by the confrontation between the poem's speaker and these "monsters" in the form of an affluent and politically powerful white family, comprising a judge, his wife, and their five sons and five daughters in the southern American state of Alabama.

Among them there is a West Point cadet, a Yale University student, a future American ambassador to Panama, a businessman, and the widow of a colonel killed in the Korean War. They are introduced with a withering contempt by the poem's speaker:

Une famille bien américaine
Participant à fond à tout ce qui
Mène l'Amérique à la catastrophe

(A properly American family
Participating wholly in all that
Leads America to catastrophe) (114–15)

Approaching barefooted while the family is dining, "in the grass of [his] négritude" (113), Depestre's narrator instantly sees through the façade of civilization which this family professes and assumes to inhabit. The coexistence of Christian and brutally reactionary values is a fact that is absolutely clear to Depestre's speaker: they are "A beautiful family standing up in its scum!" (115). In a manner that recalls Césaire's *Discourse on Colonialism*, the narrator is overcome with disbelief and anger that the family can reconcile Jesus, the Ku Klux Klan, the H-bomb, the electric chair, and the Statue of Liberty. It is a poetic reshaping of Césaire's argument from the *Discourse* that Western society has for so long chosen to avert its eyes from its descent into savagery. Like Césaire, what Depestre and his speaker hold against the "pseudo-humanism" of Western society is its nature—"narrow and fragmentary, incomplete and biased and, all things considered, sordidly racist."[16] All of the poem's surreal qualities do not destabilize this foundational and highly rational analysis. In fact, *Un arc-en-ciel* indicates that when noncapitalist society comes into contact with the internal contradictions of Western capitalism, this enables them to produce a revolutionary surrealism.

It is an incendiary manner with which to begin as Depestre's speaker proclaims his blackness, his coming to consciousness, and a new humanism all drawn from black history, vodou, and his own lyrical inventiveness. Like Césaire's narrator in the *Cahier*, Depestre's narrator repeatedly, boldly, and at times comically reverses and manipulates race stereotypes in order to celebrate indigenous and black histories and cultures that have been denigrated by the Christian West's project of colonialism. The cruelties of the bigoted Christian West become comical and lose their power to oppress; and as they are rendered absurd, the greatness of black cultures, the source of which, the poem makes clear, is

Africa, asserts itself. Depestre repeatedly evokes the power of Africa through images of the continent's landscape, wildlife, and minerals:

> Je fais sauter mes ténèbres
> En mille matins de lions.
>
> (I blow up my shadows
> Into a thousand lion mornings) (108–9)

And:

> Moi-même dans la géometrie de mes lions
> Moi-même dans la violence de mon diamant
>
> (Me in the geometry of my lions
> Me in the violence of my diamond). (110–11)

Part II. "Epiphanies of the Voodoo Gods"

At the opening of the poem's second part, "Epiphanies of the Voodoo Gods," the narrator's journey has taken him to Johannesburg, where his bear crowned with thorns has been thrown into prison. His escape route and savior is the sea, which assumes a potent symbolic significance of instability throughout the poem. At times it is invoked to recall the Middle Passage, and at other times it is the source of regenerative possibilities, and it is also deployed in order to reconnect the global black diaspora to Africa. The sea connects the American, European, and African continents, and as a metaphor it allows Depestre's speaker access to a triangular transcontinental black solidarity that is communicated most clearly later on in the poem in the "Seven Pillars of Wisdom": Patrice Lumumba, representative of Africa, is heralded alongside five West Indians and an African American. Depestre's attribution of power, significance, and complexity to the sea via his poetic imagery is thus much more than an emotive symbol in *Un arc-en-ciel.* The sea, specifically the Atlantic, is transformed from being a negative symbol that connects the Americas, Europe, and Africa through plantation slavery, into a site of complex possibilities. At various points in *Un arc-en-ciel* the sea is Makandal's personal domain and universe; it is Toussaint's muse, violent like Dessalines; it is the resting place of untold numbers of slaves who perished during the Middle Passage; it is a source of revolution and divine inspiration. Rescuing his bear from prison in apartheid South Africa, the sea also becomes part of a chain of events in which the surreal and revolutionary possibilities of the imagination are celebrated. Depestre's narrator draws a little sailboat in the soil of the cell and then releases "the wind of innocence in its sails," and the bear and narrator make good their escape. Even "all the salt of the sea hailed" them, and "even the worst monsters of the sea opened the way" for them on their surreal escape:

> La patience de la mer était avec nous! La beauté de la mer était avec nous! Les merveilles de la mer étaient avec nous!
>
> (The patience of the sea was with us! The beauty of the sea was with us! The marvels of the sea were with us!) (134–35)

The second part of *Un arc-en-ciel* also includes the poem's first reference to the Haitian Revolution. In the section subtitled "Azaka-Médé," named after the vodou *loa* (god) of agriculture, Dessalines's victory at Vertières, the final major military battle in the Haitian Revolution, is invoked at a high point of poetic rage (141). It is in this second section of the poem, entitled "Epiphanies of the Voodoo Gods," that Depestre's narrator is inhabited by the male vodou *loas*.

While possessed with the spirit of Azaka-Médé, who as the *loa* of agriculture connotes the twin themes of fertility and fecundity, Depestre's narrator embarks on a boisterous wordplay in which sexual freedom becomes subversive and anarchic; Dessalines's victory over General Rochambeau at Vertières is recalled, linking sexual freedom and political freedom:

> Conillons avec nos douleurs
> Conillons avec nos colères
> Comme Dessalines à Vertières
>
> (*Conillons* with our sufferings
> *Conillons* with our fury
> Like Dessalines at Vertières). (141)[17]

Then, later in the poem's second section, the narrator is inhabited by the *loa* Ti-Jean Sandor, who characteristically is represented as having only one foot, or no feet at all, but who is extremely agile in climbing trees (251n44). As Depestre's narrator is possessed by Ti-Jean, he undergoes an imaginative journey that initiates a movement from slavery to resistance and revolution. The example of the Haitian Revolution and slave resistance in general is never far away: "In front of me I explode / Charges of gunpowder / Behind me I leave / A long wake of chains" (157). Depestre also injects a blackly ironic and subversive humor into the recuperation of resistance that is simultaneously imaginative and rooted in historical memory:

> Je change mon cadet de West-Point
> En un beau chien de race
> Que je mords à l'oreille
> Je suis un grand mangeur
> De chiens blancs . . .
>
> (I change my West-Point cadet
> Into a beautiful pedigree dog
> Whose ear I bite
> I am a great eater
> Of white dogs . . .) (157)

The cunning image recalls the slave hunting dogs that were used by Rochambeau in the latter stages of the Haitian Revolution, and in particular, the image of "a beautiful pedigree dog" is a means of ridiculing colonial Saint Domingue's racial classification system that was applied by law to the slave and free populations of Saint Domingue.[18] Depestre's narrator, as a "great eater / Of white dogs," comically reverses and avenges history.

Part V. "Seven Pillars of Innocence"

Un arc-en-ciel recalls the Haitian Revolution directly in its fifth part, "Seven Pillars of Innocence," which is comprised of seven odes: to Makandal, to Toussaint Louverture, to Dessalines, to Antonio Maceo, to Charlemagne Péralte, to Patrice Lumumba, and to Malcolm X. As Césaire had done earlier in his triptych of plays which invite comparison between Henri Christophe and Patrice Lumumba, Depestre mobilizes the memory of the heroes of Haiti's independence within the context of two hundred years of global black resistance. Written in 1967 with the murders of Patrice Lumumba and Malcolm X still in the foreground of memory, the Haitian Revolution, and the virtues of its vanguard, is recuperated with a renewed and immediate political relevance. A part of the challenge in such a bold move thus becomes how such different individuals can be recuperated into a single story, or how to illustrate the relevance of the Haitian Revolution to the mid-twentieth century.

The voices of the female *loas*,Ayizan, Aida Wedo, Erzili, Caridad, Guede Mazaka, Grande Brigitte, and Simbi are the means by which the virtues of the seven human "Pillars of Innocence" are recuperated and presented. In the preceding section of the poem, "Cantata for Seven Voices," the female *loas* exclaim their ambition to "make / The black race's / Pearl-sun / Explode over life!" (189) in telling the legends of the seven heroes:

> Caridad:
> Sept légendes solaires
> Sept piliers de l'innocence
> Pour féconder la marche
> Ovarienne de l'univers!
>
> (Caridad:
> Seven solar legends
> Seven pillars of innocence
> To fertilize the ovarian march
> Of the universe!) (190–91)

Thus introduced, each ode celebrates its hero of black revolutionary struggle and resistance and imbibes each one with the power to inspire Depestre's narrator to deliver his message to the white southern family and the Christian West.

"Ode to Makandal"

Aziyan's "Ode to Makandal" begins the sequence and represents the rebel maroon whose legend endured throughout the Haitian Revolution. Makandal is presented as drawing his strength from the elemental forces of the earth; he is a supernatural being. The sea, which is figured as a means of resistance, is his kingdom: Aziyan is required to summon him "back from the bottom of the sea" (193), and its power is represented as being at his disposal. The poisoning campaigns that Makandal orchestrated as a maroon leader in prerevolutionary Saint Domingue are recalled as having been "The first poison the first tidal wave" of resistance, and he is celebrated for being "The first maroon" and a founding pillar in the genesis of black revolutionary resistance. He is the "first volcano," an "all-powerful fire," "the first in his green progeny":

> Le premier à souffler sur nos tisons de haine
> Le premier qu'habitèrent les complots de l'orage

Et la grande santé de la mer

(The first to blow on our fire-brands of hate
The first one to harbor the plots of the storm
And the sea's great health) (192–93)

Depestre's representation celebrates Makandal's extraordinary, and violent, achievements, reiterating Césaire's argument that it was in Haiti that négritude first stood up. Above all, Makandal is heroized as an emblem of fierce and total resistance, and his bravery is emphasized by his disfigurement, having lost an arm in an accident while working a sugarcane press (192–93).

"Ode to Toussaint Louverture"

The contrast between Makandal and Toussaint's representations is striking. Aida Wèdo's "Ode to Toussaint Louverture" picks up many of the common visual images that have survived of Toussaint and poetically develops them in highly original ways. For example, the figure of Toussaint on horseback has stood the test of time in terms of its frequency and popularity, and here it is majestically reworked. It is an image that adorns the cover of Madison Smartt Bell's *Master of the Crossroads*, and it has long fascinated visual artists. Jacob Lawrence's *The Life of Toussaint L'Ouverture*, a series of forty-one tempera paintings, contains a number of examples of the dramatic visual potential of a triumphant and uniform-clad Toussaint astride his white horse, Bel Argent.[19] Perhaps it has much to do with the power the image generates by virtue of its comparability with Jacques-Louis David's arrestingly powerful neoclassical 1801 painting of Toussaint's nemesis, Napoleon, astride his horse, Vizir, *Napoleon at the Saint Bernard Pass*. However, in Depestre's hands the configuration suggests the light of Toussaint's vision, driving him to a future in which the incompleteness of the European Enlightenment will be surpassed:

Regardez-le sur son cheval qui galope encore vers la lumière

(Look at him on his horse still galloping towards the light) (194–95)

Whereas the "Ode to Makandal" emphasized the maroon's warlike and uncompromising qualities, Depestre highlights Toussaint's more saintly virtues. Nature imagery, especially that of trees, is employed in order to praise Toussaint's attribute of tolerance and his penchant for diplomacy. Thus, Aida Wèdo sings of Toussaint "the star-negro" whose "tree-patience" leads toward a glorious springtime (195). The image of Toussaint's tree-like patience recalls his famous address to his French captors on the inevitability of black freedom in Saint Domingue that is later quoted in full in the Ode:

> En me renversant, on n'a abattu à Saint-Domingue que le tronc de l'arbre de la Liberté des Noirs; il repoussera par les racines, parce qu'elles sont profondes et nombreuses!
>
> (In felling me, you threw down in Santo-Domingo only the trunk of the tree of Black Freedom; it will shoot up again by the roots, because they are deep and numerous!) (196–97)

In common with Makandal however, Toussaint has the ability to shapeshift and to assume the form of animals: "Sometimes his walk is a tortoise carrying on his back an olive branch" (195). Toussaint also has the supernatural ability to commune with the sea that acts as his counsel:

> Le mer un jour se brisa à ses pieds et lui dit
> "Mon Toussaint tu verras désormais par mes yeux
> Tu entendras par mes oreilles
> Et par la force de mes vents tu sortiras de toi-même
> Pour donner à ton pays tout le soleil qu'il y a en toi."
>
> (One day the sea broke at his feet and told him:
> "My Toussaint from now on you will see by my eyes
> You will hear by my ears
> And by the strength of my winds you will emerge from yourself
> To give your country all the sun that there is in you.") (194–95)

The final celebratory image in the Ode is not one of resistance or violence, but a highly unusual image that conjoins maleness and fertility: black freedom is "planting fruit trees" (197).

"Ode to Dessalines"

With Erzili's "Ode to Dessalines," there is a return to some of the earlier images that were associated with Makandal in Aziyan's Ode. Erzili's duty is to tell of Dessalines, who is a "torrent of black flames" (197). Dessalines is a powerfully sexualized figure ("Dessalines carried away my body in his current" [197]), and his strength is likened to "the sea on a stormy day" (199); however, Dessalines is presented above all as a courageous *voice*, and the latter half of the Ode is given over to a recital of Dessalines's own words. He demands unceasing revolution, and his rhetoric sounds more reminiscent of Che Guevara than what we might have expected from a late-eighteenth-century rebel slave. Dessalines's enduring command to the masses is: "Be an incendiary people" (199).

The Odes to Antonio Maceo, Charlemagne Péralte, Patrice Lumumba, and Malcolm X

The celebration of three of the heroes of the Haitian Revolution in Depestre's *Un arc-en-ciel* is made more unusual for the context and company in which they are placed, particularly with regard to their relationships to vodou. There are some intriguing tensions: the female *loas* sing their odes of praise, and yet it is interesting to note that Toussaint was hostile to vodou—although there is conflicting evidence on this matter. Michel S. Laguerre in particular, has written on the subject of Toussaint's ability to juggle both vodou and Christian beliefs and practices in a nonexclusive manner.[20] The later revolutionaries Maceo, Péralte, Lumumba, and Malcolm X certainly regarded it as little more than primitive superstition.[21] The case of Dessalines is a good deal more complicated, however. He is thought to have been a vodou adept, and he is also the only one of the revolution's triptych of revolutionary leaders, Toussaint, Christophe, and Dessalines, to have been resurrected by the Haitian people as a *lwa*, and there are accounts of him heading into battle covered in amulets and vodou charms. However, he is also known to have massacred vodou leaders and their followers.[22] Thus, only Makandal, about whom the historical record is rather thin, appears to fit, in an unproblematic sense, his own place in a vodou celebration. Yet these tensions did not appear to strike Depestre as problematic, and the use of vodou to celebrate revolutionary heroes was something that he would attempt again in his poetic tribute to Che Guevara in 1968, *Cantata de Octubre a la vida y a la muerte del Comandante Ernesto Che Guevara* (October cantata for the life and death of Commandant Ernesto Che Guevara).[23]

One of the most intriguing aspects of the "Ode to Antonio Maceo" is the manner in which a teleological view of Caribbean revolution is traced from Haiti in 1804 to Cuba in 1959. Depestre's move here is similar to C. L. R. James's argument in the essay "From Toussaint L'Ouverture to Fidel Castro" appended to the 1963 edition of *The Black Jacobins*. Depestre finds in the story of Caribbean revolution the exemplar of the multiracial progressive "rainbow" that fits his embrace of all races and cultures, black, white, mulatto, and indigenous Indian:

L'homme-maïs de la montagne: Fidel Castro!
Marti est avec eux plus joyeux que jamais
Toussaint et Bolivar, O'Higgins et Juarez
San Martin et Lincoln, John Brown et Péralte
Héros noirs, héros blancs, et les héros indiens
D'Amérique les voici tous les porteurs de joie
Qui tiennent Cuba haute et forte en leurs vagues!

(The corn man of the mountain: Fidel Castro!
Marti is with them and happier than ever
Toussaint and Bolivar, O'Higgins and Juarez
San Martin and Lincoln, John Brown and Péralte
Black heroes, white heroes and indian heroes
Of America here they are bearers of joy
Holding Cuba high and strong in their waves!) (200–201)

The "Ode to Charlemagne Péralte" celebrates the Haitian nationalist leader with some of the poem's most daring poetic imagery, taking two hallowed American symbols—the Stars and Stripes and the American eagle—and comically ironizing them both. Péralte is represented as a victim of the piracy of "*la loi yankee*" ("yankee law") (202–3) that marched not under the American national flag, but under a flag of skull and crossbones, while Péralte and rebels are figured as eagles (202–3).

The Odes to Lumumba and Malcolm X are also noteworthy for the manner of their representation with regard to their iconic statuses and the way in which they are connected to the Haitian revolutionaries Makandal, Toussaint, and Dessalines.[24] The characteristic that Depestre chooses to connect all seven of these black nationalist figures is innocence. Thus, Lumumba is shown as having stood for freedom in not just the Congo but in all of Africa, and his affinity with nature suggests a connection with an African essence—he was, like Toussaint, "*Un négre-arbre-fruitier*" ("a fruit-tree-negro") (208–9). The representation of Malcolm X is also remarkable for its tenderness: Malcolm X is a "Harlem-lamb . . . / Weeping" who was motivated by his loathing of "tears, chains and hatred" and who was murdered for trying "to tell the world's story" (209). The portrayal of Malcolm X, the most famously militant of black nationalists, as a gentle lamb is a stunningly subversive representative gesture. Moreover, it is a move that links Malcolm X to Christ, and it also parodies a long history of the trope of the lamb of God in the poetics of race discourse. The most famous example in this tradition can be found in William Cowper's 1815 antislavery satirical poem, "Epigram (Printed in the *Northampton Mercury*)." This poem conflates the acts of purifying wine with lamb's blood and the purifying of sugar with slaves' blood as a means of lampooning slaveholders:

> Now lambs and negroes both are harmless things.
> And thence, perhaps, this wondr'ous Virtue springs,
> 'Tis in the blood of Innocence alone –
> Good cause why Planters never try their own.[25]

Cowper's "Epigram" thus equates the innocence of the lambs with the innocence of slaves and thereby represents the slaves as sacrificial victims. Depestre's image of Malcolm X as a lamb however, does not rob his subject of agency as occurs in Cowper's representation. Instead, Depestre's Malcolm X is a radical black subject whose revolutionary zeal is informed by a Christ-like compassion.

Revolutionary Heroes, Vodou Gods

When *Un arc-en-ciel* was first published in 1967, Haiti was firmly in the grip of the Duvalier dictatorship, which used vodou as one of its tools of repression. Thus, Depestre's recuperation of vodou's qualities as a liberating force in the poem is a particularly bold move. By mapping onto vodou the possibility of radical liberation, Depestre recognized its original status as a liberating force for the early revolutionaries of Saint Domingue. The evidence that vodou played a strategic, religious, and ideological role in the Haitian Revolution is compelling. It encouraged the politicization of the rebel slaves and operated as an organizational tool that the revolution's leaders could use to their advantage.[26] Thus, Depestre's "Voodoo Mystery Poem" is not merely romantic fantasy located in the celebration of a revolutionary spirit, but an important recuperation of the intricate relationship between vodou and the achievement of Haiti's independence. It is Depestre's lasting achievement that in *Un-arc-en-ciel* he created an aesthetic with which to connect vodou to past, contemporary, and present oppression, and an enduring demand for revolution. *Un arc-en-ciel pour l'occident chrétien* remains one of black francophone literature's most original and politically infused works that recuperates the past in order to engage with the contemporary world.

The Afterlives of Decolonization

Given the radicalism of Depestre's stance, it becomes a matter of interest to the intellectual history of revolutionary thinking to consider

Depestre's renunciation of left-wing politics. Charles Forsdick has accurately surmised that Depestre's disenchanted late style and politics should be regarded as an emphatic eschewal of "the revolutionary politics of his youth in favour of exoticist *métissage* and apologies for *la francophonie*."[27] I now examine and contextualize this conservative turn.

In a 1993 interview with Joan Dayan, Depestre declared that henceforth he desired to operate only within depoliticized aesthetic boundaries: "I don't give a damn about politics; turn the page."[28] Even more explicitly, Depestre has recently remarked: "If the notion of revolution itself has failed, it would be illusory of me to continue to sleep with a phantom. The great zombi of modernity is revolution, alas. The great zombi."[29]

Renouncing revolutionary politics coincided with being lionized by the French literary establishment: Depestre is now a Gallimard-published author who is regarded as a key Franco-Haitian spokesperson for *la francophonie*. Considering these unavoidable facts, Silvio Torres-Saillant has remarked, "One feels tempted to say 'yes' in response to Dayan's question: 'Has Depestre been zombified by French fame?,'" before adding: "Perhaps it is even gloomier that his market success has come precisely after he ceased challenging the ways of the Christian West and the workings of empire."[30]

A 1997 interview with Depestre in the *UNESCO Courier* that gently probed the subject of his renouncing of Marxism and négritude begins with the following remark: "Your life as an adult and as a poet began with what you later called 'A triple badge of rebellion'—proud négritude, impassioned surrealism, and the idea of revolution. Today only the surrealism part seems to have survived."[31] In his response, Depestre willingly accepts the observation, and he recounts how he came into contact with surrealism without making his current stance on Marxism and négritude clear until later in the interview. When he broaches the subject, he first blames Marxism for deadening his poetic voice: "The Marxist utopia, with all its lies and repressive nightmares, took over my work and my life as a poet until the moment I broke with Stalinism."[32] And then he continues, explaining that his commitment to revolution "nearly destroyed my integrity as a citizen and a writer. The ideal of revolution seriously impoverished my personal stores of poetry and tenderness. . . . The treasure islands invented by the utopias and mythologies of revolution went up in smoke with the great dreams of our youth—uniting the idea of transforming the world (Karl Marx) with that of changing life (Arthur Rimbaud)."[33]

Here, Depestre, appears implicitly to attribute an anti-aesthetic Stalinism to the idea of revolution that négritude imaginatively conceives of and calls for. The fact that Depestre's own major works were *enabled* by négritude would at the least suggest that it cannot be as easily dismissed as Depestre attempts here:

> I've always mistrusted the idea of négritude because I did not think it was possible to constitute an anthropology which is the exact opposite of the one which devalued us and downgraded us as "Blacks." You can't just transfer to a Black context what is said and done in terms of Whites. Aimé Césaire referred to this phenomenon as turning Gobineau upside down. I realized we had to create our own aesthetic and ideology without falling into "anti-racist" racism.' That's why I said goodbye to négritude at the same time as I dropped Marxism. I've only stuck with surrealism, which is still one of my working tools.[34]

Thus, Depestre has latterly misrepresented the movement to which he contributed so much himself. In particular, Depestre's critique of négritude obfuscates its universalism by ignoring the historicizing phenomenological use of the concept in the hands of Césaire, and by reductivly equating Césaire's use of the term with Sartre's identification of it as "antiracist racism."

Nick Nesbitt's analysis of négritude makes clear the inadequacies of Depestre's attempt to justify his dropping of the concept by dismissing it as an identity trap, which merely involves "turning Gobineau upside down." For Nesbitt, the universal and utopian qualities of négritude remain largely unexplored, but they imply "a developmental model of enlightenment that sustains and advances the transformational project of black liberation, pointing beyond the circularity of identity politics toward the elusive instantiation of a fully realized utopian freedom."[35]

Edward Said is also among those critics who have admired in négritude its valorization of the principle of universal freedom, and discerned in it the kernel of a concept of universal human rights. Said's analaysis of Césaire's *Cahier* in his seminal text *Culture and Imperialism* alerts us to the fact that within Césaire's concept of négritude there is no giving in to "the rigidity and interdictions of self-imposed limitations that come with race, moment, or milieu," but, instead, there is a moving through them to the concept of Fanonian liberation that moves beyond a *national* consciousness and toward a *universal* consciousness.[36]

It also seems appropriate to counter Depestre's unsatisfactory recycling of Sartre's much-misunderstood phrase "antiracist racism" with

Sartre's own words: "I should like to show that this poetry—which seems racial at first—is actually a hymn *by everyone for everyone*."[37] Though Sartre used the phrase "antiracist racism" with reference to the négritude poets in his essay "Black Orpheus," he used it in the context of his argument for the recognition of the solidarity that exists "beyond the nuances of skin color.[38] For Sartre had recognized that capitalism was color-blind: "Like the white worker, the negro is a victim of the capitalist structure of our society."[39]

However, no matter how inadequate the intellectual justification that Depestre has offered for dispensing with négritude and Marxism, it is essential to contextualize his conservative turn post-1977 and to see his move as part of a general trend. It was at this time that the notorious (and celebrated) "nouveaux philosophes" Bernard-Henri Lévy and André Glucksmann were affirming a turn to the right. Consider Depestre's recent political interventions: these include his clamorous support for the 2004 *Debray Report* to the French foreign minister Dominique de Villepin on French-Haitian relations,[40] and his 2003 speech "What Can Toussaint Louverture Do for the Haitians of 2004?," in which Depestre identifies Jacques Chirac and Dominque de Villepin as true successors to Toussaint for resisting the coming 2003 invasion of Iraq:

> Here, at the Château de Joux, so close to the destiny of Toussaint Louverture, I believe I can feel a *Louverturian* sensibility, as I thank France for its exemplary conduct in the debates that have accompanied the tragedy of the Middle East. By the blood that flows there, President Jacques Chirac and the minister of foreign affairs, Dominque de Villepin, strengthened by the almost unanimous support of the French people, plead with nobility and determination, for a reconfiguration of the planet which will be enriched by the respect for law, peace, happiness and wisdom of humankind.
>
> Honour to Toussaint Louverture!
>
> Honour to the French nation, which is once again his friend![41]

The capitulation to the establishment is so complete, the dismissal of socialism and revolution so unequivocal, and the intellectual integrity of the adopted position so questionable, that it is to be hoped the power of Depestre's radical poetry will outlive his renunciation of the ideals upon which it was based, and will continue to sustain more than a purely historical interest. The poetry's utopian dimension, its determined advocation for human dignity and for freedom for men of all races, has not aged, and its renewal of Césaire's earlier poetic declaration of remaining unreconciled to racism and injustice has not become any less relevant with the passing of time. The humanism, tenderness, and clarity of Depestre's radical poetic voice that brought the past alive again and invested it with the power to liberate the present, continues to illuminate the path to a new and free postcolonial future.

4 The Haitian Revolution and Radical Visual Politics

Jacob Lawrence, Kimathi Donkor, and the Cultures of Philately

I HAVE IN THE FIRST SECTION of this study sought to argue that a radical and original ensemble of writings, heterogeneous in medium, voice, and tenor, can be read as consistent in their ambition to recuperate the Haitian Revolution by mobilizing history as the carrier of their transformational, revolutionary messages. To elaborate the argument further, I now turn to the visual arts, in full knowledge that a proper discussion of the more than two centuries of iconography relating to Toussaint and the Haitian Revolution merits a book-length study of its own.[1]

I have therefore chosen to focus on two radical artists—one well known, the other less so—whose original and radical works contest the inheritance of overtly racist images of Toussaint and negative misrepresentations of the Haitian Revolution and its consequences—as well as representations of Toussaint and the revolution on commemorative stamps. These images, which are among the most important visual images generated by the Haitian Revolution, form a radical constellation of artworks that elucidate newly revealed affinities between the aesthetic-historical objects with which this study is engaged, and they enhance our understanding of how the tradition of imperial denigration has been contested.

The first part of my discussion in this chapter focuses on the renowned African American artist Jacob Lawrence, whose work thematically, temporally, and politically complements the quartet of Black Atlantic radicalism inspired by the Haitian Revolution: Aimé Césaire, C. L. R. James, Langston Hughes, and René Depestre. In particular, the aesthetic creations of Lawrence and Césaire can be seen to share an ideological kinship. Lawrence, born in 1919, and whose early development took place within the milieu of the Harlem Renaissance, also demonstrates affinities with Langston Hughes as well as the impact of Haiti on Harlem. Then, the visual language in the paintings of the lesser-known, but highly accomplished, contemporary black British painter Kimathi Donkor is discussed, since his paintings of Louverture and the revolution speak so powerfully to the major themes of this project and are particularly relevant to the current cultural currency of the memory of the Haitian Revolution in contemporary Britain.

Finally, the chapter addresses the subject of memorializing Toussaint on commemorative postage stamps, a medium that has for too long been unjustifiably ignored in serious scholarly work on visual representations of black power and slavery. In his discussion of the six stamps produced in Britain in 2007 to commemorate the bicentenary of the Slave Trade Act, the critic Marcus Wood claims that the commemorative stamps "were without doubt the most widely viewed and widely disseminated visual art connected with the slave trade ever to be produced. They have been seen by both sexes and all ages, they have penetrated every continent, and given the prevalence of electronic messaging for most of the world's population, they have been sent to many of the most underdeveloped parts of the globe, where email and the cell phone have yet to arrive."[2] Thus, taking my cue from this statement of the ubiquity, availability, and global reach of the postage stamp, and acknowledging that stamps have always been used to market nation states in particular ways, I comment in the final part of this chapter on the idea that the iconography of Toussaint and the Haitian Revolution generated within the genre of philately, contributes to the semiotic field accreted around the cultural legacies of the Haitian Revolution.

The discussion of commemorative postage stamps also brings into focus some of the overarching questions this project raises: How, why, and in what contexts might Toussaint and the Haitian Revolution continue to be silenced or overlooked in scholarship and public awareness? Why might the historical fact and concept of the self-liberation of slaves remain *invisible* in some quarters even if it is not any longer *unthinkable*?[3] I am proposing that contrasting Toussaint's representation on the commemorative postage stamps of Haiti, Cuba, and Dahomey (Benin), with the striking nonrepresentation of black agency on the 2007 British postage stamps celebrating the bicentenary of the British abolition of the slave trade, goes some way to answering these questions. I argue that Toussaint's presence on (and absence from) commemorative postage stamps from diverse locations within the twentieth- and twenty-first-century Atlantic world highlights both Toussaint's privileged status as an icon of the Haitian Revolution, and the enduring constraints on his international portability and acceptability. Thus, Toussaint's absence from the United Kingdom's 2007 postage stamps, I argue, is indicative of the need to write Haiti and a black revolutionary out of British history, in order to retain the hallowed reputation of white abolitionists in the official narrative of slavery and its ending.

Finally, the discussion of images of Toussaint in this chapter is intended to emphasize the absence of an authenticated original drawn from life, since despite the recent claims of Jacques de Cauna, likenesses have necessarily been invented and recycled.[4] This fact has prompted Madison Smartt Bell to remark that "portraits of Toussaint from his own time are reminiscent of drawings of American buffalo by European artists working from descriptions and without ever having seen a buffalo."[5]

Thus, although the works discussed in this chapter constitute only a fraction of the two centuries of iconography on the Haitian Revolution of which they form a part, I focus on them in particular in order to develop my argument that radical recuperations and mediations of the narrative of the Haitian Revolution form a conduit to a properly historicized understanding of the past and how this has been construed and received.

Jacob Lawrence's Radical, Modernist Toussaint

Jacob Lawrence, an African American artist, is considered to be one of America's most significant twentieth-century painters. Lawrence, who often worked in the format of narrative and serial imagery, was throughout his career repeatedly drawn to projects of representing narratives of slavery and slave resistance, and in 1938 he completed a masterful series of forty-one tempera paintings entitled *The Life of Toussaint L'Ouverture* that he had begun the year before.[6] The narrative ambition of the series is greater than the production of a pictorial biography of Toussaint, however, since this frames the story of Toussaint's life within an epic portrayal of the story of Haiti: from Columbus to the institution of plantation slavery, to the revolution and many of its battles, to the achievement of independence. The series also represents a foundational moment in the history of African American art: it was exhibited in February 1939 at the Baltimore Museum of Art, where it was the first one-man show by an African American artist outside Harlem, and singled out in *Newsweek* as "a discovery."[7] The series gained further exposure and praise in May 1939, when, thanks to the efforts of Claude McKay, it was exhibited at the De Porres Interracial Council headquarters on Vesy

Street, New York. There, it was seen by Alain Locke, who described Lawrence as an "intuitive genius."[8]

The Toussaint series was the first of four completed by Lawrence dealing with slavery. The others were: *The Life of Frederick Douglass* (1938–39), *The Life of Harriet Tubman* (1939–40), and *The Life of John Brown* (1941). Much later, between 1986 and 1997, Lawrence, in collaboration with the silkscreen artist Lou Stovall, recast the 1938 *Toussaint L'Ouverture* series and reproduced fifteen of the earlier paintings as serigraphs.[9] In the serigraphs, earlier paintings representing scenes prior to his birth were excluded, and the focus was more narrowly on Toussaint's life, his military and strategic exploits during the revolution, and his heroic status. Patricia Hills has argued that it was the radicalism of the Haitian Revolution and Toussaint's status as a revolutionary that most appealed to Lawrence, a proposition particularly apparent in painting number 20 in the 1938 series and in its corresponding 1986 silkscreen print entitled *General Toussaint L'Ouverture*, which I suggest must be seen as a radical contestation of racial denigration in earlier pictorial representation.[10]

From his earliest works in the 1930s, it was clear that Lawrence's highly individual modernist style, somehow simultaneously both nonrepresentational and figurative, was not derivative in any way, although the diverse influences of Mexican mural painting, cubism, the aesthetics of collage, and social realism can all be noted. It is a style that Ellen Harkins Wheat later dubbed social realism "flavored by more abstract styles."[11] Lawrence himself explained his conception of the abstraction process in his work in 1945: "My work is abstract in the sense of having been designed and composed but it is not abstract in the sense of having no human content."[12] It was, however, Lawrence's relationship to Harlem, his close bond with its community, and his formation within its particular cultural, political, and aesthetic environment that must properly be considered as the most important influence on his work. Leslie King-Hammond has put it thus: "Harlem was his universe and his university."[13] Lawrence learned from, studied with, and worked alongside many of the key visual and literary artists of the Harlem Renaissance. and he can thus correctly be regarded as "the first major artist of the twentieth century who was technically trained and artistically educated within the art community of Harlem."[14]

King-Hammond has also written that the inspiration for the *Toussaint, Frederick Douglass,* and *Harriet Tubman* series, all completed in rapid succession from 1938 to 1941, was Lawrence's exposure to the

Figure 1. Jacob Lawrence, *The Life of Toussaint L'Ouverture, No. 20.* "General Toussaint L'Ouverture, Statesman and military genius, esteemed by the Spaniards, feared by the English, dreaded by the French, hated by the planters, and reverenced by the Blacks." 1938. Tempera on paper, 19 × 11 ½ in. (Aaron Douglas Collection, Amistad Research Center, Tulane University, New Orleans)

oral historians of Harlem. Lawrence benefited from the community-wide effort in Harlem to provide public education on African American and African Diasporic history, despite the acute material hardships of the time. One of these grassroots educational projects in particular, the lectures on African and African American history given at the 135th Street Library, was a particularly important step in Lawrence's developing understanding of Haiti.[15] However, both Ellen Harkins Wheat and Maurice Jackson credit *Haiti*, a drama by a white southern playwright and journalist named William DuBois, for most directly inspiring Lawrence to produce a series of paintings based upon the Haitian Revolution.[16]

During his preparation for the *Toussaint* series, Lawrence researched voraciously.[17] This research was to provide more than just the information that Lawrence needed to paint the series, as painting number 20, the most magnificent in the series, is based upon what is probably the most frequently reproduced image of Toussaint, the best-known version of which is François Séraphin Delpech's 1832 engraving of Nicolas-Eustache Maurin's *Toussaint L'Ouverture*. Lawrence would have undoubtedly discovered the Maurin image of Toussaint in his researches.

The immediately striking thing about Maurin's image of Toussaint is its racism. Toussaint's profile is crudely ape-like, adhering to the conventions of scientific racism and the "facial angle" theory developed by Petrus Camper.[18] It thus becomes surprising that Maurin's image continues to be reproduced widely, and it is even more surprising that it was used as the cover for Aimé Césaire's 1981 *Présence Africaine* study of Toussaint.

The origins of the Maurin image are shrouded in mystery. Madison Smartt Bell has speculated that Maurin's portrait was done from life as a watercolor,[19] while Philippe Girard has speculated that the portrait "is most likely accurate since it was given by Toussaint Louverture to Philippe-Rose Roume de Saint-Laurent and includes some physical characteristics (such as a prognathous chin) mentioned by contemporaries."[20] Meanwhile, the French historian Jacques de Cauna has claimed to have unearthed the only existing portrait of Louverture from life, an 1802 drawing by Pierre-Charles Baquoi that de Cauna claims was drawn between July 12 and July 23, 1802, during which time Toussaint, having been captured and deported to France, was awaiting his transfer to his imprisonment in the Fort de Joux near the Swiss border.[21] Despite de Cauna's claim, debate as to which of the

Figure 2. François Séraphin Delpech's 1832 engraving of Nicolas-Eustache Maurin's *Toussaint L'Ouverture*. (© National Portrait Gallery, London)

portraits that we have of Toussaint might be faithful to their subject has not been halted.

I now suggest that Jacob Lawrence's painting based upon the Maurin image offers a solution to the problem of recuperating an "authentic" image of Toussaint, by dismissing the quest to corroborate somehow the "truthfulness" of any particular image from the archive. Rather than portraying Toussaint as a recognizable individual, Lawrence creates a universalizing image of Toussaint as a black hero. Deconstructing the stereotypical racial attributes of the Maurin image, Lawrence creates a magnificent and strikingly beautiful portrait that refuses to Europeanize his subject's profile, thereby defiantly disregarding the proposed correlation in racist theory between facial angle and intelligence. Thus, Lawrence's modernist style, confident in its use of color and dramatic in its composition, and unburdened by any concern to render accurately a study of an individual subject, creates an elegant and empowering symbol of black agency, lending the painting a powerful mystique.

I want to suggest that this mystique and power can be seen as analogous to the quality of Césaire's Toussaint as a transcendental force in the *Cahier*, since Lawrence has created a visual artwork that deploys something akin to the ideology of Césaire's négritude—negating racist with affirmative imagery of the liberation of black subjectivity. In the poetry of Césaire and the painting of Lawrence, Toussaint thus becomes more than even a great historical figure: he is an existential refusal of the world that formed the historic individual Toussaint, and an irrepressible force that dares to assert a counterreality to denigration.

Kimathi Donkor's Caribbean Passion

Kimathi Donkor's recent series of large-scale oil paintings for his first major solo exhibition, entitled *Caribbean Passion: Haiti 1804,* was originally shown at the Bettie Morton Gallery in Brixton, London, in 2004, and it has since gone on tour within the United Kingdom. The series, comprising five oil paintings, was conceived as a celebration of the bicentenary of the Haitian Revolution, and it offers us the opportunity to examine in detail the way in which the still-evolving cultural currency of the Haitian Revolution has in part been shaped by and continues to speak to radical artists and intellectuals working in the contemporary black British art scene and further afield. And just as I attempted to show affinities between the works of Césaire, Hughes, and Lawrence, I now propose that Donkor's works share a common ideology with C. L. R. James's radical recuperation of the Haitian Revolution.

Kimathi Donkor, who is also an art teacher, community activist, and human-rights campaigner, has become known for artworks that explore the themes of race and class conflict in a historically grounded manner. During the 1980s, Donkor exhibited alongside artists associated with the BLK Art Group.[22] More recently his 2005 exhibition of large oil paintings, also shown at the Bettie Morton Gallery in Brixton, entitled *Fall/ Uprising*, marked the twentieth anniversary of the conflicts between the residents of the Brixton and Tottenham districts of London and the London Metropolitan police force. Donkor's paintings in this series stress the police brutality that caused the conflict and that remained prevalent throughout the unrest. The paintings also raise important questions in relation to the issue of the representation of black empowerment and black victimhood. This is also a major theme in his *Caribbean Passion: Haiti 1804* series.

It is a matter of interest to note how similar Donkor's motivations for his *Caribbean Passion: Haiti 1804* project were to C. L. R. James's ambition to convey a narrative of black agency rather than of black victimhood in *The Black Jacobins*. Donkor explains: "I was interested in the concept of African women and men from that period in heroic roles, because we're used to seeing and understanding Europeans in heroic roles, such as Napoleon Bonaparte and George Washington: and, we're also used to seeing Africans portrayed in less than heroic roles, as most peoples' view of slavery is simply a story about repression."[23] Thus, for Donkor, the value of the narrative of the Haitian Revolution predominantly resides in its ability to challenge the dominance of the narrative of black victimhood. As was also the case for Lawrence, Toussaint is central to this conception of a counterhistory.[24] Kimathi Donkor's paintings, however, draw on a very different tradition than that of Lawrence, that of grand history painting, in order to evoke black dignity and regeneration. This discussion addresses two paintings from Donkor's *Caribbean Passion: Haiti 1804* series in relation to this issue.

Toussaint L'Ouverture at Bedourete

Donkor's grand canvas, the second largest in the series, *Toussaint L'Ouverture at Bedourete*, depicts a heroic Toussaint on horseback surrounded by ex-slave revolutionaries on foot following Toussaint into battle and to victory. The only white body in the painting is a dead French soldier who has been killed in battle, and he lies alongside a black man who has also been slain. Above both these prostrate figures towers Toussaint, who is adorned in the colors of the French tricolor. The scene is one of unabashed heroism and triumph, and it is the centerpiece

Figure 3. Kimathi Donkor, *Toussaint L'Ouverture at Bedourete*, 2004. Oil on linen, 136 × 183 cm. (Collection of the artist)

of Donkor's series. In *Toussaint L'Ouverture at Bedourete*, in order to depict his heroic Toussaint, Donkor has very clearly drawn on the traditions of European grand history painting as expounded by the works of Diego Velazquez, Anthony Van Dyck, and Jacques-Louis David. Given the rarity of representations of heroic black subjects in this medium, Donkor's canvas also evokes Girodet's famous portrait of Jean-Baptiste Belley, and constitutes a bold statement of intent and the colonization of an elite form. It is important to note that Girodet's *Citizen Belley* transcends the genre of portraiture, traditionally defined, and exhibits characteristics of grand history painting. Girodet does not portray Belley as a static subject, but recalls his actions and experience at the level of metadiscourse: the smoking buildings in the bottom right-hand corner of the painting depict the devastation of Le Cap, in which Belley had taken part, thereby evoking abolition as a black, rather than a white, achievement. In common with Girodet's masterpiece, Donkor's painting also depicts its subject dynamically, representing the cavalry skirmish at Bedourete recounted in James's *Black Jacobins*. Significantly, Toussaint is not the largest figure in the painting because of the fixed-point perspective technique Donkor employs. Thus, although Toussaint is represented as a great and imposing figure, in accordance with Donkor's Jamesian project of fashioning him into one of history's great and imposing individuals, Donkor does not deify his Toussaint. Instead, Donker's adroit manipulation of the tradition of European grand history painting enables him to construct an inspiring Toussaint who still remains among the people.

The painting is highly accomplished, and it displays a strong sense of visual harmony that is derived from its precise composition. The painting orchestrates a snapshot view of a dynamic scene abounding with energy and movement. The pose in which Donkor has painted Toussaint could be held only for an instant, but it is here preserved in the stillness of Donkor's oils. Toussaint is astride his horse, which is rearing on its hind legs, and with an outstretched right arm holding his drawn sword, his pose is flamboyantly heroic. The painting thus also communicates a revolutionary fervor that recalls Delacroix's iconic painting of revolutionary uprising, *Liberty Leading the People*, in which a topless woman—part rebel of the people, part allegorical classical goddess—holds the tricolor aloft and strides over barricades and dead bodies, leading her fellow revolutionaries onward in the French July Revolution of 1830.

Like Delacroix's canvas, *Toussaint L'Ouverture at Bedourete* depicts the turbulence of a battle scene with multiple figures running, fighting, or collapsing around an inspiring single hero. Also, like *Liberty Leading the People*, the Toussaint painting superbly conveys the sense that what is being offered is a freeze-frame of a moment of historic upheaval in society. However, when the painting's elegant composition is examined, it becomes clear that although the canvas conveys the chaos of battle, the painting itself is in fact meticulously composed. The arrangement of the painting's subjects along a diagonal line that runs from the canvas's bottom-left to top-right corners helps to convey this sense of order. Starting with the black man in the left foreground and his left arm that points toward Toussaint, a diagonal line can be traced across and up the canvas that extends through the body of Toussaint's rearing horse and through the alignment of the rifle being aimed into the distance off the canvas in the painting's upper-right quadrant. This diagonal is interrupted by Toussaint's sword, which arcs from the painting's top-left quadrant to the figures in the lower-right foreground. Furthermore, the sense of motion that sweeps across the canvas, from bottom

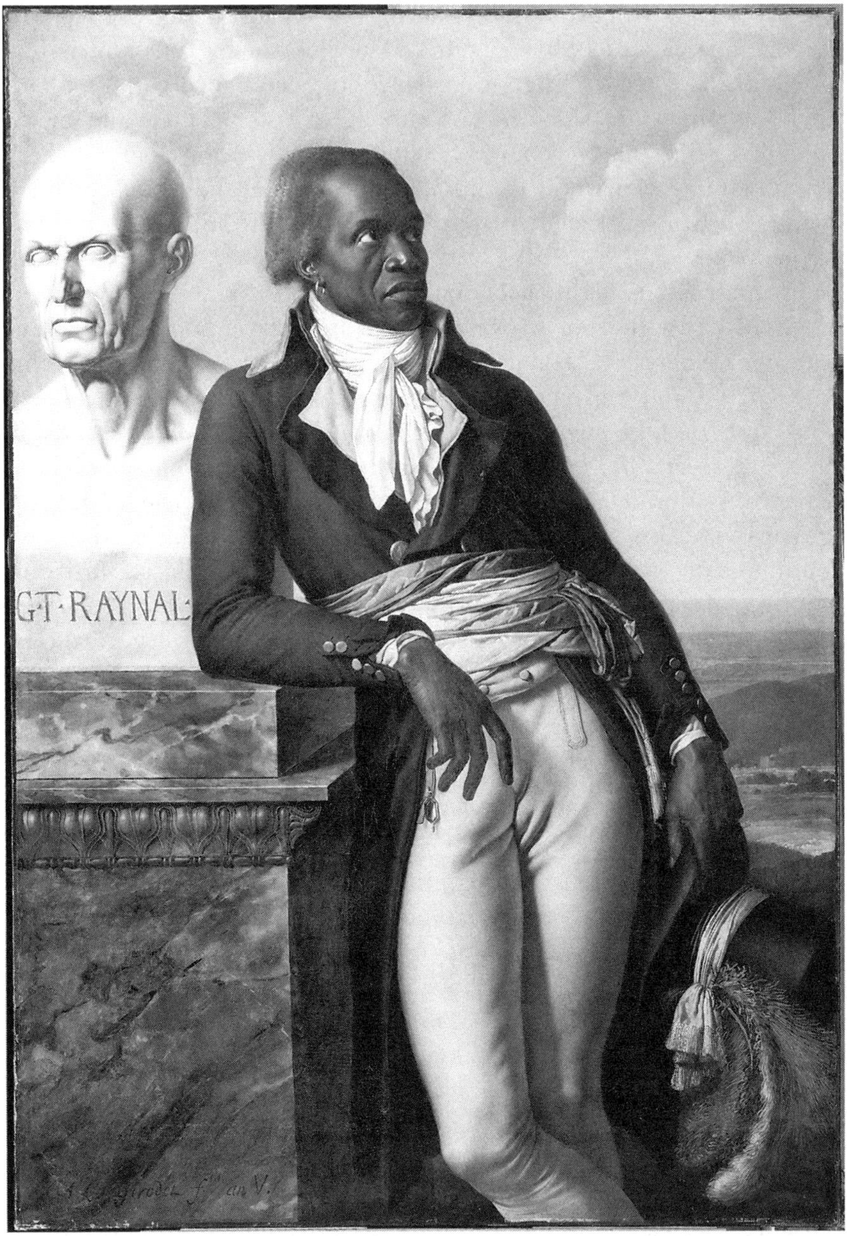

Figure 4. Anne-Louis Girodet, *Portrait of Citizen Belley*, 1797. Oil on canvas, 158 × 111 cm. Châteaux de Versailles et de Trianon, Versailles. (© RMN-Grand Palais [Château de Versailles] / Gérard Blot)

Figure 5. Eugène Delacroix, *Liberty Leading the People*, 1831. Oil on canvas, 325 × 260 cm. Musée du Louvre, Paris. (© RMN-Grand Palais [musée du Louvre] / Hervé Lewandowski)

left to top right, aids this composition and is reinforced by the gradient of the terrain, which inclines toward the top right. This carefully managed composition, although somewhat busy with bodies, attests to the artist's steady control over his subject.

The composition of *Toussaint L'Ouverture at Bedourete* also shares strong similarities with Jacques-Louis David's *Napoleon at the Saint-Bernard Pass*, which shows the French leader in a dramatic pose on his rearing stallion. The painting is also reminiscent of the final scene from Gillo Pontecorvo's 1969 film *Burn!,* in which the character of the heroic slave leader, who is loosely based on Toussaint, is also on horseback surrounded by his enthusiastic and determined allies on foot.[25] However, unlike in David's painting of Napoleon, Donkor chose not to show Toussaint as an all-conquering hero in splendid isolation. Instead, Donkor's painting is notable for its inclusion of the youthful ex-slave revolutionaries surrounding Toussaint. It is thus a painting that seeks also to accommodate the masses that made the revolution fighting at Toussaint's side.

Figure 6. Jacques-Louis David, *Napoleon at the Saint Bernard Pass*, 1801, 259 × 221 cm. Malmaison, Châteaux de Malmaison et Bois-Préau. (© RMN-Grand Palais [Musée des châteaux de Malmaison et de Bois-Préau] / Gérard Blot)

The Small Axe

The Small Axe is the most ambiguous painting in Donkor's Haiti series, and it makes a striking contrast to *Toussaint L'Ouverture at Bedourete.* Whereas the Toussaint painting is forthright in demonstrating its subject, its narrative, and its sense of place and occasion, *The Small Axe* is by contrast an equivocal work. It does not represent a specific or notable historical event, it is impossible to attribute to it a specific location or date, and it is unclear who the three subjects actually are. However, these features grant the painting a rewarding indeterminacy while complicating traditional notions of black agency and victimhood. *The Small Axe* thus goes to the heart of this book's argument.

In the foreground are two women, one white and one black; standing immediately behind the white woman is a black man. There is no white male figure present. The black man is holding the white woman by the back of her neck in order to direct her gaze toward the black woman's back. The black woman, who is holding the eponymous small axe in her right hand, has revealed her brutally scarred back by carefully lowering her red dress, but in such a way that she is still able to preserve her modesty. The black man is pointing at her scarred back with his left index finger in a gesture that recalls the apostle St. Thomas's act of poking his index finger into Christ's open wound in Caravaggio's *Doubting Thomas*. The black man's head and torso are both partially hidden from our view, but, from what can be seen, he is either unclothed or topless. Thus, with the black woman's back bared in the center of the canvas, and the black man not wearing any visible clothing, the painting achieves a strong sense of shared intimacy between the three figures and also between the figures and the painting's viewers. This intimacy in depicting the white woman's moment of visual confrontation with the black woman's horrendous scars heightens the sense of shock that the painting communicates.

The composition is highly assured: a diagonal runs from the canvas's upper-left quadrant through the gaze of the black man and the white woman through to the black man's left hand, and onto the black woman's right arm to her hand clasping the axe. This, and the use of space—three of the four corners are empty—gives the painting depth and impact. The themes of vision and looking are developed in a number of intricate ways crucial to the painting's complexly ambiguous narrative: for instance, by evincing the connection between sight and power, it challenges the received notions of the social hierarchies of Saint

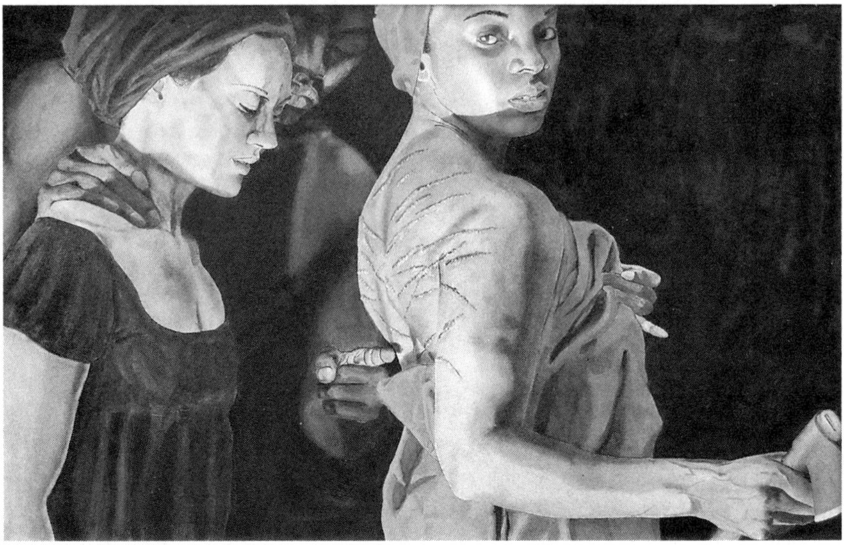

Figure 7. Kimathi Donkor, *The Small Axe*, 2004. Oil on linen, 70 × 100 cm. (Private collection)

Domingue. The scarred woman looks out from the painting not with a full stare but askance over her right shoulder, while the other two figures' heavily lidded eyes are shielded from view. The black male appears somber looking down, but ultimately, with his eyes hidden, his emotions cannot be determined with any certainty.

The white woman's eyes are also hidden by her eyelids and by the tilt of her head. They may be shut, but it is not made clear. The effect of keeping the white woman's eyes from our view is even more dramatic. Is she refusing to look or is she too traumatized to look at the black woman's scarred back? Is she wracked by guilt for her responsibility in savagely scarring this slave woman? Or is she distraught by her powerlessness? Has the white woman just seen the scarred and disfigured back and now her eyes are closed as she recoils in horror? Her body position suggests that she has been forced forward against her will. Her face, taut with tension, suggests great pain and anxiety, and perhaps also guilt and shame. The painting conveys a moment of shock superbly. The absence of a white male deepens the painting's quality of intimacy, which is derived not just from the representation of the three figures' ambiguous relationship, but also from the painting's understated composition. Unlike the busy Toussaint canvas, this painting harnesses the

Figure 8. Caravaggio, *Doubting Thomas*, ca. 1602–3. Oil on canvas, 107 × 146. Sanssouci, Potsdam.

elegant power of unfilled space. A considerable area of the canvas's right-hand side is blackly empty. This emptiness further focuses attention on the dynamic of the three figures' relationship, intensifying the painting's quality of intimacy.

The painting's sophisticated control of the symbolic act of seeing—who is looking at whom, or at what—and of who holds power over whom, is the painting's central dramatic question. None of the three figures seem to be in control of the situation: there is no direct eye contact between them. The black woman is the only figure with whom the viewer can make eye contact. Thus, although she might be considered the victim of the scene by virtue of her status as a torture victim, she is the only one of the three who is proactively looking. However, her look conveys worry—with her back turned she is vulnerable, and the painting also conveys the embarrassment of the public sharing of her private trauma. However, her scars have the power to shock, as the white woman's horror indicates, and they ensure that she holds a perverse power over the white woman. Thus, by staging a scene in which the drama of looking, or being looked at, is the main act, the painting communicates a scene of profound instability; power is balanced precariously, and serves as a metaphor for slave society in revolutionary Saint Domingue.

The Small Axe also poses a number of important questions: Why is the white woman in a headdress—does this suggest that she is, in fact, a light-skinned "mulatto"? If she is, how does this change the way we read the painting? Furthering the analysis of reading the painting in terms of its resonance to Caravaggio's *Doubting Thomas* leads us to note that the white woman is also clad in blue, thus evoking the color traditionally used for the clothing of the Virgin Mary.[26] Thus, if the black woman is being figured as Christ—they are both torture victims whose scars are pointed at and viewed—is the white woman's clothing a hint that she is being figured as Christ's mother? If so, the white woman's pain at looking at the brutally scarred back of the black woman is also the pain of a mother forced to look upon the brutal result of abuse suffered by her own child. In this scenario, the painting also comments on how their mother-daughter relationship cuts through the hierarchical racial divisions imposed on them by French colonial law. Whether we read the painting in such a manner or not, the intimacy between the white woman and the black woman nevertheless challenges our preconceptions about the relationship between white and black women in Saint Domingue, which has typically been constructed by novelists and playwrights in terms of enemies and as rivals for the sexual attention of the white male planter class.[27]

Furthermore, reading the black woman as Christ elevates her suffering to that of a religious martyr, rather than secular victimhood. As Marcus Wood has pointed out, this constitutes a bold and rare move: "The presentation of the black as the afflicted subject within the visual conventions of Christian martyrological iconography was, and is, exceptionally rare."[28] The painting further complicates traditional notions of black victimhood and powerlessness by giving the black woman a small axe. What is the black woman doing, or about to do, with the axe? This cannot be ascertained, but from Yoruba mythology to Bob Marley, axes are powerful symbolic signifiers. In Yoruba mythology, a double-headed axe symbolizes Shango Orisha, the god of thunder and lightning, and it is also representative of swift and balanced justice. Bob Marley's "Small Axe," on the other hand, is symbolic of resilience, creativity, and the dogged determination of the downtrodden. Either way, the black woman's clutching of a small axe is not an innocent symbol, and she cannot simply be read in the terms of a powerless victim.

In portraying the moment of shock in which the black woman's scarred back is seen and recognized for what it is, *The Small Axe* also recalls Toni Morrison's remembrance of slave torture and whipping in *Beloved*. In Morrison's novel, the moment at which Sethe's whipped and horrifically scarred back is also looked at and then recognized for what it is is one of the novel's most arresting passages. When Paul D., Sethe's friend, looks upon her back, he sees an unspeakably painful relic of suffering but also beauty. First he sees and feels the scars and imagines them to be the trunk, roots, branches, ridges, and leaves of a tree. However, when the illusion vanishes and he is confronted with the reality of "a revolting clump of scars," the moment is profoundly shocking.[29]

Like Morrison, Donkor's painting communicates the fact that the scars of being whipped are only a partial testimony of the suffering endured. Like Morrison, Donkor refuses a narrow representation of the site of torture as mere fact, as the photographic technique of forensic documentation does. Instead, by refusing to paint the black woman as a victim, by hinting at her status as a Christ-like redeemer, by forcing us to meet eyes with her, through the symbolism of the small axe, and without denying her suffering, *The Small Axe* turns the narratives of black victimhood and torture on their head. In their place, *The Small Axe* posits a complex story of black resistance. Thus both *Toussaint L'Ouverture at Bedourete* and *The Small Axe* demonstrate two very different ways of using the Haitian Revolution to convey the historical fact of black agency.

Philatelic Approaches to the Haitian Revolution

Most of my heroes don't appear on no stamps.

—Public Enemy, "Fight the Power"

Scholarly research that has considered postage stamps as ideological and cultural artifacts is scarce. Marcus Wood's chapter "Stamping Out the Memory of Slavery" in his recent monograph *The Horrible Gift of Freedom: Atlantic Slavery and the Representation of Emancipation* is the only extended discussion of the cultures of philately and Atlantic slavery.[30] Together with Wood's work, Nick Nesbitt's analysis of French Caribbean paper money in *Voicing Memory: History and Subjectivity in French Caribbean Literature* is notable for engaging with a comparable medium in which pictorial forms bear a highly concentrated ideological density.[31]

However, the fact that postage stamps are used by governments to promote and convey certain symbolic messages that are seen both nationally and internationally makes them useful primary sources. Commemorative postage stamps are a particularly good indicator of national identities, histories, and official cultures. Thus, the incorporation of the postage stamp into the spectrum of historical and cultural analysis is well overdue. This discussion provides an analysis of the design, imagery, and symbolism of a range of postage stamps issued to commemorate Toussaint and the revolution, including those issued by Haiti in 1904, 1954, and 2003, the West African Republic of Dahomey (now Benin) in 1963, and Cuba in 1991. The discussion also extends its frame of analysis to include the postage stamps that were issued by the British Royal Mail on March 22, 2007, to commemorate the British abolition of the slave trade by the Slave Trade Act of 1807.

It is also significant to this discussion that postage stamps are of particular interest to scholars of modern colonialism and imperialism. This is because of the deep connection between the postage stamp and imperialism. Soon after the British "Penny Black" became the world's first postage stamp in 1840, imperial enthusiasts and agitators petitioned for the penny rate to be made not just nationwide, but empirewide. In 1898, the campaigners got their wish, and two Canadian "Imperial Penny Postage" stamps bearing the slogan "We hold a vaster empire than has been" and showing a world map with Britain's possessions marked in red were issued to inaugurate the event.[32] Some twenty-six years later, the world's first commemorative postage stamps were issued for the 1924 British Empire Exhibition. Thus, from the beginning, postage stamps have been used by imperial nations to celebrate their colonial possessions. However, postcolonial and Third World nations have long since used stamp design to commemorate their independences and to communicate their national and shared histories of anticolonialism. Toussaint Louverture has been celebrated as a symbol of black heroism on commemorative stamps brought out in other parts of the Caribbean and countries of the francophone slave coast of West Africa. The symbolism and implications of Toussaint's appearance on a number of these commemorative stamps will be contrasted with Toussaint's nonappearance on Britain's 2007 commemorative stamps of the abolition of the slave trade.

Figure 9. Haiti, "Centennaire de l'independence." Toussaint Louverture commemorative postage stamps, 1904. (Maureen Bourne)

The Haitian Commemoratives of 1904, 1954, and 2003

While the 2- and 5-centimes stamps that Haiti brought out in 1904 to celebrate the centennial of independence depict Toussaint, he was by no means afforded the most privileged status in the series. In fact, the higher-value stamps in the series were devoted to some of the revolution's other heroes. Dessalines appears on the 7- and 10-centimes stamps and Pétion on the 20- and 50-centimes stamps, while the 1-centime stamp carries Haiti's revolutionary coat of arms as its centerpiece. Each stamp in the series is beautifully engraved and was printed in two strikes: the center portrait of each stamp is printed in black and framed with a striking single color. On the 2-centimes stamp, Toussaint is framed in red. and on the 5-centimes stamp he is framed in blue. However, the detail of the decorative frame remains constant for each stamp in the series: two young female figures—one European and one African or Indian—stand either side of each stamp's oval portrait of its heroic subject holding laurel branches aloft. The bottom center of each stamp displays Haiti's coat of arms and slogan, "Union fait la force"—Unity makes strength.

Figure 10. Haiti, 5-centimes stamp depicting Toussaint Louverture and commemorating the 150th anniversary of independence, 1954. (Maureen Bourne)

Figure 11. Haiti, 2-gourdes stamp commemorating the bicentennial of Toussaint's death, 2003. (Maureen Bourne)

It is notable that the portrait of Toussaint is also based on the Maurin image—Toussaint is clad in the same military uniform complete with a Napoleonic bicorne with plumage—although Toussaint's facial angle has been dramatically altered. Thus, the Haitian 1904 centenary stamps mimic traditional European philatelic modes of representing national figureheads, even down to the fact that Toussaint's profile has been Europeanized.

The stamps Haiti brought out in 1954 to commemorate the 150th anniversary of independence are more radical in their approach. However, once again Toussaint does not occupy the most privileged

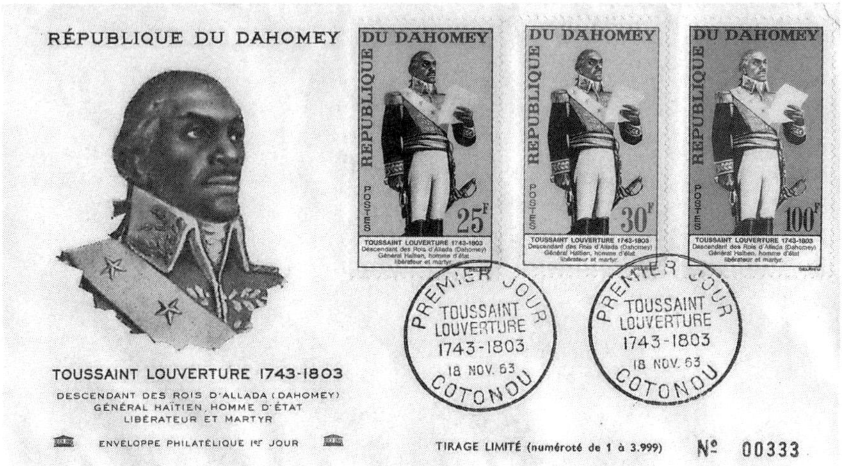

Figure 12. Republic of Dahomey, Toussaint Louverture commemorative postage stamps, First Day Cover, November 18, 1963. (Maureen Bourne)

position within the series. Toussaint's stamp is a 5-centimes stamp, whereas higher-value stamps in the 1954 sets commemorate legendary battles from the latter stages of the revolutionary war. The 25-centimes stamp celebrates the heroic actions of "Capois Death," a black officer in the revolutionary army who led a decisive assault on the French despite a bullet knocking down his horse.[33] The 50-centimes stamp celebrates the Battle of Vertières, at which, under the leadership of Dessalines, the Haitian Revolutionary Army decisively defeated Rochambeau and the French army. The day following the battle, November 19, 1803, Rochambeau settled terms of submission with Dessalines. Thus, while the higher-value 1954 stamps are given over to emphasizing black military heroism, the Toussaint stamp is once again based on the Maurin image. This time, however, unlike in 1904, Toussaint's profile is not Europeanized. Although the portrait does not carry the same conviction as Lawrence's remarkable subversion, the stamp is nevertheless notable as a visual statment of historicized racial pride.

Unlike the 1904 and 1954 stamps, the 2003 stamp was brought out in order to mark the death of Toussaint, not to commemorate the revolution itself, and it is based on a famous nineteenth-century equestrian portrait of Tossaint.[34] Here, Toussaint is depicted in splendid isolation as a military hero astride his rearing white stallion, Bel Argent. The 2003 Toussaint stamp's radicalism is to be found in its proud usurpation of "the position otherwise exclusively reserved in European portraiture for white monarchs, artistocrats, generals, and, of course, Napoleon himself."[35]

The Dahomey 1963 Toussaint Stamps and the Cuban 1991 Toussaint Stamp

Having established that postage stamps are cultural symbols that can shape identity discourses, it is also necessary to clarify the two key items of information that all commemorative postage stamps communicate. First, they must indicate a country of origin. Second, and this is their iconic role, they must represent a chosen aspect of that country.[36] Thus, one of the most striking things about the Dahomey 1963 Toussaint stamps is that they claim Toussaint as one of Dahomey's own. On each of the three different stamps as well as on both variations of the First Day Cover envelope design, Toussaint is described by the following words:

> Descendant of the Kings of Allada (Dahomey)
> Haitian General, statesman
> Liberator and martyr

Thus adopting Toussaint as a son of Dahomey, this representation of Toussaint connects Dahomey to Haiti, Africa to the Caribbean, and Haiti's independence of 1804 to Dahomey's independence of 1960 via blood kinship. The pictorial design of each of the stamps visually reinforces the message of Toussaint's inspirational status. Toussaint stands upright in three-quarter profile, erect and tall, reading an emancipation declaration. He is clad in a military uniform, complete with a sash, tassels, and stars.

The Cuban 1991 Toussaint stamp was issued not to commemorate Toussaint Louverture, but to commemorate the bicentenary of the outbreak of the Haitian Revolution. That the Cuban stamp celebrates the revolution, whereas the Dahomey stamps celebrate Toussaint the individual, is the critical ideological difference between these two First Day Covers. The Dahomey stamp and envelope do not bear the word "*Révolution*" anywhere; on the Cuban stamp, the word "*Revolucion*" is unmissable—it is used on the envelope design, in the postmark, and in the stamp design itself.

The envelope also depicts a battle scene, with burning houses and a crowd of revolutionaries running into battle and toward the mountains.

Figure 13. Republic of Cuba, bicentenary of the Haitian Revolution commemorative postage stamp, First Day Cover, November 20, 1991. (Maureen Bourne)

This is significant: whereas in all of the stamps that have been issued in France to commemorate the French Revolution the subject of violence has been carefully avoided—not even the storming of the Bastille features on any French stamp—the Cuban stamp does not sidestep the task of remembering violence.[37] The Cuban stamp thus evokes historical memory of revolution with great fervency and implies a great empathy with the taking up of arms against outrageous oppression.

Toussaint appears on the Cuban commemorative First Day Cover as the subject of the stamp itself and also in the postmark. The postmark presents a version of the well-known equestrian portrait of Toussaint in which he appears in full military uniform on a rearing horse and holding a curved sword, an image that as we have seen would later inspire artists including Kimathi Donkor. In the three-quarter portrait on the stamp, Toussaint is represented in military uniform with his feather cockade in the colors of the French tricolor, and these are also used to frame the portrait. The social realist style of the portrait has been adopted from Soviet art.[38] Toussaint's messianic gaze in the portrait recalls the intensity of Che Guevara's steely expression in the famous photograph of him that was captured by Alberto Korda in 1960, and which has since become probably the most reproduced iconic image of revolution anywhere.

The propaganda function the Cuban stamp performs seems to be that it was designed to draw out certain similarities between Cuba at the time of issue and revolutionary Haiti. Issued in 1991, after the collapse of the Soviet Union, Cuba's key ally, this commemorative stamp was issued as Cuba entered a new period of economic uncertainty, and with its sovereignty looking ever more fragile. It certainly seems probable that during this difficult period the Haitian Revolution was invoked by the Cuban government to provide an example of revolutionary success that was achieved despite a lack of international support and in the face of powerful counterrevolutionary forces. Whereas on the Dahomey stamp Toussaint was figured as a Pan-African icon, connecting Africa with the Caribbean, on the Cuban stamp Toussaint is instrumentalized as an icon of revolution and the universal desire for freedom.

The British 2007 Abolition of the Slave Trade Stamps

Amid the official fanfare, state ceremonies, and self-congratulation that characterized the British government's orchestrated celebrations of the bicentenary of the 1807 Slave Trade Act, the Haitian Revolution was conveniently sidelined. The Royal Mail commemorative stamps that were issued to memorialize the event reveal the way in which Britain would like to remember the history of slavery and her involvement in bringing about its end. The British stamps belong to a long tradition in which the British campaign to abolish the slave trade has become a national myth in which the work of a handful of Christian dissidents has usurped the role of black agency generally, obfuscating and erasing the historical reality of slave revolutionaries in Haiti, and other slave rebels and maroons throughout the Caribbean, United States, and Latin America. It is a discourse that has developed widely, including within academic and popular publishing, as Philippe Girard has noted: "Books on England's Caribbean policy in the 1790s—arguably not its finest hour—are far outnumbered by the outpouring of research on its abolitionist movement."[39] However, thanks to the work of scholars such as David Geggus, the profound and indisputable impact that the Haitian Revolution had on the process of British abolition has been made abundantly clear.[40] Yet, Toussaint's absence from Britain's 2007 Abolition of the Slave Trade commemorative stamps signals the incompatability of the Haitian Revolution with the British national memory of Atlantic slavery, in which a mythologized narrative about abolition has displaced trauma, guilt, and black agency.

Figure 14. United Kingdom, abolition of the slave trade commemorative postage stamps, Royal Mail First Day Cover, March 22, 2007. (Maureen Bourne)

In order to understand better the propaganda function of the 2007 stamps, they need to be placed in the broader context of the bicentenary of the abolition of the slave trade as a national event in Britain.[41] In his recent article "Interpreting 2004: Politics, Memory, Scholarship," Charles Forsdick has reflected on the presence and absence of references to Haiti in the events surrounding the 2007 bicentenary, observing: "In Great Britain, the bicentenary of the abolition of the slave trade has had such an influence—as a result of media, literary, and cinematic representations, as well as through prominent acts of public commemoration, the opening of new institutions and associated debates—questions of slavery, of its abolition, and of its persistence have achieved a prominence they are often systematically denied in Europe."[42] However, Forsdick also noted that within the preponderance of media, cultural, and state-sanctioned attention that was given to the bicentenary of the abolition of the slave trade, Haiti was very effectively marginalized. Forsdick noted that Haiti "remains for the British press an exotic anomaly, still routinely associated with Graham Greene and the Duvaliers [and tending to] exemplify and even permit the accentuation of certain pejorative assumptions about postcolonial cultures."[43] Remembering the Haitian Revolution as a foundational moment in the stuggle for universal freedom in such a context remains strictly off-limits, whether in the design of commemorative stamps or any other format. Thus the 2007 celebrations were successfully passed off without, for example, any acknowledgment of Britain's disastrous military intervention in Saint Domingue in the 1790s or the military expedition's purpose, and without any discussion of Haiti's emblematic status as the site at which the processes of decolonization and neocolonialism first emerged.[44] Forsdick isolates a fine example of this process of marginalizing Haiti in the Michael Apted film *Amazing Grace*. The one scene in the film in which Haiti is granted a fleeting mention manages to make Wilberforce the catalyst of the Haitian Revolution and thereby deny and disavow the agency of enslaved people: "In 1806, as Wilberforce's campaign entered its final phase, Apted's film shows the abolitionist lawyer James Stephen, author of an early biography of Toussaint Louverture, referring to events in Saint-Domingue. Stephen describes a scene in which an enslaved mother tells her child about 'King Wilberforce' coming across the sea to free them."[45]

All of this fits into the pattern that has been identified and analyzed as processes of silencing and disavowal in the works of Michel-Rolph Trouillot, Sibylle Fischer, and Susan Buck-Morss and also discussed in the introduction to this volume. However, some dissident voices did manage to make themselves heard above the din of "Wilber-mania" and national self-congratulation that so characterized the 2007 celebrations. These dissident voices highlighted Haiti's absence from the public debate by raising questions about the absence of black resistance, rebellion, and revolution generally in the commemorations. Some critics memorably dubbed and dismissed the bicentennial as a "Wilberfest" or "Wilberfarce," and their high-profile interventions included Toyin Agbetu's disruption of the official bicentenary service in Westminster Abbey in March 2007; and the Truth 2007 campaign, a grassroots initiative that developed in Bristol, whose members disassociated themselves from all events that heralded the actions of abolitionists such as William Wilberforce as the primary emancipators of enslaved Africans in 1807.[46]

It is in this context that the 2007 commemorative stamps must be placed. Their conservatism in every detail is impossible to overlook when one scrutinizes the stamps themselves, the First Day Cover envelope design, and the postmarks.[47] The six stamps bear portraits of William Wilberforce, Olaudah Equiano, Granville Sharp, Thomas Clarkson, Hannah More, and Ignatius Sancho. Thus, although two black faces do appear in the commemoratives, the collection gives the overall impression that these two figures of fundamental significance to black British history have simply been slotted into an elite abolitionist club. Although

Olaudah Equiano's writings contributed so much to the abolitionist cause, the success of which he did not live to see, it should be pointed out that Ignatius Sancho was only rather tangentially connected to abolitionism.[48] Notwithstanding the facts of Sancho's extraordinary life, it is also worth remembering that for the British establishment Sancho represents the acceptable face of black freedom: rescued by an aristocrat, loyal to the monarchy, and supportive of the British during the American Revolutionary War.[49] The sad conclusion that must be drawn from the analysis of the 2007 British commemoratives can only be that their failure to represent black agency, their graphic conservatism, and their dedication to supplanting the memory of slavery with the British national myth of abolition make them poor relations indeed to the radical sets already discussed from Haiti, Cuba, and Dahomey inspired by the Haitian Revolution.

Part Two

Conservative Visions

Pessimism, Seduction, and Fantasy

5 Edouard Glissant's *Monsieur Toussaint*

Conservatism Hidden in *Relation*

EDOUARD GLISSANT'S ONLY PUBLISHED PLAY, *Monsieur Toussaint*, suggests that there is no one "true" account or interpretation of the Haitian Revolution or of its most celebrated figure, Toussaint Louverture.[1] In *Monsieur Toussaint*, Glissant's representation of Toussaint cannot be seen as a dramatic attempt to portray him realistically, but instead, Toussaint is used as an exemplar of the Glissantian concepts of *Relation* and *créolité*. In the preface to the 1961 first edition, Glissant claimed that the work is not politically inspired, and that rather it is linked to what he calls, paradoxically, "*a prophetic vision of the past*."[2] This chapter examines the aesthetics and politics of Glissant's play, paying particular attention to the means by which the play articulates or departs from Glissant's own theoretical work, arguing that the play offers incipient glimpses of the deradicalized political position that Glissant would adopt more fully in his later career. I make the argument that Glissant's recuperation of Haitian history in *Monsieur Toussaint* reveals the ambiguity and ultimate impossibility of any Glissantian politics. As such, I suggest that there is a puzzling discordance between Glissant's radical activism of the 1960s and the political pessimism *Monsieur Toussaint* betrays. For this purpose, I draw upon Peter Hallward's *Absolutely Postcolonial* and Chris Bongie's *Friends and Enemies*.

Hallward's study tracks what he finds to be the increasing depoliticization of Glissant's work, and in so doing, Hallward argues that not one, but two Glissants exist, an early radical and politically engaged one, and a later one who withdraws his works from political engagement. Thus, Hallward writes that whereas "Glissant's early texts narrate the constitution of the nation," the later texts generally celebrate a "global post-national reconciliation" and the dissolution of the nation.[3] Beginning with an argument that Glissant's early work is compatible with the radical anticolonialism of Fanon and Césaire, Hallward provides persuasive readings of Glissant's first two novels—*La Lézarde* (1958) and *Le quatrième siècle* (1964)—as being wholly engaged in a nationalist project, and illustrative of its most optimistic phase.[4] Hallward then develops a devastating critique of Glissant's later work, in which the 1990 text *Poétique de la Relation* plays a crucial role. The analysis makes clear the extent to which Glissant's *Poétique de la Relation* trades nationalist politics for a new project of "planetary coherence": "Glissant's new conception of Relation announces an age *beyond national itineraries*—the age, in a sense, of places without or beyond nationhood."[5] Thus, for Hallward, Glissant's postnational turn is a prominent example of the broader intellectual focus on culture, rather than on economics or politics by the post-1968 Left (a shift clearly reminiscent of Depestre's conservative turn discussed earlier).[6] For Hallward, since "institutional alternatives to the national state remain hypothetical at best," the limitations of Glissant's postnationalist cultural politics are revealed in sharp relief.[7] Finally, Hallward argues, Glissant's work from the *Poétique de la Relation* of 1990 onward can only obstruct one of the great political tasks of our time: "the articulation of fully inclusive, fully egalitarian political principles."[8]

Chris Bongie's recent work *Friends and Enemies: The Scribal Politics of Post/Colonial Literature* develops Hallward's critique of Glissant, and strategically amends Bongie's own earlier reading of Glissant in *Islands and Exiles*. In *Friends and Enemies*, Bongie argues that in his late writings Glissant effectively abandoned emancipatory politics, replacing it with a "utopian insistence on an all-inclusive poetics of Relation" that constitutes a "recantation of the once trenchant political commitments that constituted one half of his lifelong, modernist project."[9] Thus, whereas the radicalism of Glissant's early work was informed by the Marxist thesis of false consciousness and draws upon Fanonian and Sartrean Hegelianism, Glissant's late writings, Bongie argues, refrain from employing this methodology for anything other than *aesthetic* critique alone.[10] Indeed, in the later works, Bongie finds that Glissant puts the case that injustice can—and even should only—be opposed through the "cultural imaginary."[11]

It is my argument in this chapter that *Monsieur Toussaint*—a key early text in Glissant's career, first written as a radio play in 1959 and published in 1961, and then rewritten as a *version scénique* in 1977 and published in 1986[12]—reveals, in incipient form, the pitfalls of an emancipatory Glissantian politics. My reading asserts that any attempt to identify a straightforward divide between the "early" and the "late" Glissant is problematic: although the initial version of *Monsieur Toussaint* chronologically appears between Glissant's two early novels of optimistic radical nationalism, *La Lézarde* (1958) and *Le quatrième siècle* (1964), it cannot be situated in their company from the perspective of a critical politics. My argument thus diverges from interventions into the discussion surrounding the periodization of Glissant's late work by Celia Britton and Charles Forsdick. In contrast to the contention that the "late" Glissant abandoned political commitment, Celia Britton argues that Glissant's later texts in fact explore possibilities of new kinds of political action that could be effective in the era of globalization.[13] And Charles Forsdick has also argued against perceiving works from Glissant's "late" period as either depoliticized or apolitical: "What remains striking about Glissant—and what distinguishes him from the disenchanted lateness of a near contemporary such as René Depestre . . . is the way in which a form of active political engagement nevertheless persists."[14]

For Forsdick, the politics of Glissant's late works are to be found in their persistent engagement in "key political debates in postcolonial France, and in the wider French-speaking world, relating to the French Empire and its afterlives."[15] However, in contrast to these critical positions, my argument is that *Monsieur Toussaint* should be read as a text that foreshadows Glissant's later conservative retreat to cultural politics, a position that becomes most clearly apparent in the 1990 work *Poétique de la Relation.*

Monsieur Toussaint, *Relation*, and Conservativism

Monsieur Toussaint has not yet drawn the extensive critical attention that Glissant's essays, novels, and poetry have. It has been widely alleged that Glissant's only play lacks the sophistication of his other works. It has frequently been dismissed as being a cumbersome and unwieldy drama that is too densely packed with historical details, too dense with dialogue, too problematic for actual stage production, and for failing to bring the historical players convincingly to life. These are criticisms mostly well placed: indeed, it must be admitted that, in common with C. L. R. James's play *The Black Jacobins*, there is a woodenness to much of the dialogue. At times the play's language strains with the weight of the history that the play recuperates for the audience to reconsider. It is also very demanding of its readers and theatergoers, both in terms of the play's form and the level of historical knowledge with which the play assumes the audience is familiar. The audience is plunged into events with no historical or narrative introduction and is required to make sense of a nonlinear, elliptical narrative form. The play is divided thematically into four acts, "The Gods," "The Dead," "The People," and "The Heroes," rather than into a straightforward chronological sequence. Nor does the play's setting help matters since it is precariously set simultaneously in Saint Domingue and at the same time in Toussaint's prison cell at the Fort de Joux in the French Jura Mountains. As the play opens, the revolution in Saint Domingue is already in its eleventh year, but historical figures long since dead from Saint Domingue and the wider Caribbean are central characters. However, as a text that casts light on Glissant's slippery concept of *Relation*, *Monsieur Toussaint* remains a fascinating work that reveals Glissant's precocious conservatism.

However, in order to sustain my argument that Glissant's abstract concept of *Relation* is housed in *Monsieur Toussaint's* formal and aesthetic framework, and that the play foreshadows the author's future turn to antipolitical critique, it is necessary to consider the major critical responses to Glissant's concept of *Relation*, which has been said to underpin the entire corpus of Glissant's theoretical work. Celia Britton defines Glissantian *Relation* as a system rather than as a number of separate, singular relations, but also as "a fluid and unsystematic system whose elements are engaged in a radically nonhierarchical free play of interrelatedness."[16] However, Britton also contends that *Relation* is "an anti-imperialist project": in opposition to the colonizers' singular hierarchies, *Relation*, it is alleged, posits a dynamic of nonhierarchical multiplicity.[17] Whether such multiplicity is something to be celebrated unambiguously is in itself a moot point.[18] Further, Britton has since modified her position, writing that although *Relation* was *originally* an anti-imperialist project, in Glissant's later works, *Relation* became "a global reality," defining identity in "relational terms rather than as the 'root-identity' that fueled colonial conquest and still fuels sectarian politics."[19] Thus, even among defenders of the concept, the attribution of any clear anti-imperialist quality to the concept appears somewhat dubious.

Monsieur Toussaint formally and aesthetically expounds the concept of *Relation* in various ways. Dispensing with realistic representative techniques of temporal and spatial dimensions, *Monsieur Toussaint* enacts Glissant's claim that "centres and peripheries are void notions."[20] And in Glissant's representation of the character of Toussaint the concept is fully realized: Glissant's Toussaint is a concept metaphor, a figure, Charles Forsdick writes, "in whom the distinction between the metropolitan centre and the peripheries has been eclipsed. . . . Glissant's refiguring of Toussaint represents a prototypical illustration of the precarious notion of *la Relation*."[21] Eschewing a *root identity* founded in a belief in the certainty of origins in favor of a *relational identity* linked to the contradictory but furtive experience of contact among cultures, Glissant's Toussaint comes to life as a symbol of a modern, creolized, and anticolonial Caribbean.

Monsieur Toussaint thus communicates Glissant's perspective of interrelationships and the new contexts and connections they produce, as well as the tensions to which their frequently contradictory forces give rise. The Haitian Revolution is presented to the reader and audience in a chaotic network of *Relation* in which the interconnectedness of world and local cultures is seen to have produced powerful and conflicting forces. Glissant sets up the character of Toussaint as the subject of these conflicting forces: Toussaint's Glissantian fate is to fail while striving to balance the cultures of Africa, the Caribbean, and Europe, which have combined to create his people and his personal context. Thus, when Toussaint is shown to be struggling to reconcile his divided affiliations to, for example, the incommensurate ideologies of *maroonage* and Jacobinism, or vodou and Christianity, he reveals his entrapment in the contradictions of a colonial French-Caribbean strand of relations. Toussaint is subject to, and the subject of, a creolized modernity, and the focal point in an anticolonial struggle of a dynamic array of cultural, intellectual, and practical contradictions and uncertainties. As well as the concept of *Relation*, the play is thus also, as Glissant himself points out in the foreword, the mise-en-scène of Glissant's political concept of historical memory, which he dubs "*a prophetic vision of the past*."[22]

Monsieur Toussaint expresses these ideas through a number of aesthetic devices. The play begins with a detailed stage direction that indicates the method through which the play structurally destabilizes our sense of place and space: "The play is set in Saint Domingue and at the same time in a cell at the Fort de Joux where Toussaint is being held prisoner."[23] By symbolically compressing space in this way, the staging of the play impresses upon the theatergoer or the reader the possibility of the transfer and movement of not just goods and commodities from the colony to the colonizing power, but of the movement of ideas from one place to the other. Neither space is hermeneutically sealed: whenever the action takes place in Saint Domingue but requires the presence of Toussaint, the stage directions inform us that Toussaint simply "moves into the space at the front of the cell. . . . There is no clearly defined frontier between the world of the prison in France and the lands of the Caribbean island."[24] Toussaint's world is always in a state of flux; both *Relation* and its theatrical counterpart in *Monsieur Toussaint* initiate a move toward a concept of globalization, demonstrating the flow of ideas, and embedding in the play's structure connections across space and time.

The play's representation of Toussaint held prisoner in his cell in the Jura also bears comparison with Césaire's description of Toussaint imprisoned in the *Cahier.*[25] In the *Cahier,* the cold, small cell in the white snow represented an affront to Toussaint's dignity and status as the heroic and upright symbol of négritude. The potent color symbolism of the *Cahier* also used the white snow surrounding Toussaint's cell to emphasize his solitude and his isolation from the final, dramatic sequences of the revolution in Saint Domingue. However, Césaire does not present Toussaint's revolutionary spirit as something that can be simply locked away: it overflows and mixes with the narrator's own subjectivity in the *Cahier.* Glissant extends Césaire's idea that Toussaint cannot be separated from the Caribbean people as *Monsieur Toussaint* makes the point that Toussaint's cell is not just deterritorialized but becomes the locus for interaction with ideas and people from both sides of the Atlantic, as well as from elsewhere in the Caribbean. And just as there is no clear demarcation between the Caribbean and France, there is no clear demarcation between the worlds of the living and of the dead. Toussaint is visited by a host of characters including a vodou priestess, the spirits of Makandal, Moïse, and other slave rebels, Toussaint's former master Bayon-Libertat, as well as Toussaint's prison guards and Napoleon's envoy. At times this approach makes for a chaotic and jumpy narrative, but it does hold the advantage that the formal quality of the play fits the twin concepts of *Relation* and creolization that the play articulates. The disorientating effect, built into the play's structure, serves to illustrate Toussaint's own disorientation and self-doubt as he suffers the consequences of living through the painful experience of being caught in between conflicting worlds, cultures, ideas, languages, and histories. With this in mind, J. Michael Dash's analysis of the play as "a somewhat surreal journey into the mind of Toussaint Louverture" that, "in formal terms, can best be seen as a stylized oratorio" seems particularly apposite.[26]

Monsieur Toussaint as a Pan-Caribbean Text

Monsieur Toussaint is also a Pan-Caribbean text, and Glissant is careful to show that Haiti's cultural formation was not a singular event in the Caribbean, even if the historical fact of the achievement of independence by revolution does make Haiti a special case. The spirit of the Martinican Louis Delgrès, the mulatto leader of the resistance against the reoccupation and the reinstitution of slavery in Martinique, is among the cast of historical characters who appear around Toussaint in his cell. Delgrès and his followers, facing certain defeat after a heroic struggle, committed suicide en masse on the Matouba volcano in Guadeloupe on May 28, 1802, a little less than a year before Toussaint's death, by detonating their gunpowder reserves.[27] Delgrès's inclusion in the play exemplifies Dash's observation that "Toussaint's deterritorialized cell is meant to be seen as an island in the New World archipelago."[28] It is indicative of the pan-Caribbean valency of Glissant's representation of Toussaint, and it is also a further element in the conflicting network of *Relation* that haunts Toussaint. Moreover, the presence of Delgrès along with Makandal also introduces the theme of revolutionary legacy into the play. Was Toussaint inspired by either the maroon Makandal or the example of Delgrès? And can we see Toussaint as the inheritor of Makandal's and Delgrès's anticolonial struggles? In their most dramatic exchange, Delgrès unsettles Toussaint as they interrogate the true worth of each other's actions:

TOUSSAINT: Colonel Delgrès, you think it is a long way from your Matouba to my prison? That I was free to choose another fate? That I was worthy of another death, a powder more glorious than this dust-like snow in which I will perish slowly, wretchedly?

DELGRÈS: Which of us has accomplished more than Toussaint?

TOUSSAINT: . . . Don't announce my death just yet, it is my turn to prevail over you, my companions.[29]

Glissant had certainly been attracted to the idea of linking Delgrès to Toussaint for some time: in his early book-length epic poem *The Indies*, which takes for its subject the entire history of the Caribbean, Glissant begins the canto entitled "The Heroes" as follows: "Thus, to evoke the obscure epic—Delgrès: fought to the death against forces far superior in number and armament. Perhaps his example sustained the will of—Toussaint: he who also died for this cause."[30]

Thus Glissant draws out the interconnected nature of Caribbean resistance to slavery: along with the news of Toussaint's capture, it was the news of Delgrès's defeat by Richepance and the reimposition of slavery that radicalized the Haitian Revolution and impelled it to its successful conclusion—Delgrès triumphed in his very defeat, but not where he thought he was fighting. It is also noteworthy that Glissant was not the first to link Delgrès's story to the Haitian Revolution. Dessalines did so shortly after independence in Haiti had been achieved, and Césaire's poem "Memorial for Louis Delgrès" draws on this, beginning with two epigraphs. One is an extract from Dessalines's "Proclamation to the Haitians" of April 28, 1804, in which he declaims the brave example of Delgrès: "Guadeloupe pillaged and destroyed, its ruins still smoking from its children's blood, women and old men put to the sword . . . the brave and immortal Delgrès blown into the air with the debris of his fort rather than accepting shackles. A magnanimous warrior!"[31] Dessalines's invocation of Delgrès serves as further evidence that we should not, as is the prevailing trend, interpret the events of the Haitian Revolution as a unique or freak event, and nor should we see the May 1802 revolt led by Delgrès as a failure.

Another key player represented in *Monsieur Toussaint* whose inclusion contributes to the recuperation of Haiti's revolutionary heritage is Makandal. Unlike Toussaint, Makandal's cultural and intellectual formation and political loyalties are a fairly straightforward matter. Whereas Toussaint is a divided and creolized figure who had some access to the philosophies and politics of the European Enlightenment, Makandal's identity is clearly formed by Africa, vodou, and *maroonage*. While Toussaint is caught between the conflicting ideologies of *maroonage* and French revolutionary Jacobinism, or idealistic revolutionary internationalism, Makandal's commitment to *maroonage* and a rejection of Western values is absolute. However, *Monsieur Toussaint* does show *maroonage* to be an inward-looking form of resistance, whereas the Jacobin ideals of the French Revolution, which had already been betrayed in the metropolitan center by the time of Toussaint's capture and imprisonment, are shown to have been attractive to Toussaint since in them he saw the possibility of their achievement in a free and postrevolutionary Saint Domingue. Thus, although Toussaint does not reject *maroonage* outright, the constant presence of the legendary maroon Makandal serves to illustrate the cultural and intellectual distance that separated Toussaint from the masses. Toussaint could not disown his affection for the Enlightenment utopianism of the French Revolution; Toussaint wished to lead Saint Domingue to an authentic freedom, in which law and order, science and knowledge, would be integral elements. This is made clear by Toussaint's words to a common soldier: "If you win in disorder and madness, you will still be slaves."[32]

The tension between Makandal's and Toussaint's different intellectual and revolutionary trajectories is clearly expressed in a conversation between the two men, Toussaint alive and trapped in his cell, and Makandal as one of the inhabitants of the world of the Dead who converse with Toussaint throughout the play. Toussaint is portayed as having been unaware of Makandal's spirited resistance against slavery—as a slave and then a coachman on the Breda plantation, he had not heard tales of the inspiring Makandal. In a scene in which Toussaint jumps to his former master's defense, Makandal pertinently points out that despite Toussaint's protestations that his former master was "good and just," he is still a man from whom Toussaint must steal his freedom as a "thief who kills and pillages."[33] Toussaint's difficulties in getting his men to relate to the principles for which he wants them to fight are exacerbated when Toussaint switches allegiance from the Spanish to the French midrevolution. It is a moment that has often been celebrated as being a diplomatic maneuver of great cunning, but in Glissant's drama, when Toussaint responds to the news that the French Republic has decreed the equality of all men by accepting the National Convention's gift of the title "Brigadier General," it is, in the eyes of Macaïa, a dead slave rebel leader, an act of betrayal that renders Toussaint "already more dead than I in this icy room":

> So, one fine morning, he hears the mass, he communes with his God. He was on good terms with his personal confessor, as they say. Then he ups and attacks his old allies, his friend and brother Biassou! They all shared each other's trust, and Toussaint was the most trustworthy of all! Betrayal made him into a Republican general.[34]

When Macaïa's words are heard by Delgrès, the complexity of Toussaint's dilemma is captured in Delgrès's simple question—"Is that true, my General, is it true?"[35] The response of Toussaint, who had placed his faith in Laveaux and in the National Assembly that had been created by the French Revolution, which had finally voted for an abolition decree, is an impassioned attempt to explain the rational basis for the actions he took. That both Delgrès and Toussaint were Enlightnement and French Revolution figures in its paradigmatic tropicalization is clear, but Toussaint's argument that he trusted the Assembly to make good on its decree, and that he trusted the French Jacobins and Laveaux, does not appease Makandal, who cannot forgive Toussaint for waging war on the early black rebel leader and ex-slave Biassou, who had continued to fight for Spain.

The Haitian Revolution created unsustainable allegiances, enemies of friends and friends of enemies, and as Glissant's play demonstrates, it pressed Toussaint into making decisions that would inevitably divide his own people. Macaïa and Makandal are not persuaded by Toussaint's pleading and protestation from his prison cell; on the contrary, in Toussaint they see a revolutionary seduced by false idols and a false god. They believe Toussaint to have been seduced by the ideals of the French Revolution, and that those ideals cannot be transported to the revolutionary struggle in Haiti. When Macaïa cries out: "Freedom cannot be taught! And there is no timetable for it! Freedom has grown in the forest ever since the slave trade began," it is a direct rejection of Toussaint's political ambition and intellectual investment.

Toussaint's embrace of Christianity is a further source of tension that the play exploits. Knowing that his faith pits him against his ancestors, Toussaint asks the question: "I know universal faith, is that my fault?" before he explains, "I love the peace this religion brings."[36] The question of the "fault" is a central one in Glissant's representation of Toussaint: he certainly feels privileged to have been exposed to Enlightenment ideals and the culture and religion of France. However, *Monsieur Toussaint* is in many ways an expression of the painful intermingling of those ideals. C. L. R. James called Toussaint a great man and claimed that "great men make history, but only such history as it is possible for them to make";[37] Glissant, on the other hand, depicts Toussaint as a man torn apart by history. Toussaint, then, for Glissant, is not a mythological maker of history, but merely *Monsieur* Toussaint, Toussaint's self-adopted surname "L'ouverture"—"the opening"—is stripped from him just as the prison guards remove Toussaint's sash and uniform, giving him instead the overalls of an ordinary peasant. From this image, however, the question arises: How can this be reconciled with Glissant's early radical politics? And what are we to read into Glissant's belittling of the capacity for self-designation and understanding? It is my contention here that these tensions are not resolvable: certainly Glissant's Toussaint is far removed from his representation as the liberator and symbol of négritude as summoned by Césaire. Whereas Césaire and James needed to mythologize Toussaint for their projects, Glissant needed to *demythologize* Toussaint for his. For Césaire, Toussaint was a bold exemplar of upright négritude, and for James, the Toussaint myth was the means by which he could fashion a "great man" of world history in the hope that he would provide a model for the twentieth-century anticolonial struggles in Africa. But Glissant's recuperation does something rather different: it reveals the man whose actions would later generate the myth and in so doing, his recuperation evokes Toussaint's human frailties whereas Césaire and James glossed over them. And yet Glissant's Toussaint is an aesthetic creation that first emerged precisely when Glissant was agitating for Martinique's independence. Perceiving Toussaint through Glissant's thesis of *Relation* does not require the invoking of a great man or a myth. Rather, it emphasizes the Caribbean region's richly syncretic heritage, in which Toussaint was a heroic, and tragic, all-too-human player.

Glissant, Césaire, and Theater

Glissant's earliest published representation of Toussaint comes in his epic poem *The Indies*. Here, the influence of Césaire's portrait of Toussaint in the *Cahier* can be strongly felt. The canto begins by comparing Toussaint to the mythological creature the centaur, and ends with Glissant borrowing from Césaire's reworking of the fertility myth in which Toussaint fills the role of the dying and reviving god. The canto begins: "Toussaint, already named, who was centaur, and came to die on the frozen sand of the empire," and concludes with: "Let him die O let him die, and let the forest grow."[38]

It is interesting to note Césaire's and Glissant's similarities and divergences when it comes to their reworking of the Toussaint myth. Forsdick has argued that in *Monsieur Toussaint,* Glissant departs from Césaire's analysis in his historical work *Toussaint Louverture*, and that, crucially, Glissant's recuperation marks an important development of the Toussaint myth in response to and away from Césaire. Both Césaire and Glissant saw in Toussaint a contradictory, multiple, and partial figure, but their different critical interpretations ensured that the way in which he was adapted to their projects was also different.

Whereas I have claimed that Césaire's recuperation of Toussaint should be considered radical, and Glissant's conservative, Forsdick has contrasted what he regards as Glissant's "open" and Césaire's "closed" interpretations. Forsdick claims that Glissant saw Toussaint's heteronomy as an opportunity to make him metonymically stand for the complexity and richness of Caribbean history. Forsdick then contrasts this by arguing that for Césaire, Toussaint's heteronomy was paralyzing, the ultimate exemplar of "le problème colonial." As such, Forsdick's analysis would seem to reinforce the mood of the general shift away from Césairean thought that can be witnessed in recent years: in this school of thought, Glissantian *créolité*'s "openness" represents a more sophisticated, politically furtive development of Césairean "closed" négritude. And yet, Césaire's position is the politically more incisive stance: the argument that Césaire's Toussaint is ultimately only a "problematic convergence of issues" overlooks Césaire's representation of Toussaint in the *Cahier.*[39] Here, Toussaint is not a dead-end of contradictions: he is represented as a Nietzschean tragic hero to whom Césaire ascribes the paradigm of primitive Greek fertility myths, and he thereby becomes the source of a revived Caribbean subjectivity.

Reading Glissant's *Monsieur Toussaint* alongside Césaire's play *La tragédie du roi Christophe*, and Glissant's own writings on theater in *Caribbean Discourse* is also a rewarding project: surprisingly perhaps, it is Césaire's play rather than Glissant's that seems to capture much more of the life and folklore of revolutionary Haiti. Whereas Césaire's play is varied in tone, tragicomic, and a dynamic blend of theater, ritual, and dance, Glissant's play remains a think-piece that never quite becomes living theater. It is thus somewhat ironic that Glissant's *Monsieur Toussaint* never quite convinces and that it carries no echo of his writing on theater. In "Theater, Consciousness of the People" in *Caribbean Disourse*, Glissant writes about theater as a necessary stage in the development of a national consciousness, and among a number of other related points that Glissant calls "scattered proposals," he argues that "theatrical expression is structured from the forms of common folkloric background" and that "this form of dramatic expression becomes that of the (entire) community because it moves beyond its folkloric origins while not undermining them."[40]

Thus, read alongside his writings on theater, the absence of folk culture in Glissant's *Monsieur Toussaint* is strongly apparent and surprising. Although *Monsieur Toussaint* presents an original recuperation of Toussaint and it is especially productive as a vehicle with which to expand his theory of *Relation*, Glissant's play's shortcomings, including its lack of folkloric elements and its failure to bring to life the narrative of the Haitian Revolution with accessibility and narrative coherence, profoundly limit the play's dramatic impact.

6 Ideological Frailty and the Marvelous in Alejo Carpentier's *El reino de este mundo*

> Carpentier's artistic enterprise in the forties became a search for origins, the recovery of history and tradition. . . . Carpentier is reaching for that elusive Golden Age when fable and history were one.
>
> —Roberto González Echevarría, *Alejo Carpentier: The Pilgrim at Home*

ALEJO CARPENTIER, THE CUBAN NOVELIST, essayist, musicologist, and communist, is widely acclaimed as having been one of Latin America's most influential writers. His innovation of the concept of "*lo real maravilloso*"—the marvelous real—gained such influence among the writers of the region who chose to affiliate themselves with the term that the particular perception of Latin American social reality it encouraged is evident throughout the writings of the Latin American literary boom of the 1960s.[1] *Lo real maravilloso* was an extraordinary and distinctive literary style and theory that was defined by the bewitching novel of the Haitian Revolution *El reino de este mundo* (*The Kingdom of This World*) and in Carpentier's landmark essays "On the Marvelous Real in America" and "The Baroque and the Marvelous Real."[2] In those essays, Carpentier called for a new and radical way of perceiving Pan-American cultures and histories with a particular emphasis on their syncretic and non-European elements; significantly, the essays also reveal the influence of Oswald Spengler's vision of the cyclical nature of history on Carpentier's conception of the nature of historical change. It is my argument in this chapter that in spite of its technical brilliance and economy, *El reino* encourages an understanding of the Haitian Revolution that obscures its most radical qualities. In failing to attribute to the former slaves of Saint Domingue a radical rational humanism in addition to a consciousness imbued with the marvelous, Carpentier, contra James and Césaire, conspicuously circumvents recuperating the Haitian Revolution as the fullest articulation of the political implications of the Radical Enlightenment. Hence, Carpentier's attribution of instinct and spirit to the actions of the former slaves of Saint Domingue, as opposed to reason and matter, becomes a problematic aspect of the novel that I suggest reveals an ideological frailty at the heart of Carpentier's deployment of the concept of the marvelous real. Thus, it is part of the argument of this chapter that although Carpentier's marvelous realism shares certain aesthetic affinities with the négritude of Aimé Césaire and René Depestre, it lacks any corresponding vision of emancipatory political action.

The roots of what Carpentier dubbed *lo real maravilloso* can be found in his reaction to his trip to Haiti in 1943. It was in this journey that he first perceived the existence of a distinct continental American sensibility that encompassed Haiti; this in turn would lead him to his "first inkling of the marvelous real." Everyday Haitian culture struck him as being deeply connected to its historical past, and "to certain synchronisms, American, recurrent, timeless, relating this to that, yesterday to today." Carpentier conceded that this reality bore certain similarities to European surrealism, which he faulted for its artificiality: "having felt the undeniable spell of the lands of Haiti, after having found magical warnings along the red roads of the Central Meseta, after having heard the drums of the Petro and the Rada, I was moved to set this recently experienced marvelous reality beside the tiresome pretension of creating the marvelous that has characterized certain European literatures."[3]

Carpentier's theory of *lo real maravilloso*, then, displayed a deep awareness of the critical differences between a manufactured surrealism and the inherent surrealism of Haiti's cultural practices, history, and geography: "if Surrealism pursued the marvelous, one would have to say that it very rarely looked for it in reality. . . . Where is it [surrealism] going? What is its purpose? No one knows. A mystery. A *manufactured* mystery."[4] However, Carpentier argued that the *marvelous real* could not be disengaged from reality since he saw it as belonging to reality itself, since it was "latent and omnipresent, in all that is Latin American."[5] Thus, although it has been argued that Carpentier's work has a more ambivalent relationship with surrealism than his denunciations would suggest, the basis of Carpentier's theory of *lo real maravilloso* can be found in the allegedly strange, or surreal, *material realities* of Haitian life.

The Origins of the "Marvelous Real"

Alejo Carpentier's essay "On the Marvelous Real in America" remains the most important key and the starting point to any interpretation of *El reino de este mundo*. This argument begins with a series of subjective case studies of cultural and artistic difference based upon his firsthand experience of traveling in China, Iran, the Soviet Union, and the Czech city of Prague. Carpentier uses each occasion to record his sense of amazement at their different cultural languages and his varying ability to connect to them. Thus, Carpentier laments the impossibility of ever truly understanding Chinese or Iranian cultures: "Upon my return I was invaded by the great melancholy of one who wanted to understand but understood only partially."[6]

True understanding, Carpentier somberly notes, would entail more than a lifetime of learning languages, texts, and history. On the other hand, Carpentier joyously discovered that Soviet culture was not alien to him, despite his inability to speak the language. Here, Carpentier's "sense of incomprehension was entirely alleviated": "the magnificent architecture of Leningrad, at once baroque, Italian, Russian was pleasing to me before I ever saw it. . . . [T]he Winter Palace, deeply blue and foaming white, with its Neptunian, aquatic baroque [*barroquismo*], spoke a language well known to me."[7]

In Prague also, Carpentier found himself at home in a city dominated by historical and cultural referents already familiar to him as a Latin American of European extraction: the legacies of the Reformation and Counter-Reformation, Faust, Mozart, and Kafka. Together, they enabled him to connect with Prague's cultural history and life in a manner that was impossible on his visits to Peking and Tehran. From Prague, Carpentier's observations move on to Latin America: he notes in its land, its people, and its ontology, a confluence of mythologies and histories, pre-Colombian, European, African, baroque, and Faustian. In a succinct and eloquent affirmation of the link that binds aesthetics to the specifics of historical materiality and cultural heritage, Carpentier writes: "Latin Americans drag a legacy of thirty centuries behind them, but in spite of a record of absurd deeds and many sins, we must recognize that *our style* is reaffirmed throughout *our history*."[8] Emphasizing the historical aspect of the marvelous, the inheritance of the Americas, Carpentier argues, is a fecund cultural fusion, and the challenge for the American writer is to find a language capable of expressing this reality. *Lo real maravilloso* was Carpentier's response to that challenge, and his representation of the Haitian Revolution in *El reino de este mundo* illustrates how and why the marvelous real could function as such a profound representative tool.

Within the corpus of writing about the Haitian Revolution, *El reino de este mundo* stands out for eschewing preoccupation with the veneration of Haiti's revolutionary leaders. The novel's historical focus is not history told from the perspective of great men—indeed the most important historical figures are glaringly absent. Instead, Carpentier narrates the events of that history as experienced by the ordinary slave. In other works—Edouard Glissant's *Le quatrième siècle* and Toni Morrison's *Beloved* are two obvious and relevant examples—the strategy of narrating through a slave yields access to a radical consciousness, and the technique also undeniably provides a solution to the elitism of narrating through great individuals, a problem we encounter in C. L. R. James's *Black Jacobins*. However, Carpentier's novel, I argue, is conservative not as a result of its focus on a slave, but because of its fatalistic, cyclical view of history into which the Haitian Revolution is subsumed. Thus, leaving Toussaint, Dessalines, Moïse and a host of the other important historical players out, Carpentier's *El reino* uses its fictional protagonist, Ti Noel, to represent the "ordinary slave," although his life story is far from "ordinary."

As a field slave in prerevolutionary Saint Domingue, Ti Noel developed a close friendship with the great maroon rebel Makandal as the two shared the same master and worked on the same plantation. Makandal's influence over Ti Noel is deep and vital to the narrative: he is the novel's most heroic figure, and his inspiring personal story of great courage, ingenuity, and resistance is felt throughout. This evocation accords with Carolyn Fick's claim that François Makandal was, by far, "the most extraordinary and awesome of the pre-revolutionary leaders."[9] Though historians have found certainties in relation to Makandal's background and biography hard to come by, it is thought that Makandal was born in Guinea, highly educated, a Muslim, an Arabic speaker, and that he displayed a talent for the arts and for medicine from an early age. Captured as a prisoner of war and sold as a common slave to European traders, Makandal was then sold and resold in Saint Domingue, where he eventually came to be owned by Lenormand de Mezy in the Limbé region of Saint Domingue before his escape to the mountainous highlands, where he became a legendary maroon leader of resistance to slavery for nearly two decades. Fick has argued that Makandal's leadership and organizational skills, his status as a great vodou priest, and great eloquence as an orator afforded him an extraordinary influence over slaves in his following and helped to perpetuate his legendary status among ordinary slaves.[10]

However, in *El reino,* Makandal personifies the marvelous realities of Latin American and Caribbean history, and by his actions, his legend, and his gift for storytelling, he exists primarily as a progenitor of an insurrectionary Haitian mythology rather than as a figure of rational agency. In stories that Ti Noel has heard of him, Makandal was able to transcend his earthly, human limitations by supernatural cunning and his ability to assume the form of animals, birds, or insects. And it is Makandal's stories of great African history and mythology that inspire the young Ti Noel: "With deliberately languid tone, the better to secure certain effect, the Mandingue Negro would tell of things that had happened in the great kingdoms of Popo, of Arada, of the Nagos, or the Fulah."[11] Makandal's stories speak of great tribal migrations, epic battles, and they celebrate Africa at the expense of the European powers. Their impact on Ti Noel is dramatic: "the deep wisdom of Macandal" [*sic*] enables Ti Noel to develop a revolutionary consciousness that recognizes the illegitimacy of slavery and colonial rule.[12]

The emphasis placed upon Makandal's extraordinary gift for the art of narrative emphasizes the manner in which storytelling fosters both a hero myth and a climate of insurrectionary potential in Saint Domnigue. Makandal's stories tend to follow a similar theme: that the European creation of the colony of Saint Domingue is culturally, architecturally, and historically a "trumpery thing compared to the great cities of Guinea," a theme that registers a defiant rejection of the inferiority of Africans.[13] Makandal's stories also frequently evoke a Dionysian spirit; they refer to "giant drums," "feasts of circumcision," rituals, and dancing youths; and they associate Africa with a deep mysticism.[14] Thus, Makandal's stories contradict the argument that a cultural void is a necessary legacy of slavery.[15]

However, while the symbolism of Carpentier's revalorization of Africa via his representation of Makandal's legend communicates a message that could be recognized as a form of négritude (about which Carpentier never wrote), it is ultimately subsumed by the novel's ideological conservatism. Thus, while I wish to suggest that although there are commonalities in Carpentier's, Césaire's, and Depestre's invocations of a primal and powerful Africa functioning as a root identity for all those subjected to the slave trade and New World plantation system, the differences in the ideological ends to which the symbolism is put must not be ignored.

Ti Noel's life story is also made unusual for a number of other factors beyond his friendship with Makandal. He experienced firsthand the Bois Caiman vodou ceremony, participated in the subsequent great slave uprising of the northern plains in 1791, after which he knew short-lived freedom as a rebel slave before his recapture and transportation to Cuba with his old master. In Cuba, he was won in a card game by a Santiago slave owner, shortly after which his first master, Lenormand de Mezy, died. Ti Noel's experience as a slave was more bearable in Cuba, and over a period of many years, he was eventually able to save sufficient funds to buy his passage on a fishing boat to the land that was by then an independent black republic and had been renamed Haiti. However, Ti Noel's travails did not end on his return to "a land where slavery had been abolished forever."[16] By then an old man, he was recaptured and put to work as a slave-laborer in the disintegrating Kingdom of Henri Christophe.

Through the character of Ti Noel, whose interiority is revealed, the novel imaginatively expounds on the role played by ordinary slaves throughout the revolution. The novel's animation of Ti Noel's consciousness thus acquires a significance that goes beyond the need to evoke an authentic self: Ti Noel's belief systems, his rational and irrational thoughts, become our way of accessing the marvelous realities of Saint Domingue's slave culture. It is important to note that in *El reino*, the revolution and its surrounding events are both explicable and inexplicable in rational terms, and that slave culture, particularly vodou, is presented as both magical and understandable in reasonable terms. For example, Ti Noel's and the slaves' faith in the power of metamorphosis—a power to which both Makandal and Ti Noel have access—is presented as being perfectly natural.

One of the great *aesthetic* achievements of *El reino* is thus its evocation of the richly detailed, seemingly strange, folk culture and intellectual and spiritual life of Saint Domingue's slave population. The novel's narration of the execution of Makandal exemplifies this point. Intended to illustrate definitively the futility of resistance to his followers, the public burning of Makandal instead ironically served to reinforce his followers' faith in his supernatural powers of insubordination. The novel thereby demonstrates an understanding of how resistance can be dependent on beliefs as well as on "reasonable" ideas, offering a counter-perspective to the primacy of the values of the Enlightenment and the French Revolution in the genesis of 1804, which, as discussed earlier, is one of the hallmarks of James's account of the revolution in both the history and play *The Black Jacobins*. The execution of Makandal occurs at the end of the novel's first part, and the scene describes the slave masters' total inability to influence a population who believe in the powers of "a man chrismed [anointed] by the great Loas."[17] With Makandal lashed to a post, and with his death by burning imminent, the crowd's certain belief in his escape is vividly conveyed by Carpentier. As the crowd had predicted, after Makandal's "howling unknown spells," and with the flames "licking his legs," "the bonds fell off and the body of the Negro rose in the air, flying overhead, until it plunged into the black waves of the sea of slaves. A single cry filled the square: 'Macandal saved!'"[18] Dramatizing how the European slave masters could find no way to stifle the sustaining spirit of the slaves' faith in vodou and in Makandal's boundless powers—"Once more the whites had been outwitted by the Mighty Powers of the Other Shore"[19]—the aesthetic form of marvelous realism is thus used in order to convey that the slaves of Saint Domingue were able to translate even the direst news of oppression into empowering stories of resistance, and even the capture and public execution of a heroic maroon leader spreads within the slave community not as a story of defeat, but of an ingenious triumph over the witless slave owners.[20]

The Mythological Drama of *El reino de este mundo*

El reino de este mundo also narrates the history of the Haitian Revolution in such a way that the story takes on an epic mythological dimension, drawing on Christian myths of Paradise and Hell. The epigraph to the novel's first part is taken from Lope de Vega's *The Famous Drama of the Discovery of the New World by Christopher Columbus*, and it is used both to contrast and to blur the relation of history to myth. The epigraph is a segment of an exchange between the Devil and Providence; the Devil declares himself to be "The King of the West" before inquiring of Providence:

> Oh, blessed court,
> Eternal Providence!
> Where are you sending Columbus
> To renew my evil deeds?
> Know you not that long since
> I rule there?[21]

Casting Christopher Columbus as an instrument of the Devil, Lope de Vega's text boldly subverts the status of Columbus as a discoverer and hero, and instead reduces him to a pawn in a grand and demonic plan. Thus the epigraph taken from Lope de Vega encourages us to see the

West's colonial project and the installation of slavery in the New World in diabolical, Faustian terms. In this context, the Haitian Revolution becomes not just a revolution against French, British, and Spanish imperial powers, but also a rebellion against evil itself. The brutal slave system of Saint Domingue can easily be seen in these hellish terms, and the novel frequently focuses our attention on the macabre horrors that could be found in colonial Saint Domingue, but without resorting to the kinds of graphic descriptions of violence and torture that we will find in Madison Smartt Bell's Haitian trilogy. Instead, the abominable and hellish state of prerevolutionary Saint Domingue is evoked in a manner that manages to be disturbing but not gratuitous. Atrocity always lurks just below the surface, suggesting the depraved nature of the colony; for example, in the novel's first chapter, entitled "The Wax Heads," the description of Ti Noel's expertise in judging horses and their physical potential is a powerful reminder of the slave markets, and the novel thereby juxtaposes the sale of horseflesh and human flesh. The purchase of the horse is immediately followed by a trip to the barber's for Lenormand de Mezy, which offers Ti Noel the opportunity to pass the time looking in at the butcher's next door. The subtle comparison of horseflesh to human flesh is thus extended by the ironic suggestion of cannibalism. In order to ensure that the reader does not miss the point, the omniscient narrator explains that Ti Noel also notices that the calves' heads in the window of the tripe shop shared the same "waxy quality" as the four wigged wax head mannequins in the window of the barber's shop, and that "it amused Ti Noël to think that alongside the pale calves' heads, heads of white men were served on the same tablecloth."[22] Ti Noel's imagination is quick-witted and grim, conjuring a "picture of an abominable feast" that alerts us to the demonic ills at the heart of Saint Domingue society.[23] With the morning, in Ti Noel's imagination, abounding with heads—human, animal, and mannequin—Ti Noel then observes how, as his master emerges from the barber's with powdered cheeks, that "his face now bore a startling resemblance to the four dull wax faces that stood in a row along the counter smiling stupidly."[24] Finally, the macabre and subversive associations reach their climax: clasping a calf's head his master has just bought from the tripe shop, Ti Noel is struck by how much "that white, chill skull" probably resembled his master's bald head underneath his wig.[25]

Figuring Saint Domingue as Hell, Carpentier was also playing with the colonists' desire to perceive their colony as a paradise. Clearly evoking the degeneracy of colonial life, as well as a fascination with the macabre and the violent, *El reino de este mundo* displays a gothic eroticism and cannibalism that is far from the only trait of depravity the novel reveals in its indictment of white settler society in Saint Domingue. Via the character of Lenormand de Mezy in particular, the novel reveals the licentiousness that was part and parcel of this community.[26] Sex was to be found everywhere, especially at the Cap Français marketplace, the sights and sounds of which are vividly evoked in a baroque jumble. "Quadroons" and "Negresses," who are treated as the sexual playthings of de Mezy and men of his ilk, clutch prayer books and parasols, mingle in the marketplace alongside sailors selling monkeys to the ladies of the plantocracy. The ubiquity of drunkenness and the coexistence of material luxury and moral laxity evoke a society wherein everything is tainted by slavery—all is rotten and infected. De Mezy's lust, in particular, metonymically represents the general libertinage of prerevolutionary Saint Domingue: with the colony on the threshold of the first major slave uprising of the revolution, Carpentier describes how "a perpetual erotomania . . . kept him panting after adolescent slave girls, the smell of whose skin drove him out of his mind."[27]

Further, as de Mezy's lust spirals out of control, so too does his habit for meting out corporal punishment. Meanwhile, Mlle. Floridor, ravaged by malaria, the bottle, and her recognition of her failure as an actress, on any pretext orders her slaves whipped.[28] The rapid degeneration of de Mezy and Mlle. Floridor is presented as a disease, and when the tables are turned on the first night of the great slave uprising in the northern plains, Ti Noel, having long since dreamed of raping Mlle. Floridor, succumbs to the contagion that had tempted him for so long.[29]

Given the acceptance of sexual depravity in Saint Domingue, Carpentier concurs with C. L. R. James's assessment of the extreme violence, particularly of the early stages of the revolution, by explaining how sexual exploitation and rape were normalized in the course of the revolution: "From their masters they had known rape, torture, degradation, and, at the slightest provocation, death. They returned in kind."[30] Neither James nor Carpentier shirked from representing the atrocities committed throughout the revolution, while never isolating the crimes from their context.

Continuing with his strategy of narrating the history of the Haitian Revolution from the perspective of lesser-known historical figures rather than from the perspective of the leaders, Carpentier chooses Pauline Bonaparte, Napoleon's sister and wife to General Leclerc, to offer the novel's most significant French perspective on the revolution. The history books provide many memorable anecdotal portraits of Pauline Bonaparte as Napoleon's silly and spoiled sister who was uncontrollably adulterous and a spendthrift. Carpentier does not deviate from the historical evidence, but he does flesh out the character of Pauline to a degree unusual compared with other recuperations of the Haitian Revolution.

Pauline's appearance in the novel is brief, occurring only in the novel's second part, but her significance should not be underestimated. Carpentier's Pauline Bonaparte is intellectually lazy and incurious about politics, although we do learn that she had been much moved by the tear-jerking antislavery novel of Joseph Lavallée, *Le nègre comme il y a peu de blancs*.[31] Pauline is characterized as a pampered and spoiled young woman used to getting her own way; thus she figures as yet another example of the novel's representation of European excess and indulgence. Carpentier reminds us that she single-handedly held up her husband's army that was being dispatched to Saint Domingue to crush the revolution and subordinate the colony to French rule once more because of "a childish whim to make the trip from Paris to Brest in a litter."[32] Pauline is also represented as a sexually predatory figure: she was, Carpentier writes, "a connoisseur of male flesh" despite her tender years.[33] Thus, despite her initial worries that the trip would be a bore, her attitude is entirely changed by the combination of the company of so many good-looking, youthful military men, and her excitement at the prospect of arriving in the lush tropical paradise of her imagination, a romantic island throbbing to the exotic rhythms of Creole *contredanse*. Initially Saint Domingue was not a disappointment to her: "the sight of the Cap and the Plaine du Nord, with the backdrop of mountains blurred by the mist rising from the canefields, delighted Pauline."[34] Surrounded by material luxury and abundance, Pauline quickly grows accustomed to a life of tropical privilege, and she feels herself to be "part bird of paradise, part lyrebird" as she spends her days being waited on by slaves and French maids, taking siestas, swimming naked, and dining on tropical fruits.[35]

However, Pauline's paradisial dream is abruptly ended by tropical disease: when her French coiffeur collapses suddenly with cholera, it immediately inspires terror in Pauline, and she flees to the island of La Tortue with her slave Soliman. Here Pauline attempts to restore herself with a daily routine of sensual massage administered by Soliman and bathing in sandy coves; this interlude of respite is, however, brief. When her husband returns from battle ravaged by tropical disease—malaria, yellow fever, and cholera—Pauline is once more struck with terror, and this time it deranges her. Finding her paradise transformed into a hell—"Now the tropics seemed abominable"[36]—Pauline abandons all faith in European medicine and rationality. Instead, she seeks refuge in the sorcery and vodou rituals of Soliman before fleeing Saint Domingue for France.

Pauline's breakdown emblematizes the dissolution of European rationality, and her departure signals "the end of such common sense as still existed in the colony."[37] The deceased Leclerc is replaced by General Rochambeau, who takes charge of the ravaged colony that has become an inferno in which the remaining colonists "gave themselves over without let or hindrance to a vast orgy."[38] Time and order disintegrate, along with any semblance of the rule of law, as Saint Domingue becomes a site of ever more abominable atrocities: sexual crimes, including the rape of infants, corruption, and prostitution, all become even more prevalent than they had been previously, while Rochambeau takes to throwing his Negroes to his dogs and sends to Cuba for mastiffs trained to kill and devour slaves.[39] Rochambeau's reign recalls the epigraph to the novel's first part, taken from Lope de Vega, and can thus be read as the final stage of the colony's descent into Hell, with Rochambeau as a latter-day Columbus, another of the Devil's unwitting instruments of destruction sent to renew evil deeds.

The Return of Repression: Christophe's Kingdom

Whereas Toussaint is entirely absent from the narrative of *El reino de este mundo*, Henri Christophe has a prominent role, and the focus on Christophe throws the novel's ideological conservatism into sharp relief. The novel's third part begins with Ti Noel's return to Haiti after the revolution, which is now Christophe's Kingdom. Haiti is now "a land where slavery had been abolished forever," but it is made clear that Haiti is free of slavery in name only.[40]

The joy of Ti Noel's return is powerfully expressed, and he falls to his knees giving thanks to "all the deities of powder and fire."[41] It is significant that Ti Noel does not feel that he owes thanks to Toussaint or any of the other leaders of the Haitian Revolution, but to the vodou gods. Ti Noel's happiness, however, is short-lived, and not long after his return he is captured by men working in the service of Henri Christophe's government, and, despite his advanced age, he is set to work as an enforced laborer in conditions that to Ti Noel evoke memories of his prior existence as a slave. This episode signifies the corruption of the ideals of the revolution. Put to work constructing Christophe's Citadel, Ti Noel's experience is of "a slavery as abominable as that he had known on the plantation of de Mézy [*sic*]", before he remarks that it was, in fact, "even worse, for there was a limitless affront in being beaten by a Negro as black as oneself."[42]

In contrast to Ti Noel's return to a harsh routine of heavy labor, punishment, and cruelty, *El reino* also evokes the splendid world of the court of Henri Christophe. This world is a breathtaking display of ball gowns, orchestras, and luxury. Christophe's adoption of French culture in his palace of Sans Souci emphasizes the gulf that separates this world from the world of the vast majority of the new citizens of Haiti. Christophe's manner of leadership is "Napoleonic," and his despotic aspect is wantonly cruel: while observing the progress of the building at the site of his Citadel, it was commonplace for Christophe to order "the death of some sluggard surprised in flagrant idleness, or the execution of workers hoisting a block of granite too slowly up a steep incline."[43]

The predictable result of Christophe's despotic regime is that he is soon regarded by the Haitian people as having ushered in a reality little different to that of the regimes of the European slavers. The radical song that Ti Noel once sung as an insult to the king of England is now adapted to abuse Christophe. Ti Noel considers that the song's important message was that the song was an insult to a *king*. Thus, Christophe is no longer regarded as a liberator by his people, but as another despot wreaking suffering on the Haitian people. Having evoked the fault lines and shortcomings of Christophe's kingdom, Carpentier narrates Christophe's downfall and suicide, all the while emphasizing that Christophe's kingdom bears no resemblance to the grand African kingdoms that Ti Noel had previously imagined. As compelling as Carpentier's portrayal of Christophe is, the representation is unsatisfactory at the level of ideology that can be inferred from the absence of historical context. Although Carpentier's portrayal of Christophe is actually quite similar to Césaire's depiction in *La tragédie du roi Christophe*, Césaire's does not skirt round the climactic events of the Haitian Revolution. Whereas Césaire's play begins in 1806, with Haitian independence established and Toussaint and Dessalines already dead, Carpentier's novel does not: the major historical events of the Haitian Revolution occur, chronologically, in the midpoint of *El reino*, but, as Chris Bongie has pointed out, these are "passed over in virtual silence.[44] Instead of an account of Toussaint's capture by Leclerc and the achievement of independence under the leadership of Dessalines, Christophe, and Pétion, Carpentier narrates the Pauline episode, distancing the reader from any sense of the achievement of 1804. The result is an unbalanced and unreservedly pessimistic view of revolution: colonial tyranny is merely replaced by Christophe's tyranny, and there is no sense of the fact that, notwithstanding the new oppression to which the Haitian people were subjected, the situation of black Haitians after 1804 was substantially improved, especially in terms of labor, living conditions, freedom of movement, sexual exploitation, and cultural production.

By way of comparison, Robin Blackburn's work also reminds us that the expansion of dominion by the English in India, the French in North Africa, and the United States across the American continent in the nineteenth century unleashed and involved violence and racism on a scale that far exceeded the state-sponsored violence that occurred in independent Haiti.[45] It must thus be recognized that the conservative logic of Carpentier's novel, in filtering the undeniably violent regime of Christophe through the ongoing suffering of Ti Noel, and by eliding all moments of revolutionary triumph, reveals a conservative antipathy for revolution.

Thus, although *El reino de este mundo*'s figuration of the project of colonialism as a hellish enterprise and its celebration of the marvelous realities of slave resistance might be interpreted as politically progressive, the novel's depiction of the return of repression under the rule of Henri Christophe forces us to recognize the novel's Spenglerian nature: Carpentier narrates history as the repetition of a futile cycle that humans are powerless to influence.

The trajectory of the novel thus leads to pessimistic despair; repression and resistance are both rendered meaningless in the novel's conception of history—and something similar to the novel's organizing structure of cyclical pessimism will be seen in Derek Walcott's recuperations of the Haitian Revolution. And as if to erase any doubt, the apocalyptic ending of *El reino* underscores the novel's conservative political vision. This refers to three disasters that all caused great destruction: in August 1831, Les Cayes was struck by a hurricane and a tidal wave; in July 1832, large sections of Port-au-Prince were destroyed by fire, and in 1842, the whole island of Hispaniola was hit by an earthquake that killed more than one hundred thousand people. Does the novel intend to imply that the Haitian Revolution was similarly responsible for meaningless destruction on a vast scale?

The novel's valorization of human toil and suffering in its final pages appears as a gesture that offers token compensation for such profound pessimism in which all political action is rendered futile. In the final pages, Ti Noel experiences an epiphanal moment of lucidity and knowledge which is beautifully expressed; as a lyrical celebration of the dignity of human struggle the passage is masterful, yet it affirms the inevitability of human suffering: "now he understood that a man never knows for whom he suffers and hopes. He suffers and hopes and toils for people he will never know, and who, in turn, will suffer and hope and toil for others who will not be happy either, for man always seeks out a happiness far beyond that which is meted out to him."[46] Thus, Ti Noel reconciles himself to the inevitability of suffering, which he makes sense of by placing faith in the idea that "man's greatness consists in the very fact of wanting to be better than he is."[47]

El reino thus concludes affirmatively, but in a manner entirely compatible with Carpentier's vision of historical pessimism. Although the ability to love and to be loved transcends individual suffering, the individual must toil for future generations who will also inevitably suffer, and there is no prospect for successful progressive political intervention. The overall movement of Carpentier's novel works toward the denial of the possibility of historical transformation; the contrast with the radical visions of Césaire, James, Hughes, Depestre, Lawrence, and Donkor could hardly be any starker.

7 The Aesthetics of Cyclical Pessimism

Derek Walcott's *Haitian Trilogy*

Derek Walcott's long-standing interest in Haitian history is revealed in a trilogy of plays that draw on the Haitian Revolution for their subject matter. The three plays—*Henri Christophe*, *Drums and Colours*, and *The Haitian Earth*—were collected into one volume and published as *The Haitian Trilogy* in 2002.[1] Until their publication in this collected format they were largely forgotten works and hard to find; even the most recently completed play in the trilogy, *The Haitian Earth*, which is now presented as Walcott's major or mature Haitian work, had never been published. Walcott wrote a new foreword to the plays for their publication in *The Haitian Trilogy* which, as well as providing a problematic and laconic consideration of Haitian history, is a useful starting point from which to begin to understand the ideological basis that underpins all three of Walcott's dramatic representations of the Haitian Revolution. In the foreword to *The Haitian Trilogy,* Walcott writes: "The Haitian revolution, as sordidly tyrannical as so many of its subsequent regimes tragically became, was an upheaval, a necessary rejection of the debasements endured under a civilized empire, that achieved independence " (vii–viii).

It is a summation that credits the revolution with having achieved no more than "independence," recognizes it as having been "necessary," although "sordidly tyrannical," and sees the event as having opened the doors to the many tyrannical "subsequent regimes" that have commanded power in Haiti since the 1804 revolution. It is a barely positive summation and suggests a deep skepticism about revolution in general, and the received historical record. It is also an interpretation that fits neatly with a reading of Haitian history as an endlessly repeating cycle of tragic violence and tyranny, and it is this that emerges as the predominant view of Haitian history throughout *The Haitian Trilogy.*

To a certain extent, the view of the Haitian Revolution that Walcott's *Trilogy* presents holds a great deal in common with Alejo Carpentier's *El reino de este mundo*, which we have seen also supports an interpretation of Haitian history as cyclically tyrannical, albeit in a more complexly qualified manner. However, Carpentier does emphasize Haiti's situation in a threatening imperial world, as represented by the sections of the novel set in Cuba. In contrast, Walcott's Haiti trilogy—in *Henri Christophe* and *The Haitian Earth,* at least—fails to evoke this external world. Also, while both authors interpret Haitian history in terms of a tragic repeating cycle, *El reino de este mundo* at least proffers Ti Noel's compensatory vision: politics are enfeebled and resistance to tyranny is futile, but there remains dignity in human frailty, toil, and aspiration. Finally, while the novel denies revolution any historical logic—the representation of resistance within the marvelous and of the powers of shapeshifting suggest that the normal avenues of political agency have been exhausted—*El reino* does not goes so far as to render all individual historical action amoral and meaningless.

Walcott's *Haitian Trilogy,* on the other hand, renders all ideological, political, and moral distinctions between historical actors meaningless via the mapping of a model of repeating tragedy onto history. The trilogy thus communicates the defeat of not just historical resistance, but it also discounts the possibility of successful future resistance: the exercise of historical agency is doomed to failure. To read Walcott's *Haitian Trilogy* is to be confronted with a series of arguments that are specific to Haitian history but also general enough to be easily extrapolated into more universal theories about colonial and postcolonial histories: that whites and blacks can both be tyrants, that revolutions corrupt themselves, that European slaveholders transported slaves to the New World but black Africans captured and sold them, and that when in power the colonized will behave as the colonists once did; all are guilty, and only oppression endures.

Thus, despite the lyrical and eloquent seductiveness with which this position emerges from the texts of the *Trilogy*, it is important to follow through the implications of this argument. Refusing the emancipatory potential of any radical politics, Walcott's *Trilogy* embraces a conservative vision in which history can only ever be malign and oppressive.

However, using the Haitian Revolution to project a pessimistic and conservative fatalism requires a complex rearrangement of history. This move, together with the mapping of cycles of tragedy onto and over the historical record, becomes the most important object of scrutiny in analyzing Walcott's *Haitian Trilogy*. Thus, the politics of Walcott's *Haitian Trilogy* depend not on the historical accuracy or otherwise of the dramas, but on how Walcott reorders "history," and how this rearrangement supports or encourages a particular perspective on the Haitian Revolution. For example, Walcott's pessimistic take on events depicts Dessalines and Christophe as being the real enemies of liberty in an independent Haiti. However, their representations are taken out of their macrohistorical context in order to make the new oppression of their regimes seem as cruel and as contrary to human rights as the governance of the colonists had been. Instead of providing historical context, Walcott evokes the internal lives of the characters to find explanation for their recourse to the same old injustices. It is a very problematic method insofar as it ensures that the reader must judge Dessalines and Christophe in a vacuum. In failing to evoke the neocolonial context of the early-nineteenth-century Atlantic world in which Dessalines and Christophe were forced to govern, Walcott's microrearrangement of history distorts his dramatic representation—what is left out of Walcott's *Trilogy* thus becomes as important as what is left in. Chris Bongie has made a comparable observation on a different aspect of the representational politics of the trilogy: Bongie finds that by focusing on Dessalines and Christophe, and largely writing out of the play the important figure of Alexandre Pétion (a mulatto who was Christophe's main political rival and who became president of the southern half of a divided Haiti while Christophe ruled in the north), Pétion largely escapes criticism. Leaving Pétion out, Bongie argues, results in a representation that colludes with what the historian David Nicholls has identified as the "mulatto legend."[2]

Thus, the representational politics of Walcott's *Haitian Trilogy* are profoundly conservative—even, it will be seen, fatalistically pessimistic—in sharp contradistinction to the interpretations offered by Césaire, Depestre, James, and Hughes, for whom the Haitian Revolution opened the gates of black liberation and served as an example to anticolonial movements. Instead, Walcott's plays carry within them a tension born of the fact that they were written and first performed during an era of optimistic anticolonialism, but that they bear a message of profound skepticism about revolution.

However, critics who have gleaned a positive reading of Walcott's plays have managed to do so by drawing attention to the fact that through the plays one can trace an arc of development in Walcott's voice and worldview.[3] This reading emphasizes that the trilogy was written over a period of around forty years, and that in them one can detect Walcott's maturation as an artist. The first play, *Henri Christophe*, was finished in 1949, when Walcott was still only nineteen years of age. It was privately published at Walcott's own expense in Barbados in 1950, and it was first performed in St. Lucia in the same year.[4] The trilogy's second part, *Drums and Colours*, an "epic" or "pageant play," was first produced as the main event of the West Indian Festival of the Arts in Trinidad in 1958. It had been commissioned to mark the opening of the short-lived first Federal Parliament of the West Indies and was performed by a cast of around eighty actors before a seated audience of three thousand. Finally, the last part of the trilogy is *The Haitian Earth*, which was originally conceived as a script for a television film, and was first performed in 1984.[5] The long periods of time that elapsed between each installment have encouraged critics to read into the trilogy evidence of Walcott's artistic growth. For example, Edward Baugh maintains: "To compare [Walcott's] treatment of the Revolution in the three is to enhance understanding of his evolution as a dramatist, both in content or world view and in style."[6]

However, while it is true that the trilogy reveals elements of Walcott's artistic maturation, an underlying conservatism is a constant. For example, the plays certainly do differ in tone, theme, and narrative mode: one can trace the diminishing importance of the "hero" and the increasing significance of "the people" from one play to the next. However, I contend that this strategy is illustrative of the fact that narrating through "the people" does not necessarily give rise to a radical discourse, just as narrating through great individuals can be considered elitist, but not necessarily conservative. Elitism and radicalism are not dichotomous, and both radical and conservative discourses might have elitist or proletarian origins. Further, it is my argument that the trilogy as a whole serves to misrepresent the achievements and tragic reversals of the Haitian Revolution, and that none of the three plays is able satisfactorily to map an aesthetic model of cyclical tragedy onto a version of Haitian history. My critique here is thus indebted to Chris Bongie's analysis, but I build upon Bongie's work by offering attention to the overall movement and structure of each of the plays, arguing that the conservatism inherent to the trilogy should be situated within a wider field of cultural contestation in which some have sought to negate the value of the Haitian Revolution as a demonstration of the possibility of self-determination.

Revolution as Endless Tyranny and the High Style of *Henri Christophe*

The first play in the trilogy, *Henri Christophe* reads very much like the work of a young and prodigiously talented writer who is still some way from artistic maturity. The play is not derivative, but it does bear strong indications of Walcott's enthusiasm for Shakespeare in particular, as can be seen in the aesthetics of the play's high style as well as its narrative mode. Of most interest, however, is that the play's recuperation and interpretation of the narrative and major players of the Haitian Revolution emerges in the form of a tragic drama.

Henri Christophe is subtitled "A Chronicle in Seven Scenes," but it might well have been subtitled a tragedy. Whereas the most obvious influences come from Shakespeare's *Hamlet* and *King Lear*, there are signs that Marlowe and Webster were also sources of inspiration. *Henri Christophe*'s portrayal of the power struggle between Christophe and Dessalines, their betrayal of Toussaint, and their deaths are easily recognizable in theatrical terms as elements of tragedy. The play bears all the hallmarks of a gifted writer who was also thoroughly acquainted with the English literary canon through a colonial education, and although not wholly transfixed under the spell of his literary idols, had not yet defined his own voice. In his 1970 essay "What the Twilight Says," Walcott wrote clearly about his fascination with the Haitian Revolution as a young man, and the terms in which he envisaged Haitian history: "Full of precocious rage, I was drawn, like a child's mind to fire, to the Manichean conflicts of Haiti's history."[7] Walcott was struck by the partial parallels of Haitian history with that of his own island of St. Lucia, which was only lacking the heroes that Haiti produced. The linguistic, religious, and folkloric otherness of Haiti was also alluring to Walcott, for whom Haitian history distorted into myth. That the young Walcott also perceived Haiti's history in the terms of Jacobean tragedy is made clear later in the essay:

> [The black Jacobins of Haiti] were Jacobean, too, because they flared from a mind drenched in Elizabethan literature out of the same darkness as Webster's Flamineo, from a flickering world of mutilation and heresy. . . . [T]hey seemed to him, then, those slave-kings, Dessalines and Christophe, *men who had structured their own despair. Their tragic bulk was massive as a citadel at twilight.* They were our only noble ruins. He believed then that the moral of tragedy could only be Christian, that their fate was the debt exacted by the sin of pride, that they were punished by a white God as masters punished

> servants for presumption. *He saw history as hierarchy, and to him these heroes, despite their meteoric passages, were damned to the old darkness because they had challenged an ordered universe.*[8]

It is as clear a statement as we have of how Walcott viewed Haitian history and the lives of "those slave-kings" in the fatalistic terms of Jacobean tragedy—harsh, violent, and hierarchical. Dessalines and Christophe are also described as fatally flawed figures having been the architects of their own despair and with it the despair of their own people. It is an important passage as it ultimately shifts the burden of moral responsibility for the decisions that they took while they were, respectively, Haiti's first "Emperor" and first "King," onto the individuals themselves. Through the lens of Jacobean tragedy, Walcott focuses on their reigns at the expense of dramatizing the neocolonial world that Haiti found itself in from 1804 onward. In fact, Dessalines and Christophe are situated within the aesthetics of Jacobean tragedy first, with the macrohistorical context of Haitian history coming a distant second.

Walcott's debt to Shakespeare is evident from the outset of *Henri Christophe*: the play's first part opens with an epigraph, taken from *Hamlet*, that is a meditation on the theme of kingship and social order, and it serves to introduce Walcott's major preoccupations in *Henri Christophe*: History, Time, and the place of Kingship in the cycles of tragedy that Walcott saw in Haitian history, all reworked from their Shakespearean sources. The play is set in Haiti in 1803, suggesting a slight inattentiveness to historical chronology on Walcott's part, since Haiti did not exist until 1804. Nevertheless, the significance of Walcott's setting holds good: Toussaint was captured and imprisoned in the Jura some time before the play's opening scene, and the Government Palace at Cap Haitien is awaiting news of Toussaint from France. The opening scene foreshadows Haiti's ill fate by demonstrating the infighting that has emerged from within the revolution's leadership during Toussaint's imprisonment. General Pétion, the second character to speak in the play, ironically remarks that Dessalines is "preparing to be valedictory" during the wait for news of Toussaint from France, but Pétion's words cast Dessalines as ambitious, secretly hoping for confirmation of Toussaint's death, and as a mortal danger:

> This country that stretched, crowing to greet
> The sun of history rising, will have its throat cut
> That's the truth. (8)

Before Dessalines has even spoken, his representation makes for an unmistakable contrast with Pétion's character: Dessalines is murderous and "would like Toussaint dead" whereas Pétion is analytical and civilized. Pétion's speech also reveals him to be a shrewd judge of character, and astutely he notes Dessalines's ambitions and predicts his fate: "He considers kingship; / Vanity will undo him" (8). Thus from the outset, even before Dessalines assumes command of an independent Haiti, Walcott, through the voice of Pétion, seeks to illustrate that Dessalines was no republican. When a messenger arrives to bring the news of Toussaint's death, the play's homage to *Hamlet* reappears. Dessalines's reaction to the news of Toussaint's death is formal and unsentimental and evokes the theme of overhasty mourning. The messenger declares that Toussaint "died, grace on his lips; / But that is no comfort, he is dead . . . / You have heard his fate" (10). Dessalines's response to receiving news of Toussaint's death is to urge his compatriots that they must "not profane his memory with idleness," but his words ring hollow and they lay bare his personal ambition (11). As Dessalines declares himself Haiti's new leader, Walcott uses the character of Brelle, a priest and later an archbishop, to drive home the *Hamlet* comparison, further readying the stage for a tragedy:

> This is a cursory mourning;
> Do tears dry up so very quickly? (12)

Although the strong presence of a Shakespearean tone and mood might be considered irksome or distracting, it does serve to illustrate the kind of recuperation of the final stages of the Haitian Revolution in which Walcott was interested, as well as his innovative literary talents. By taking the story of Dessalines's and Christophe's power struggle into the vacuum that had been caused by Toussaint's death, and telling it in a high style, Walcott's play is an attempt to elevate their story to a level of grandeur that had been reserved for stories from the European traditions. Thus, Walcott's *Henri Christophe* has something in common with James's history *The Black Jacobins* in terms of style and representation. But whereas James communicates the radical history of the Haitian Revolution via a recuperation of Toussaint as a great man worthy of comparison with Napoleon, Walcott recovers Dessalines and Christophe as protagonists worthy of a Shakespearean stage without their specific historical context. There is thus a certain irony to Walcott's representational tactics: whereas the power of the language in the play, together with characterization and aesthetic register, illustrate that the Caribbean's indigenous history is rich enough to sustain a literary imagination equal to any European art, *Henri Christophe* nevertheless demeans the history it enacts by presenting it in the terms of fatalistic tragedy.

The ambivalent outcome of Walcott's rewriting of the historical record in this manner is particularly clear when the recounting of the notorious episode of the 1804 massacre of Haiti's white population is examined. In *Henri Christophe,* the rewriting of this historical event has the effect of confirming that Haiti has entered an endless cycle of recurring tragedy: "The cycle will never end. Blood grows / Where blood is uprooted" (15). Furthermore, in *Henri Christophe* culpability for the atrocity rests with Dessalines and his sadistic desires alone. It is here worth juxtaposing Walcott's rewriting with C. L. R. James's recuperative work on this notorious episode and noting that James presented a very different version, which recognizes that the truly tragic quality of the atrocity emerges only after the way in which Dessalines was held hostage to political manipulation by British imperial diplomats who threatened Saint Domingue with a trade embargo until "the last of the whites had fallen under the axe."[9] Thus, Dessalines's massacre was for James not an "example of black savagery," but of "the calculated savagery of imperialism."[10] On the other hand, in *Henri Christophe*, the writing out of the political background to the massacre has problematic consequences. Rather than showing how his hand was forced, *Henri Christophe* shows Dessalines eagerly anticipating the massacre and looking forward to creating a new aristocracy: "Think, gentlemen, a black nobility, the white flower / destroyed" (20).

This caricature of Dessalines as the epitome of evil is reiterated throughout, and there is nothing to counter Pétion's opinion that: "He is a model / Of horror. Dessalines is only a beast; / He goes to blood with the joy that I go to a feast" (41–42). Thus, although Walcott makes a Jacobean protagonist of Dessalines, in emphasizing his bloodthirsty character his representation reworks the many demonizing imperial figurations of his character.

Walcott's representation of Christophe is also problematic for its subtle reinforcement of colonial stereotypes; however, it must be noted that the play's finest and most romantic lines are reserved for him. Christophe's speeches, which frequently contain references to European Classical antiquity, are delivered with innovative lyricism. Lamenting

Toussaint's death, for example, Christophe compares the ingenuities of his military leadership to the Greek triumph in Troy—"The duplicity of the horse"—serving as a metaphor for his ability to keep his enemies guessing (25). Christophe is also the character who most frequently elaborates on the play's "big" themes of History, Time and Fate. For example, his reaction to Toussaint's death expresses the idea that Haiti itself has been betrayed: "The man is dead, history has betrayed us" (24).

Christophe also perceives himself as a Greek tragic hero, and the analogies that he uses to describe the situation that Haiti finds itself in are often based on the ancient Greek fertility myth of seasonal birth, death, and resurrection—a move that was also made by Césaire in his representation of Toussaint in his *Cahier.* In the play's first half shortly after Dessalines has assumed command of Haiti but while the men in Christophe's camp are awaiting news on Toussaint, Christophe delivers a rousing speech to his camp in which he pronounces himself the true successor to Toussaint, and a leader who will reenergize Haiti. At the same time, he concedes he is unable to break the tragic bonds of birth, death, and resurrection: "Under that winter death / I will perform the rites of spring" (25).

Fearing that with Dessalines in command he may have missed his political opportunity, Christophe declares, "We have slipped the chance to hold time by the / tail" (26), alluding to Marvell's "To His Coy Mistress," before invoking history again as an ill fate that has robbed him of the opportunity of power:

> History has duped me; I, who was leader,
> Shall now play school to a pawn, a breeder
> Of petty hates in which I am part. (27)

In these speeches, there are hints of the self-delusion, egomania, and paranoia that were to haunt Christophe when he eventually did assume power, and a little later he declares that he *is* history: "You are fools; I do not tie the shoelaces of history; / I am the history of which you speak" (28).

Some of the play's critics have found the elegance of Christophe's speeches to be problematic and somewhat above his station, but Christophe's high speech is important in order for Walcott's play to sustain both its impetus as high tragedy and his understanding that Haiti's Black Jacobins were also Jacobean.[11] Furthermore, they also reveal Walcott's ability to tackle major themes though drama. The power, tempo, and rhythms of Christophe's blank verse give the play a literary vitality unique among the Anglophone representations of the Haitian Revolution. Thus, however problematic Walcott's desire to map a repeating cycle of tragedy onto Haitian history might be seen to be, *Henri Christophe* does succeed where many other plays about the Haitian Revolution have fallen short. For example, whereas C. L. R. James's play *The Black Jacobins* is plagued by woodenness, and Langston Hughes's *Emperor of Haiti* lacks the poetic imagination that is commonly associated with its author, Walcott's play is replete with technical accomplishment and linguistic virtuosity. However, of the plays discussed in this volume, it is my suggestion that it is only Aimé Césaire's *La tragédie du roi Christophe* that successfully combines a magnificent poetic symphony with a progressive-critical analysis of political decolonization.

Ultimately, *Henri Christophe*'s ideological and aesthetic structure demands that it ends in a manner befitting a Jacobean tragedy. The Jacobean themes of human weakness and corruptibility, violence and revenge, and an obsession with rulers and tyrants were particularly apposite for Walcott's purpose, and all are present in *Henri Christophe*. The failure of Christophe's kingship, which is caused by his hubris, megalomania, and corruption, is the fundamental driving force to the play's tragic end. Because he is unable to balance the forces of "darkness" and "light" that combine in his personality and ultimately tear him apart, Christophe's regime condemns the legacy of the Haitian Revolution to failure and his obsession with the construction of his Citadel becomes the most important symbol of his failure:

CHRISTOPHE: I will build my cathedral in a month,
Then break or build this kingdom. (73)

His final speech, addressed to a skull and recalling Hamlet's melancholy monologue evoked by Yorick's skull, reaffirms the play's debt to a Shakespearean concept of tragedy. It also echoes Gloucester's despair with the malign gods, although this is replaced by Christophe's despair at "History," which has proved resistant to his vainglorious attempt to make an individual mark of greatness. Moreover, recalling *King Lear*, in *Henri Christophe,* "History" combines with a tragic wheel of fortune to emphasize the collapse of the ideals that had once defined the Haitian Revolution:

CHRISTOPHE: History, breaking the stalk she grew herself, Kills us
like flies, wings torn, held up to light,
Burning biographies like rubbish. (106)

It is a speech of a failed leader, and it neatly summarizes Walcott's early representation of the Haitian Revolution. "History" is captive to tragedy, and the revolution's leaders are nothing more than actors in its inevitable unraveling. *Henri Christophe* sees nothing worth celebrating in the achievement of black independence in Haiti. And ironically, for all its talk of "History," the real, confusing, messy and tragic-historical context in which Dessalines and Christophe had to govern is almost entirely absent. In its place, the aesthetic reconstruction of Dessalines and Christophe as tragic heroes dominates.

Drums and Colours: The Great Tapestry of Caribbean History

Drums and Colours was commissioned to mark the opening of the first West Indies Federation, and the play's premiere took place in Port of Spain, Trinidad, on April 25, 1958. Thus it is fitting that it does not narrate the story of the Haitian Revolution in isolation. Instead, the event is the centerpiece to a play that functions as a grand, transnational Caribbean historical pageant. The play focuses on a few iconic episodes in Caribbean history ranging from Columbus's arrival on Hispaniola in 1492, to Sir Walter Raleigh's expeditions in search of the mythical golden city of El Dorado, to 1830s Jamaica.

The cast includes some fifty-nine characters, although the play's episodic structure does allow for some actors to take on more than one role. In addition to Columbus and Raleigh, there are many iconic and infamous historical figures, European and Caribbean. Among them are the major players from the Haitian Revolution, including General Charles Leclerc and his wife, Pauline, and the revolutionaries Toussaint, Boukmann, Henri Christophe, and Jean-Jacques Dessalines. In addition there are Bartolomé Las Casas, various conquistadors and sailors, a Jewish emigrant to the New World, a carnivalesque Chorus, a Crowd that frequently sings and dances, and Mano, who is described as being "a masquerader" and "leader of a Carnival band," and who is accompanied by his band members, Pompey, Yette, Ram, and General Yu (115).

Mano's troupe also emphasizes the play's metatheatrical framework, with Mano serving as an onstage director of sorts as well as a narrator. The play opens with a prologue in which Mano leads his band's "War and Rebellion" performance march, and the theme is also introduced by Pompey in song. The play's dynamic opening, making use of music, dance, and dialogue that reverberates with resonances of patois and creole, makes for a powerful contrast with the elevated, sometimes pompous language of the earlier play *Henri Christophe*. This suggests Walcott's attempt to write a drama that is more evidently rooted in the Caribbean; however, the difficulty of synthesizing so many different historical strands into a single work includes the particular problem of how to incorporate sufficiently developed and differentiated linguistic registers. Although Pompey's Caribbean voice contrasts with those of the play's mainly European historical characters, it is noteworthy that there is little in the play's language to distinguish Las Casas, Columbus, Raleigh, or Le Clerc. Ironically, it is the fictional characters that are the most fully realized as Mano's onstage casting illustrates. Picking out members of the Crowd to act the roles of the historical characters, Mano's speech reveals his characterization as quick-witted, intelligent, and eminently likeable: "No Horatio Nelson? He ain't in Mass this year? Well, we going take what we get [*sic*]. Toussaint L'Ouverture and his Haitian rebellion. In front brother" (121).

The "casting" concludes with Mano's final instructions to his "actors" in which he makes clear that the purpose of the performance is to "act the history of this nation" (122). Mano leaves the audience and his own actors in no doubt as to the intended sense of unification that his story is intended to inspire. Furthermore, the Brechtian direct addresses to the audience and to other characters enable Walcott to dispense with the need to create characters with genuine emotional and mental depth—a task that would have been impossible given the size of the play's cast and its epic historical sweep. In fact, many of the characters serve as signposts for an audience that could not be expected to have a level of historical knowledge sufficient to follow a narrative that condenses four hundred years of history into just nineteen scenes.

The prologue is used as a device to assist the audience as much as possible, and it concludes after the Chorus has summarized the historical background to the play's first scene: it is 1499, the setting is a crowded beach in Santo Domingo, and the focus is on the fate of the disgraced Christopher Columbus, who is about to be sent back to Spain in shackles following the failure of his governorship of Hispaniola. However, despite the foregrounding of Columbus, the subject that is shown to be of real significance is the genocide of the Indians. Drawing freely on supernaturalism, the opening scene sees ghosts of murdered Indians descend through trap doors, figures of slaughtered Indians emerge from shadows, and on one occasion awaken a panic-stricken Columbus, as the play ingeniously establishes the starting point of Caribbean history with the islands' indigenous populations.

The action of the play then proceeds to flit, somewhat abruptly, between Spain and the "New World." The second scene, after eleven years have elapsed, is set in Cádiz, which was the destination of the ship carrying Columbus. This pictures Cádiz as a rough, unevenly developed town, a place of seediness and depravity that had a new importance thrust upon it by virtue of its position as a crucial port to the Americas. The characters through which Walcott chose to represent the life of Cádiz include sailors, drunks, idlers, whores, and the young Taino Indian Paco, who was also present in the play's first scene. However, the Paco of the play's second scene is a corrupted version of his formerly innocent self who now works as a pimp. There is certainly little evidence in Cádiz of a glorious "Old World" culture that was to be exported to the colonies.

The next two brief scenes, which are set on board a Spanish slave ship, strive to represent the indignity and violence of the Middle Passage, and although punctuated with horrific episodes, the worst atrocities are left to the imagination. The presence of an unnamed Jew onboard the slave ship implicitly recalls the similarities and dissimilarities of the Jewish and African Diasporas, and the unnamed Jew speaks for Africans and Jews alike:

> Because they have wrenched my people from the roots,
> I am like a shattered timber cast adrift. O God,
> The shores of the new lands will soon be known.
> Preserve my faith, O Lord, comfort Thy people. (167)

The subsequent two scenes then jump forward in time to tell the story of Sir Walter Raleigh. The Indian, Paco, is again the common link between the different narratives and scenes. This time Paco appears as a native who is useful to Raleigh's imperial ambitions as he claims knowledge of the reality behind the Spanish legend of El Dorado. Raleigh's two failed searches for El Dorado and his execution in the Tower of London in 1618 are included to show the imperial conquest of the "New World" for what it really was: a violent quest for riches that placed the imperial powers in competition with each other. A somewhat superfluous scene set in the British colony of Barbados is interspersed in between the Raleigh scenes, in which there is an altercation between a drunken sailor and a steward. Not before the eighth scene does the play turn to the subject of revolutionary Saint Domingue.

The Haitian Revolution is the play's most developed narrative, and it is in the story of the Haitian Revolution that Walcott seems to try to tie together all the play's thematic threads. The message communicated to the audience is that four hundred years of genocide, exploitation, robbery, and murder all reach an endpoint and a definitive rejection in the Haitian Revolution. Yet the play also unambiguously conveys the point that the Haitian Revolution, inspirational though it was, did not usher in a new era of postcolonial utopianism. The representation of the Haitian Revolution in *Drums and Colours* is drawn to a poignant close, with Dessalines and Christophe about to betray Toussaint to the French, signifying the political infighting that was to plague the newly independent state of Haiti. *Drums and Colours* provides a representation of the revolution that, while refusing to romanticize the event, encourages us to view it as a foundational Caribbean happening.

The play's Haitian section begins with Leclerc's arrival in Saint Domingue to suppress the slave revolution that is already well under way. Walcott eloquently conveys the atmosphere of the French courts and the customs of the French aristocracy transported to a self-styled tropical colonial paradise in a scene set in Leclerc's colonial mansion. Fine wine and food is served in a tropical garden, and the idle chatter of colonial high society is particularly well evoked:

LECLERC: It's not quite as terrible as one had imagined,
This heat, I mean, General. In France one had heard
That Haiti was a plague of fevers and sweltering heat,
Yet your garden is cool, and the view is excellent. (215)

The scene also quickly establishes Leclerc's view of the situation in French Saint Domingue that he had been instructed to deal with. For Leclerc it was clear: he had orders "to subjugate a province of France" where neither a war nor a revolution was taking place, but simply a "large-scale civic action" (218). In the year of the play's first production, 1958, four years into the Algerian War of Independence, Leclerc's words would have sounded frighteningly apposite, since the French government refused to concede that the military operations in French Algeria constituted a "war" and it preferred to look upon events in Algeria as the pacification of a province of France.

In *Drums and Colours*, Leclerc's voice is not just the official voice of the French government, but he appears to be the character closest to the pessimistic view of the Haitian Revolution that the trilogy as a whole promotes. For Leclerc, revolution ushers in not liberty, but "mere patterns of revenge" (220).

Leclerc's sense that the situation in Saint Domingue cannot be called a war can be contrasted with Dessalines's very different consideration. The Dessalines in *Drums and Colours* defines his entire self in relation to the extent of the destruction of the violent revolt that he is waging. For him, the revolution is "more than a war"; it is "the black man's turn to kill" (240). Although his ideological grasp of the revolution is not nearly as developed as Toussaint's, *Drums and Colours* does represent a Dessalines who has a sense of Haiti's regional role, and he speaks of exporting the revolution throughout the Caribbean. Thus he is shown to have developed a pan-Caribbean anticolonial sentiment, a quality particularly apt for celebration, given the play's original performance context:

> The flame is catching in the unharvested canes,
> Not only in this island, but through the Antilles.
> We have sent agents to stir up this violence. (239)

However, Dessalines does not speak of Haiti's future; his vision is dominated by a project of destruction and his ceaseless thirst for destruction is tiresome for his ally, Christophe (241). Walcott's Dessalines is consumed by a desire to drive the whites out of Saint Domingue and a quest for personal power. It is one of the curiosities—and disappointments—of Walcott's play that this representation is so unreconstructed.

In *Drums and Colours*, it is Toussaint alone who articulates a project greater than revenge, and, as we have seen, this resonates strongly with James's analysis of Toussaint and Dessalines. Toussaint's anticolonialism is informed by his knowledge both of the necessity of driving out the colonists and his sense that the rebuilding process will be more difficult than the winning of the war: "Revenge is nothing . . . peace is harder" (241).

The Haitian segment of *Drums and Colours* ends with the reinforcement of Walcott's characterizations of Toussaint, Christophe, and Dessalines. As Christophe and Dessalines plot to turn Toussaint over to the French, there is a dramatic exchange involving Toussaint and his former master Calixte-Breda, who is now a prisoner. Toussaint is shown to have retained respect and affection for his old master, but Walcott reveals how the revolution has now driven an insurmountable distance between them. Finding themselves on opposite sides of a war which Calixte-Breda refuses to acknowledge as legitimate, Calixte-Breda accuses Toussaint of being "blood drunk" before their argument reaches boiling point when Breda accuses Toussaint of murdering Anton, Calixte-Breda's mulatto son or "nephew" (245). When Toussaint orders Calixte-Breda's execution, the line symbolizes the tragic impossibility of a middle way for the Haitian Revolution: "Shoot him. Monsieur Calixte, it is the times" (249). With a bloodthirsty Dessalines on one side, and Toussaint's moderate conscience on the other, the execution of Calixte-Breda also serves to illustrate the divided nature of the revolution's leadership, a point that finds its analogue for both James and Césaire in the execution of Moïse. As the scene comes to a close with Toussaint walking into the trap laid for him by Dessalines and Christophe, the Haitian Revolution is left to an uncertain fate in the hands of a vengeful Desssalines. Ending the Haitian narrative at this juncture leaves the audience with a sense of precarious incompleteness, and a powerful sense of the vulnerability of the revolution.

The first scene after the play's Haitian narrative is a brief one set in Jamaica in 1830 and begins with Yette, a slave "housekeeper," being thrown out of her home by her master, a white planter. Jamaica is *Drums and Colours*'s final location, and as with the play's earlier scenes, the narrative leaps forward in time rapidly, sometimes making the story hard to follow.

The play's final scenes focus on the story of George William Gordon, the mulatto advocate for the rights of the emancipated, but poor and excluded, Negro peasantry in Jamaica. Walcott uses Gordon to reinforce his view of the cyclical nature of Caribbean history. In Gordon's final speech before his execution, he claims that "there can be no last battle. For the history of man / Is continual conflict, with himself, with his enemies," before the final pessimistic analysis of Caribbean history:

> The history of these islands has been tragic from birth,
> Their soils have been scoured, their peoples forgotten,
> While the powers of Europe struggled for possession.
> And when that wealth has been drained, we have been abandoned. (259–60)

The Haitian Earth: Independence Discredited

The Haitian Earth is the last play in *The Haitian Trilogy,* and it was Walcott's last attempt to dramatize the events of the Haitian Revolution. Written to commemorate the 150th anniversary of the Slavery Abolition Act of 1833, it was first produced in St. Lucia on August 1–5, 1984. It marks a point of total departure from the high style and court language that was so prevalent in *Henri Christophe,* and it emphasizes a different side of the story of the Haitian Revolution from both preceding plays. The intense preoccupation with heroic historical figures that was so prevalent in these is tempered somewhat, and *The Haitian Earth* strives to make the Haitian people the play's major subject. Walcott does this by telling the stories of Toussaint, Dessalines, and Christophe alongside the stories of a black Haitian peasant, Pompey, formerly a slave from the Breda plantation, and Yette, a mulatto prostitute from Le Cap. Pompey's and Yette's lives are profoundly marked by the events of the revolution, and in particular by the revolution's injustices and shortcomings. Through the story of their romance, *The Haitian Earth* reemphasizes a pessimistic recuperation of the Haitian Revolution as tragedy, tyranny, and senseless cruelty and violence that leads directly to dictatorship and a failed postcolonial state.

The Haitian Earth frequently reads like a film or television drama script. There is great attention to detail with regard to visual and acoustic directions that would only be realizable in cinematic form—and Bruce King has discovered that this was the medium in which Walcott himself envisioned working.[12] The play's opening images are certainly ripe with visual drama that would translate into film very successfully: a Caribbean dawn on a wide, wild beach with the sound of the sea heard through the noises of hungry cattle, providing a powerful auditory ambience. On the beach, Dessalines, dressed as a buccaneer, confronts a wild boar that rips his calf with its tusk before he wrestles the animal to the ground and cuts its throat. It is a scene that memorably introduces us to Dessalines as a physically imposing warrior, while his speech in this opening scene emphasizes this representation of him as a fighter rather than as a thinker. Although not uncharismatic, his speech is composed of short sentences that convey his meaning simply and directly. Walcott's skill as a playwright is particularly evident in Dessalines's dialogue, since his deft manipulation of unrhymed verse creates a voice for this figure that is frequently poetic, yet still allows a representation of a brutish but remarkable military leader to emerge. His speech reeks of anger, and it is also notable for the prominence of the motif of the sea and declarations of supernatural gifts:

> I'll tell you, *cochon*, the sea frothed like your mouth.
> And I have magic in me, and power, to kill the sea. (302)

His opening monologue continues with an intensity derived from the adrenaline of having tangled with and killed the wild boar as well as his already crazed personality. His belief in his own powers is entirely free of self-doubt, and he stridently declares his belief in his own immortality:

> Nothing can kill me. My name is Dessalines.
> Jean Jacques Dessalines. Nothing can kill me. (302)

And a few lines later he shouts out a proclamation of his intentions:

> The next time you see me, I will be a king!
> The hills, the sea, will echo with my name.
> DESSALINES! DESSALINES! (303)

However, the echo that he hears immediately after his cry comes from the play's two Choruses, one a "Chorus of Peasants" and the other an unnamed Chorus, and they operate together in the manner of call-and-response. As he exits the scene, the Chorus of Peasants chants the names of Toussaint, Dessalines, and then Christophe, while the other Chorus directly poses the question of individual revolutionary heroism and memorialization, asking, "When that big drum, / The thunder shake Haiti . . . / What man we does remember?" (304). Drawing attention to the question of who has been forgotten in the memorialization of the Haitian Revolution, the Chorus provides an early hint of the significant roles that Pompey and Yette will have to play.

In the second scene, we meet Anton, a young mulatto, through whom Walcott represents the discontent of that community. Anton is well read in the texts of the European Enlightnement, but he has absorbed the racial discourse of slave society. For Anton, "White / Is the colour of thought, black of action," and he speaks of being paralyzed "between thought and action." Anton has no wish "to go back to the bush," and he thinks "African nostalgia is rubbish," but he is also "very tired of Western culture," which he perceives to be a failure (305–6). Anton's characterization thus alludes to the clichéd négritude of its post-Senghorian reception: its admonishment of Western culture as a failure recalls négritude's condemnations of the West's duplicitous humanistic project of civilization and progress; yet it also warns against a reactionary sentimental attraction to "African nostalgia." It also summarizes the sense of social exclusion that was one of the identifying traits of the mulatto class in Saint Domingue. However, Anton does more than merely highlight the legally codified isolation of Saint Domingue's mulatto group. He also draws out, through punning on "Entitlement" and "Enlightenment," his sense of lethargy when it comes to Western culture, and his equal disdain for a naïve Africanism, and he thus evokes the limited cultural, political, or intellectual locations to which he could attach himself. The mulattos' vulnerable position is reinforced the moment that Yette makes her first entrance into the drama.

Denied freedoms and status by the whites and also despised by the blacks, Yette becomes a prostitute. Significantly, when we first meet her she is not being abused by a *grand blanc*, but by one of the revolution's own leaders, Henri Christophe, who cruelly taunts and insults her during their brief encounter:

> Wouldn't it be nice if your children were white?
> But making children is not a whore's business,
> Any more than making revolution
> Is a mulatto's. (319)

Christophe's ill treatment of Yette ensures that the audience quickly dispenses with any rose-tinted concept of the revolution's leadership. With the exception of the ever-moderate Toussaint, who plays only a relatively minor role in *The Haitian Earth*, the revolutionary leaders Dessalines and Christophe are represented as being wholly inadequate to the challenge of uniting a fractiously divided and war-torn society that has been deeply scarred by the legacies of slavery and colonialism. Dessalines is shown to be a womanizing, cruel, illiterate, and anti-intellectual bully, and Christophe shares many of Dessalines's qualities, such as ineffectual political leadership and a weakness for women.

By representing Dessalines and Christophe in such despicable terms and by giving Toussaint only a minor role, *The Haitian Earth* looks beyond the revolution's leaders to find qualities of heroism. Instead, the fortitude and strength of the Haitian people in the face of appalling conditions is imagined. Yette and Pompey represent this neglected but heroic story of the Haitian Revolution. After the burning of the city of Le Cap by the slaves during the course of the revolution, Yette finds herself one among many refugees who have been forced to evacuate their homes and flee the town, and her only option in order to survive is to learn to plant in order to live off the little piece of land left to her by her auntie (333).

Attempting to work as a subsistence farmer, Yette's story becomes representative of true heroism in the play, and it recalls Ti Noel's celebration of dignified toil in *El reino de este mundo*. Alone on her small allotment in the mountains, Yette reveals, in a monologue addressed to her father, her awareness of the dignity with which she has chosen to confront her difficulties: "Papa . . . if I could write you, you would laugh now to see your daughter, who you say would be nothing, bending down on the earth . . . trying to plant something" (334). Her determined attempts to adapt to a new, rural lifestyle are part of a binary division that *The Haitian Earth* sets up between the country and city: the countryside and a rural way of life is presented as being authentically Haitian, whereas the city is associated with vice and the colonists. Moreover there is a racial quality to the contrast that is captured in Yette's lines of self-analysis: "The white part of me is the town, / The black part of me is the country" (355). *The Haitian Earth* thus contributes to the long line of tradition in which Haiti's peasant economy is associated with dignity. And notably, Toussaint also demonstrates a deep attachment to the earth that he recognizes as being crucial to Haiti's future as he laments that "The soil itself / Is bleeding, and I can't stop it" (352).

However, even in her newly adopted rural community that she shares with Pompey, Dessalines and Christophe continue to be a threatening force. In one ominous scene, a peasant woman working in a cane field screams on finding a snake in her patch of corn. Amid the cries of panic, Pompey runs to the scene with his musket ready, but when he arrives, what emerges from the corn is not a snake but Dessalines, who explains that he "was just sleeping" (336). Later, Dessalines fulfills the villainous role suggested by his appearance as a snake when he abuses his powers as "King of Haiti" and asserts his authority over Pompey by using Yette for sex against her will. When Yette resists Dessalines, antimulatto racism emerges in plain speech: "Yellow bitch . . . you sweet / Yellow bitch" (417). Representing the founder of Haiti, Dessalines, in such unrelentingly negative terms seems to justify Walcott's assessment of the Haitian Revolution in general in the trilogy's foreword: "as sordidly tyrannical as so many of its subsequent regimes became" (vii).

As the play reaches its tragic denouement, even Christophe now confronts Dessalines, as he recognizes that with the French defeated, Dessalines is the progenitor of a new misery that is being inflicted upon the Haitian people. Christophe's speech to Dessalines is remarkable for the terms in which it praises and condemns Dessalines. Christophe speaks of how during the course of the military stages of the revolution Dessalines seemed to him "like a panther" with a "black scream" for a banner (423). Christophe then describes the influence he exerted on the revolutionary slave-soldiers fighting alongside Dessalines in battle: to them he was "like a black centaur," "African, magical" (423). Of his own reaction, Christophe states that he lost himself

> In utter and unutterable admiration
> Like a man wandering through a forest
> Whose compass is the moon, and when the moon went,
> I took an even deeper pride in blackness,
> In the night's skin; for us, you were the night,
> The constellations were your medals,
> The clouds, your plumes, you were a forest
> Where our ancestral spirits lived, you were,
> Jean Jacques. (423)

The pathos and richness of Christophe's speech is an aesthetic highpoint of *The Haitian Earth*: its similies and powerfully descriptive language imagine and describe Dessalines during the revolution as having been like a force of nature and the very essence of blackness. He is a source of racial pride—"I took an even deeper pride in blackness"—and Walcott seems to have seen in his character certain qualities that also found expression in the négritude movement, especially in Dessalines's inspirational "African, magical" aura.

Yet, the Dessalines that Christophe sees before him today is a betrayal of all that he once stood for, and makes Christophe turn away his eyes that had once "watered with admiration" for Dessalines, as if he were now "a curse" and a betrayal of himself (424). Dessalines's fall from greatness, and the suffering that he inflicts upon Yette and Pompey and the Haitian people at large combine to make *The Haitian Earth* the most unequivocally pessimistic recuperation of the Haitian Revolution in Walcott's *Haitian Trilogy*.

The play's two final scenes occur many years after Christophe's confrontation with Dessalines. It is 1820, and Christophe has assumed power after the murder of Dessalines. Yette, still haunted by her suffering and despairing at the succession of abusive dictators the revolution has produced, is now shown as a *vodoussaint* who uses a *vodou* ritual to inflict upon Christophe a mysterious and paralyzing stroke. For this, Yette's fate is to be hanged, and her execution represents the final betrayal of the Haitian people by the revolution's leaders. In her final speech before her execution, Yette proclaims her pride in Pompey and she expresses her disgust at where the path of the revolution has taken them all. Her words are the clearest indication of the play's celebration of the Haitian people, and its condemnation of Haiti's leaders: "He love his country more than all of you! / He is the sweat and salt of the earth, this man. / And I am prouder of him than if he was a king" (433).

The final words of the play fall to Pompey, the Chorus, and Haiti's peasants, who sing in unison:

> They cannot take our faith from us,
> We, who suffered many things,
> All the soldiers, guns, and drummers,
> All the emperors and kings. (434)

Thus, the play ends with Yette executed, Pompey bereaved, and the revolution's leadership corrupted and disgraced, leaving behind only a legacy of terror. It is an ending that presents little hope for an independent Haiti trapped in a tragic cycle of tyranny and misery. *The Haitian Earth*, having muddied the historical reasons for the ostensible failures of the Haitian Revolution, ends with discrediting the momentous achievement of independence.

8 Fantasizing the Haitian Revolution with Madison Smartt Bell

Madison Smartt Bell's trilogy of novels on the Haitian Revolution and Toussaint Louverture are discussed in this chapter in order to assess their productive capacities and limitations.[1] The limitations are manifest when the novels are examined in the context of the contemporary historical novel of slavery and the genre's antecedents, as well as when they are contrasted with the fertile radicalism of the works considered in this book's first part. Despite an extensive documentary basis and an apparent progressive interpretation of events, Madison Smartt Bell's trilogy undermines itself by emphasizing an exotic setting, insufficiently individualizing its characters, and producing a fictional-historical account of revolutionary Saint Domingue that is reliant on horrific accounts of slave torture and violence, together with frequent interludes of mild erotica centered on the familiar racial stereotype of the beautiful mulatto woman.[2] A desensitized voyeuristic consumption of the trilogy as escapist adventure fiction is thus encouraged, and the ideological radicalism of the Haitian Revolution is supplanted with a superficial representation that reduces history to, in Lukács's famous phrase, "a world of historically exact costumes and decorations,"[3] and gory descriptions of horror, carnage, and mindless violence.

It is noteworthy that of all the writings this book examines, only Bell's trilogy can be regarded as an attempt to produce writing in the mold of the classical historical novel that aspires to the tradition of the towering literary figures of Walter Scott, Balzac, and Tolstoy. While Alejo Carpentier's *El reino de este mundo* undoubtedly represents a starting point for metahistorical fiction, Bell's Toussaint Louverture trilogy is something of a throwback to the premodernist literary tradition of the historical novel as defined by Georg Lukács: real historical figures are interwoven with fictional characters, the varied and dramatic experiences of the fictionalized protagonist create a social context that mediates the appearances of "great" world-historical individuals, and the novel's underlying narrative of progress conveys the idea of a journey to national independence.

In his recent essay "From Progress to Catastrophe," Perry Anderson surveys the rise and fall of the historical novel, as well as the subsequent evolutionary "mutation" of the metahistorical novel in the peripheries in the era of postmodernity. Following Lukács, Anderson links the etiology of the historical novel to an exercise in nation building, but he also notes the contrast formed by the fact that postmodern re-creations of the past transcribe "the ravages of empire" rather than the emergence of the nation: "not progress as emancipation, but impending or consummated catastrophe."[4] Thus, Anderson concludes that the persistent backdrops to historical fiction of the postmodern period—"military tyranny; race murder; omnipresent surveillance; technological war; and programmed genocide . . . are at the antipodes of its classical forms."[5] It is thus implied that the contemporary historical novel has been forced to navigate the guilt associated with the act of aesthetic construction out of historical trauma. This problem of aesthetic creation and the inheritance of trauma has been memorably defined by Nick Nesbitt in the context of a discussion of Edwidge Danticat's writings: aesthetic language is condemned to "pretend to the humanity from which its rigid forms and structures are unavoidably alienated."[6]

However, when considering Bell's Haitian trilogy of novels, it is striking that they combine an aspiration to the historical novel in its classical form but with a backdrop—race murder—more readily associated with postmodern historical fiction. Furthermore, Bell's writing, replete with detailed descriptions of brutality for its own sake, appears oblivious to the guilt of its representation of historical trauma. A critical reading of Bell's Haitian novels thus prompts a consideration of Lukács's critique of the failings of the post-1848 bourgeois historical novel and its applicability to Bell's works.

In his seminal work *The Historical Novel*, Lukács argues that the revolutions of 1848, which witnessed the defeat of the proletariat and the bourgeois betrayal of its own earlier revolutionary ideals across Europe, resulted in a widespread change of attitude to history. Whereas the most notable writers of the period before 1848 offered a sophisticated historical analysis of the contradictory concept of the idea of human progress, the events of the class struggle of 1848 "presented to the ideologists of the bourgeoisie so threatening a prospect for the future of their society and class, that the disinterested courage with which the contradictions of progress has been disclosed and declared was bound to disappear."[7] This, in Lukács's argument, then marked the aesthetic of the historical novel with the tendencies of archaeologization and modernization. After 1848, with the notable exception of Tolstoy, history as presented in the historical novel was decisively disconnected from contemporary society and statically lacking the dynamics of historical change. The presentation of such a past emptied of sociohistorical significance, Lukács contended, gave rise to a "longing to escape from the triviality of modern bourgeois life," which found expression in the historical novel in the themes of exoticism and explicit brutality.[8]

Lukács thus reveals how an emphasis on exoticism and brutality merely produces "pseudo-monumentality" and the attempt to achieve by these means the significance of the pre-1848 historical novel—Walter Scott's *Waverly* is the primary exemplar—is doomed to failure. Lukács takes Flaubert's historical novel *Salammbô* and its description of the suffering of the population during the siege of Carthage to make the argument: "Flaubert takes delight in giving detailed and cruel pictures of the sufferings of the masses in and around Carthage. There is never any humanity in this suffering; it is simply horrible, senseless torment."[9]

Whereas writers in the tradition of Scott "were only interested in the cruel and terrible happenings of previous history insofar as they were necessary expressions of definite forms of class struggle," or insofar as they made intelligible the cruel processes of social development, Flaubert's writing began a trend wherein the inhumanity of subject matter and the presentation of "atrocity and brutality become ends in themselves."[10] However, instead of producing outrage in the reader over the cruelties of the past, their explicit narration only numbs and brutalizes the reader. It is my argument here that Bell's trilogy must be regarded in the tradition of historical fiction that Lukács traced to Flaubert, in which atrocity and the exotic acquire a central position.

It is thus instructive to preface the discussion of Bell's narrative style by contrasting it with two (post)modernist historical novels of slavery, which developed sublimely original methods of navigating the essential unrepresentability of the horrors of the past. Toni Morrison's *Beloved* and Edouard Glissant's early radical novel *Le quatrième siècle* will be taken as a priori models.[11] Of concern here is the fact that torture, violence, and sexuality in slave conditions have been represented with reticence, turning "the partial guilt of artistic representation"[12] back upon the total guilt of slavery, torture, and the Middle Passage.

At its core, Toni Morrison's *Beloved* is engaged with the production of a profoundly responsible aesthetic with which to negotiate the inheritance of the trauma of Atlantic slavery. Sethe, the novel's central character, is haunted by memories of having suffered the brutalities of slavery, and this frames her explanation for killing her baby daughter. The harrowing and long-term trauma inflicted by sexual abuse that was innate to colonial slavery is also conveyed without prurience and in sparing language that makes clear the link between sexual abuse and the institution of slavery. Morrison's work thus prompts us to ask what the role of aesthetics might be in recalling the sexual power of whites in slave society.

Glissant's novel *Le quatrième siècle* also develops startlingly original aesthetic strategies in order to represent the trauma and suffering of the Middle Passage. The first two chapters of the novel relate a fictionalized slave narrative of the Middle Passage in "poetic, delirious free-indirect prose."[13] Through the character of Papa Longoué, a descendent of maroons, and a *quimboiseur*—a healer, seer, and storyteller—Glissant finds a language with which to communicate the horrors of the Middle Passage that does not numb the reader into a state of intellectual or emotional paralysis:

> For he would have preferred, oh barge I the barge and he I on my belly the powder I the boat and beating on my back the current and the water each foot I the rope sliding for and dying the harbor country and so far faraway nothing I nothing nothing to end falling the water salty salty salty on the back and blood and fish and eating oh country the country[14]

This disorienting language, Christopher Miller has argued, conveys the message that the trauma of the Middle Passage "cannot be represented in transparent language. Normal grammar cannot do it justice."[15] Instead, *Le quatrième siècle*'s radical recuperation of the Middle Passage finds expression in a modernist and radical linguistic aesthetic form. The discretion with which the conditions in the hold are communicated, and the means by which clear impressions of terror, agony, and violence are filtered through the consciousness of a tormented participant in the inflictions of cruelty, conveys a profoundly unsettling message without any descent into sensationalism.

The critique of Bell's trilogy that follows is thus not a moral complaint, but an investigation into the limits of language and a question of genre: I argue that Bell's attempt to revitalize the historical novel in its premodernist form fails to cope with the burdens of a specifically Caribbean modernity which irrupted within and out of slavery. And, placing the novels within the schema of the conservative depolitizization of the historical novel via Lukács, I argue that the novels' exoticizing and brutalistic qualities should be identified as characteristic of an archaeological presentation of the past isolated from the currents of history.

Suffering and Exploitation in *All Souls' Rising*

All Souls' Rising is the first installment of Bell's trilogy of novels that tell the story of the Haitian Revolution in considerable detail and with mostly commendable historical accuracy. The trilogy as a whole was published between 1995 and 2002 to near universal acclaim, although so far the trilogy has attracted only limited academic criticism.[16] The *New Yorker* found the novel to be "meticulously researched" and with "the feel of a tableau by Delacroix"; the *Oregonian* felt that Bell had learned well the lessons of Tolstoy and produced a "brilliant blend of history and fiction"; and Harold Bloom considered *All Souls' Rising* to be "a beautifully composed, eloquent, grand nightmare of a book. With it, Bell becomes as remarkable a historical novelist as we have in this country."[17] However, Bell's meticulous and lengthy enterprise—the trilogy amounts to more than two thousand pages—is remarkable for its extended descriptions of torture, violence, and sexual exploitation under the guise of truthful historicism. The novels combine depictions of extreme violence and sex with such fluency that they are evocative of Hollywood sex-horror movies, particularly "horror teen-pics" and "slasher" films. Such films have routinely been examined for the ways in which they combine erotic imagery with extreme and/or graphic violence that is frequently directed at women.[18] A novelistic equivalence to this technique is present in *All Souls' Rising*. Further, although the novel presents itself as an attempt to recuperate the story of the Haitian Revolution in order to bring to life a decisive moment in the history of race, class, and colonialism, it is easily consumable as soft-core erotica.[19]

The novel's principal fictionalized character is Antoine Hébert, a French doctor, who has traveled to Saint Domingue in order to find his sister, the wife of a recently deceased planter. Like a hero from a Scott novel, Hébert becomes caught up by events when the revolution breaks out and he fortuitously comes into contact with the key players of the revolution. In his review for the *Times Literary Supplement*, Zachary Leader ironically summarized this narrative conceit: "In the course of his travels, he [Hébert] befriends a troop of Royalist soldiers, falls in love with a mulatto prostitute, is seduced by the imperious wife of a rich *grand blanc*, travels into the mountains with

Toussaint, Riau [the fictional slave] and other rebels, and only just escapes with his life."[20]

The novel mechanistically alternates its focus of attention between the rebellious slaves, the mulatto factions, and the *grands blancs* planter class in an attempt to bring to life the political and cultural complexities of revolutionary Saint Domingue. However, despite the attention to historical detail, nothing more than a historical gloss is achieved—this is history as ornament. Furthermore, the novel's principal characters are only superficially conditioned by their material and historical circumstances. Instead, Hébert's affairs of the heart, which play on erotic race stereotypes, assume center stage in *All Souls' Rising*.

Hébert's first meeting with the exotic mulatto prostitute Nanon occurs during the interval of a theater performance in Le Cap, and it foreshadows the lubricious tenor of the encounters to come. When Nanon is present, the Saint Domingue of *All Souls' Rising* seems to exist only in order to arouse Hébert's and the reader's concupiscent imagination with florid accounts of sexual encounters. These encounters are littered with descriptions in which Nanon is likened to animals and a crass African exoticism is linked to impulsive sexual energy:

> The doctor turned in time to see her [Nanon] touch herself cunningly just above the breastbone. The cotton wrap came undone spontaneously and whispered to the floor. The necklace winked at him, her bare skin changed its surface like a leopard's coat as she moved forward under the white-hot dots and bars of light that leaked through the weave of the blind. Her bracelets softly belled together as she reached out, and wherever she touched him a piece of his clothing fell away as though cut with a hot knife.[21]

Nanon's ethnicity, it is implied, makes her a "natural" sex object. That mulatto women were highly prized sexual objects by white men in the early French Caribbean is not in dispute, as studies such as Doris Garraway's have made clear.[22] But the endorsement of this perception via the construction of a female mulatto character by an omniscient narrator in a contemporary historical novel that creates linkages between stereotypical racial characteristics and sexuality, African imagery and sexual energy, and mulatto women and animal traits is clearly problematic. Consider the description of Nanon's physical characteristics: her legs are long and "ivory" (although the exact tone of her skin color varies throughout the novels), her lips are "large and cushiony" and "muscular," her body is "lithe" and like a "stoat," during sex she tantalizes by uttering "some phrases of Creole," and her sexual prowess is accentuated by her racial identity.[23]

Furthermore, the novel pays scant attention to Nanon's particular material conditions. She remains only a mulatto body, and her characterization lacks personal history and individuality. Her past experiences as an abused prostitute make little impression on her character; she remains throughout merely a late-twentieth, early-twenty-first-century fantasy image of eroticism, otherness, and excitement. The fact that Nanon would likely have been as attracted to Hébert for her own security and personal safety at least as much as for any other reason barely surfaces in the novel. Nor does the novel encourage an understanding of the development of Nanon's feelings and their complexity in a relationship that is inherently uneven due to her racial classification in a slave society.

It is remarkable that in the many reviews of Madison Smartt Bell's Haiti trilogy, none of the critics noted this problematic depiction of the interaction between the novels' principal characters and the society that they inhabit. While some found fault with Bell's troubled and wooden dialogue, especially when it came to creating a convincing voice and consciousness for the novel's black characters, and also with the pomposity of the novel's antiquarian voice, very little has been said about the reduction of revolutionary Saint Domingue to a scene of tropical erotic fantasy for a middle-aged Frenchman's sexual adventures. The novel thereby meretriciously transforms the history of slave society in colonial Saint Domingue on the eve of revolution into an escapist paperback sex tour for the early-twenty-first-century reader.

The fact that slave girls and women and free and unfree mulatto girls and women were raped, abused, and otherwise sexually exploited in a society which propagated and systematized the uneven power relations of racial hierarchy and classification has been documented and is well known. However, the conversion of this historical knowledge into sensational fiction requires slave society to be imaginatively recalled as a place of unparalleled erotic encounters. The *grand blanc* Captain Maillart tells Hébert that the mulatto woman Nanon is "made for love—and yours for the asking," and her characterization in the novel suggests little to contradict Maillart's statement.[24] She is likened to a number of animals (leopards, lionesses, and stoats, among others), normally in order to highlight her sexual athleticism and drive, as well as her sensual connection to nature; of course, there is nothing new in such erotic racist cliché—it is, for example, reminiscent of the treatment inflicted upon

Josephine Baker in the 1920s. However, it is notable that Bell's revivification of colonial sterotypes of black eroticism has gone entirely unnoticed in popular reviews and academic critique. Indeed, one reviewer of *All Souls' Rising* even claimed that "the novel's racial politics are impeccably liberal."[25] The reader is also subjected to a great deal of description concerning Nanon's skin tone, her odor, her hair, her breasts, and her body, and the minutiae of her bathing and boudoir customs, but precious little else. In this respect, *All Souls' Rising* is the kind of cheap literary trick that more than 150 years ago the great nineteenth-century Haitian antiracist and radical intellectual Anténor Firmin would have condemned as pandering to a foreign market by "evoking the charms of the frisky Creole woman."[26]

Fantasizing Slave Torture and Violence

Bell's Haiti trilogy has been noted for its obsessively detailed representations of slave torture and violence. In the *Times Literary Supplement*, Zachary Leader observed the effect of this litany of described horrors: "we get an infant impaling, or a blinding (with a corkscrew). The effect is numbing, especially since the horror is extreme from the start, beginning with a hideous episode involving a pregnant slave. . . . [T]he extremity of the violence seems related to the exotic setting."[27] There are a number of important points to be drawn out from the descriptions of torture and violence in the trilogy. The first is the desensitizing effect produced by the interweaving of erotic scenes and forensic descriptions of torture and violence. Second, the novels reveal an obsession with recalling slave torture through an emphasis on torture and punishment equipment. In his study of English and American visual representations of slavery in the period 1780–1865, Marcus Wood noted a "Western obsession with representing the memory of slave torture through objects."[28] Bell's Haiti trilogy provides ample evidence of this continuing obsession: the trilogy's first chapter, from the very first sentence, describes in extreme detail the torture and murder by crucifixion of a female slave who had just given birth. In the description, we are informed of the precise shape and thickness of the nails used, the appearance of the wood, and a careful, quasi medical-scientific description of the effect these instruments of torture have on the slave body, with particular attention paid to describing the slave's sexual organs. Bell's description seems to reflect a desire to possess, to recuperate absolutely the memory of slavery, to "face up" to the horrors of the past no matter how terrible without shirking, with the object of containing or ordering the memory of slavery. However, the strategy misfires badly, and Bell's trilogy illustrates the pitfalls of an ordered, realist memorialization of slavery.

In contrast to Césaire's, Depestre's, Glissant's, or Carpentier's nonlinear strategies of memorializing the Haitian Revolution, Bell's trilogy strives to re-create what it was like to live through the turbulence, uncertainty, and trauma of the Haitian Revolution from a myriad of different perspectives dictated by race, class, and political allegiance. This appears to be the implicit justification for the inclusion of the many detailed descriptions of slave torture, punishment, and sexual abuse: the novels strive to leave nothing out. To that end, each of the novels in the trilogy makes the use of a preface, a chronology of historical events, and appendices that include translations of original historical letters and documents, a great number of which are translations of Toussaint's letters. This desire to leave nothing out might be termed a "cabinet box" approach to the memorialization of the Haitian Revolution: Bell's Haiti trilogy is at one level a novelistic museum of the Haitian Revolution. However, the problematic effect of this approach can be made clear by a close reading of any number of the passages that describe torture and violence.

In one scene, Claudine Arnaud, the disturbed wife of a depraved *grand blanc*, exacts her revenge on a hapless slave girl, Mouche, one of the many slave girls with whom Claudine's husband had been having sexual intercourse. Claudine, plagued by *delerium tremens*, craving a return to France, and an end to her husband's infidelities, suffers a nervous breakdown before she brutally tortures and murders the pregnant Mouche. The process begins with a whipping, and the instrument of torture is precisely detailed: a "riding crop, tan leather braided around whalebone."[29] The ritual of torture by whipping is faintly eroticized: Claudine, riven with jealousy, strips Mouche down "to the swell of her buttocks," and as Claudine's hand comes back with the riding crop for the first time, she momentarily pauses, "as though she anticipated a touch of love."[30] Although Claudine tries to "flay the bitch to the bone . . . [t]he crop could barely scratch the surface of Claudine's deepest indignation."[31] The torture scene thus continues for a further four pages: Claudine, finding the riding crop insufficient for her purpose, and now drunk with white brandy and power, then takes a razor blade to the naked Mouche. In the final denouement to the torture, Claudine slices Mouche open "down the plumb line to her center" before the scene finally ends with a shower of blood and with Mouche's entrails and unborn child lying on the floor.[32]

In an interview published in *Bomb* magazine, Madison Smartt Bell sought to defend such representations of torture and violence:

> I'm probably lucky not to have heard the splatterpunk accusation more often than I did. Most readers seem to have seen the violence as something you had to go through in order to get to the essential point. . . . [I]t is a story about attempted genocide and the inherent violence that goes along with that. As far as the intended total effect, the game plan is straight out of Aristotle, where pity and fear produce catharsis. Or as Flannery O'Connor put it, the shock of violence is used to turn the mind of the audience toward the moral issues.[33]

Yet, despite Bell's protestations, the extreme violence of the novel subsumes its cultural and political context and ignores the fact that the violence and torture described are often eroticized. Far from directing the reader "toward the moral issues," the trilogy's representation of violence and torture propogates not a cathartic or critical reiminagination of the violence of the Haitian Revolution but a reification of colonial stereotypes about black savagery and eroticism. This trilogy's representations of atrocities committed by the rebellious slaves once the revolution has broken out are especially problematic. In such scenes, the slaves of *All Souls' Rising* become monsters as they joyously swig the blood of their former masters from drinking bowls crafted from the scooped-out craniums of white men.[34] Racist stereotyping prevails in the portrayal of the slaves as if they were a collection of Tolkien's orcs on the rampage rather than as human beings: the black slave masses in revolt are not just violent, as no doubt they were during the outbreak of the revolution, but also unfeeling and senseless brutes.

Master of the Crossroads, the second installment in Bell's Haiti trilogy, picks up where the first volume left off: with regular Mills and Boon–style interludes and action-packed battle sequences to provide a light diversion from the heavy and serious matter of "history" and political and military strategies. As in *All Souls' Rising*, the most fully realized scenes are those that deal primarily with the novel's tableau of characters of European descent rather than those scenes that involve the rebel slaves. The quickly established sexual tension that is prevalent in *Master of the Crossroads* produces a dispiriting sense of déjà vu for the reader who comes to the novel fresh from a reading of the trilogy's first installment. In one scene, Captain Maillart, while cooling himself from the steamy tropical climate in an outdoor bathing pool, finds his mind wandering as he recalls past erotic encounters with Isabelle, a married white who belongs to the planter class. Predictably, who should promptly appear on the scene but Isabelle, conveniently clad in "a tightly laced bodice," who on seeing the naked Maillart in the shallow water notices that the water is indeed so shallow that Maillart's "rampant gallantry" is plainly on display.[35] There is a good deal more "rampant gallantry" that quickly becomes tiresome: the grandiose language does little to conceal the smuttiness from which the novel never quite escapes. A little later another water scene provides some more erotic entertainment. This time Moustique, another Frenchman caught up in the maelstrom of the revolution, notices a group of black girls, just in his field of vision, playing in the stream in which he himself is bathing. It is not long before his mind also wanders, as he lazily contemplates with disappointment that if the girls had not noticed him they "would have been free to strip off the dresses they were wearing and scrub them clean and then swim naked while their clothes dried on the rocks." Moustique's fantasy problematically ascribes to the girls an Edenic primitive quality: he imagines them unclothed, naïve, and insensible to their nakedness. Unable to voyeuristically observe the girls nude, Moustique finds some satisfaction in noticing that the splashing game the girls were playing "had soaked the whole pack of them to their necks, so that the wet fabric clung transparently to the rich chocolate flesh, breast and buttocks and belly and the shadowy cleft between the thighs. "[36] And with Moustique ablaze with titillation, some of the novel's most pompous lexicon arrives: "his wicked thoughts were concentrating in the arrow shaft of sin, which sprung forward and strained against the cotton of his breeches."[37]

As with *All Souls' Rising*, the chief erotic interest of *Master of the Crossroads* is the mulatto former prostitute Nanon, mistress to Doctor Hébert, and prior to that the lover of the mulatto Choufleur, the most sadistic character in the trilogy. While Hébert is busy serving as a volunteer military doctor to Toussaint's forces, Nanon is paid a visit by Choufleur. Choufleur rapes Nanon, kidnaps her, and then keeps her as his sex slave after sending her son by Hébert away to Le Cap.

However, there is an extremely strange quality to the narration of this part of Choufleur's relationship with Nanon. What their relationship signifies, and what it might be symptomatic of, are both troubling questions, and there is a sense that the novel has opened up a subject that it is not able to deal with. When Nanon demands to know what Choufleur has done with her son and attempts to resist him, Choufleur turns her into a bondage slave. He binds her hands and gags her with torn bedclothes before returning with an iron slave collar, which he shuts around her neck, bruising her in the process, before locking the other end around a bedpost. With his victim bound, chained, and gagged, Choufleur then grabs Nanon by her hair, twists it until she gasps, and rapes her, using her "as brutally as his father ever had."[38]

Choufleur's brutal sexual abuse of Nanon lasts for three days in its initial phase. How Nanon manages to cope with her ordeal during the times in which she is left alone is described: sometimes standing naked in front of a mirror Nanon poses and drapes herself in the iron chain. On the fourth day, Choufleur releases her from her bondage and removes the iron slave collar around her neck. At this point the novel reaches a high point of inexplicable melodrama: having released Nanon there is a moment of silence and calm that is broken by Choufleur's words: "If you had left me . . . I would surely die," before he attempts to commit suicide by driving his sword into his heart in front of Nanon.[39] Nanon, however, manages to knock the blade away, and they both begin to weep uncontrollably, and with Nanon now comforting Choufleur as though he were a "hysterical child," they cling "to each other like two drowning people," yet because of their bland characterizations, the scene does not manage to communicate their trauma in any meaningful way. And the paragraph that immediately follows the episode further exposes the problem: it includes a strange meditation on slavery and freedom and begins with deeply unsatisfactory simplicity: "Afterward everything returned to normal."[40]

With Nanon and Choufleur now inhabiting the latter's plantation house and living as a colonial couple, Choufleur goes out to work and Nanon directs the house slaves in his absence. However, when Choufleur rivets "the collar around her neck again, Nanon did not try to run or resist."[41] Enslaved once again, Nanon is left alone until she is visited by one of the slaves who works Choufleur's plantation. Bringing news of the decree issued by the French Assembly that slavery had been abolished throughout France and her colonies (a decree that Napoleon would later overturn), the disbelieving slave Salomon announces to Nanon, "My dear, slavery is finished in this country" before freeing her from her slave collar.[42] Nanon's response is to take the collar in her hands before closing it around her neck once again and motioning to Salomon that he must fasten it as it had been before. With its wildly overblown symbolism, the freeing and enslaving of Nanon and the trauma that she suffers is a frustratingly ambiguous subplot in the trilogy. This is particularly true since the trauma that Choufleur subjects Nanon to does not make any real impression on the reader since the novel communicates acts of abuse with no real understanding of how the legacies of trauma might shape an individual. Soon after Choufleur's death, Nanon finds her way back into the arms of Doctor Hébert, and their lives essentially pick up where they left off. For all of the trilogy's eroticism, violence, and torture, the emotional impact the trilogy makes is distinctly slight. In *Beloved*, Toni Morrison writes that "anything dead coming back to life hurts."[43] This pain, which surely would have been experienced by Nanon after her sexual abuse and torture as a bondage slave, is not something that Bell's Haiti trilogy ever manages to find an artistic language to convey.

The Representation of Toussaint

Although he deceptively appears to be a marginal character for long sections of the trilogy, Toussaint emerges as erudite, compassionate, a skilled medical herbalist, and a master military tactician, thus possessing the full range of attributes that have often been ascribed to him. As Forsdick writes: "It is undeniable that the character Bell elaborates over his three volumes shares a series of characteristics with other fictional or historiographic constructions of the same figure. Bell's Toussaint is an abstemious, taciturn figure, requiring little sleep, capable of rapid displacement and skilled at disguise."[44] Despite this, Bell's refiguration remains remarkably vague; he smiles knowingly, or smirks and produces a witty or a cutting line of dialogue, but he remains an incomplete, shadowy character. Bell himself explains that the reason for his character's opacity stems from his refusal to fictionalize anything to do with his character: "Particularly in the case of Toussaint Louverture, I was very reluctant to falsify or invent anything at all. Obviously he is fictionalized to some extent. But there is almost nothing he does and particularly nothing that he says or thinks that I cannot justify from my reading of the historical record."[45]

Bell's strict refusal to invent thus may be the reason for Toussaint's unreadability in the novels. But Bell's determination not to invent also indicates perhaps too strong a faith in the recoverability of historical characters and events. This is perhaps the major flaw in his Haiti trilogy. In the end, no amount of archival work examining the letters of Toussaint helps us to understand the experiences of the Haitian Revolution or the conflicting forces it released in individuals. The epic scope and form of Bell's Haiti trilogy attempts to present the Haitian Revolution in the form of a coherent narrative: the novels are, in Toni

Morrison's terminology, "loaded" with documents that attest to the trilogy's authenticity: an envoi, an eighteen-page chronology of historical events, as well as a glossary.[46] However, it is a presentation of the past that is really little more than a pretense to historical authenticity. Bell's Haitian trilogy demonstrates that taking the sensational novel as a vehicle for telling the story of the Haitian Revolution is a dangerous folly indeed. The end product is a lifeless, violent trilogy, replete with stereotyping, masquerading as a liberal take on a seminal moment in world history.

Addendum: Bell's *Toussaint Louverture: A Biography*

Madison Smartt Bell's biography *Toussaint Louverture*—the first English-language biography of Toussaint in more than fifty years—is a peculiarly strange work, in which, as he admits, his elusive subject escapes representation: "Toussaint walked so very softly that he left next to no visible tracks at all."[47] Whereas C. L. R. James justified writing a history of the Haitian Revolution that was also a political biography by observing the extent to which the individual leadership of the Haitian Revolution "was almost entirely the work of a single man—Toussaint L'Ouverture," Bell's microscopic view of Toussaint's life and achievements suffers from a narrowness of focus.[48] Much of the narrative depends upon guesswork and supposition, limitations that are evident in attempts to explain the motivations behind Toussaint's political and military decisions in the course of the revolution. Like many before him, Bell concentrates on Toussaint as a freed slave, as an owner of slaves and property, and as one who had been a successful participant in the economy of the ancien régime. However, the attempt to analyze Toussaint's political formation in the early stages of the revolution relies on psychoanalytic conjecture as to why an individual who had profited from the colonial slave system came to fight so vigorously against that same system. Was it an inherent personal radical humanitarianism? Or was it the influence of the Enlightenmnt ideology of the French Revolution to which Toussaint may have been partially exposed? Or was it that Toussaint, being "ever a proud man, though skilled in camouflaging his pride . . . would have been as galled by the virulent racism of colonial society as [the leader of a mulatto uprising] Vincent Ogé and his kind"? Or perhaps he "may have expected from the very beginning that the first insurrection on the Northern Plain would inevitably lead to the abolition of slavery"? Or was it that "he may have been radicalized by the course of events from 1791 to 1793"?[49] No references are cited that make or refute either case.

Bell's Toussaint biography thus serves as a case study in the difficulties of representing Toussaint without recourse to fiction or myth.

Bell's biography begins with an introductory gloss of the historical background to the Haitian Revolution and Toussaint's rise to prominence. On the matter of Toussaint's legacy, Bell takes as a starting point the paradox that some two hundred years after his death, Toussaint, whom Bell describes as "the highest-achieving African-American hero of all time," remains an enigma, a little-known and poorly understood figure.[50] Contrasting Toussaint's cultural and political currency within Haiti, where he remains publicly renowned and highly honored, with his status in the rest of the Americas, where he has been largely forgotten, at least in terms of public memory, Bell draws on his understanding of Haitian vodou, a subject on which Bell possesses a rare knowledge for a non-Haitian and considerable firsthand experience in order to locate Toussaint and decipher his memorialization. For example, vodou allows Bell to analyze Toussaint's decision to award himself the surname "Louverture" as a cultural and religious symbolic act with a modern political resonance, alluding to a subject highly aware of and attempting to control his political personality.[51]

While recognizing the importance of Bell's work in recuperating the place of vodou in the revolution, I want to note the negative effect of his reviving the old and discredited conspiracy theory concerning its origins and outbreak in a plot hatched by white royalist *grands blancs*. The theory puts forward that the *grands blancs* manufactured a "secretly controlled uprising of the slaves on the Northern Plain" in order to "frighten the *petit blanc* faction back into submission . . . according the old sociopolitical rules of the ancien régime."[52] Although acknowledging that twentieth-century scholars—notably C. L. R. James, Aimé Césaire, Carolyn Fick, and Michel-Rolph Trouillot—have dismissed it, and conceding also that the theory "seems to belittle the achievement of Saint Domingue's revolutionary slaves in winning their own freedom and founding their own nation," Bell goes on to reiterate a conspiracy theory without engaging with the arguments of those who have refuted it.[53]

Moreover, Bell's assertion that "the strongest argument against the royalist conspiracy theory is its sheer preposterousness" does not accord with Bell's own analysis, which demonstrates how a large-scale slave uprising could have occurred without the need for any inside help.[54] In the biography's introduction, Bell paints a picture of a highly destabilized colony in which political tensions, the illegal but widely accepted movements of slaves at night, the huge annual importation of slaves from Africa, the destabilizing influence of the existence of large maroon communities, the mountainous terrain, the high number of absentee plantation owners, the unusually harsh conditions for Saint Domnigue's slaves relative to other Caribbean slave colonies, and the existence of vodou as a political and organizational tool all made for an atmosphere "infinitely more volatile than in other slave regimes like the United States" and combined to enable the possibility of a successful slave revolt.[55]

Bell's methodology, following the precedent set by James and many others since, is to rely on the surviving letters of Toussaint and his contemporaries, including the various French, British, and Spanish major players during the revolution. These include letters to and from Napoleon; General Emmanuel Leclerc, who was given the task of reinstating slavery and reconquering the colony for France; and Toussaint's trusted aide in the colony, the French officer Etienne Laveux. I have already noted that Bell's reliance on a significant number of original letters, both in the text and in appendices, lent his novels a specious authenticity. Indeed, the conflation of historical documents with erotic and macabre fantasy is a disturbing combination that impedes an ability to understand Toussaint and the events of the Haitian Revolution. In the biography, hints of the same obsession with violence and eroticism persist, albeit in a more understated fashion.

Toussaint's seductive prowess, virile sexuality, and his numerous (unsubstantiated) extramarital infidelities with both mulatto and high-society *grands blancs* also feature prominently in the biography without enhancing a perspective on a historical figure. Consider: "[Toussaint's] Port-au-Prince residence was a bachelor's paradise. An affair with Madame Desdunes, a *femme de couleur* of the Artibonite region, produced children whose descendants survive to this day. Another special favorite was 'la Dame Fissour,' the mixed-blood wife of a wealthy *blanc* from Léogane."[56] And earlier Bell notes in describing the familiar relationship Toussaint enjoyed with his old master, Bayon de Libertat, that Toussaint accompanied his master on "various escapades," some of which "were probably amorous," before concluding that "Toussaint's own youthful prowess with the ladies was proved by the number of his extramarital children."[57] What is to be gained from these speculations on Toussaint's love life? It is enough to remind one of Gilles Deleuze's remark, "la Biographie, c'est l'imbecilité".

Moïse's Story

Another problematic issue in Bell's biography is the story of Moïse, Toussaint's adopted nephew and general in the revolutionary army, particularly well known for heading the most radical wing of the revolution, and whose fate was to be executed on Toussaint's own command. One of the first brief mentions of Moïse in the biography occurs in the context of a discussion about Toussaint as a slave owner, listed in a 1779 document as the leaseholder of a plantation, sixty-four acres of coffee and staples, and responsible for the thirteen slaves who lived and worked on the plantation. One of these slaves was called Moïse, an uncommon name leading Bell to speculate as to whether this slave would become one of Toussaint's key corevolutionaries, and if this might explain Toussaint's subsequent particularly close relationship with Moïse—a supposition that cannot be validated, even if the key role of one named Moïse in the revolution is sufficiently well documented.[58]

By 1801, some ten years after the initial outbreak of the revolution, with Toussaint acting as de facto ruler of the colony, Toussaint had implemented his policy of returning the former slave revolutionaries to the plantations as a matter of economic necessity. However, although James describes the new system as "infinitely better than the old slavery," it cannot be overlooked that Toussaint's move meant that the former slaves were again working for white masters whom Toussaint judged to have the necessary expertise to manage the plantations.[59] It was a revival of an old system that predictably proved to be unpopular. As James has claimed, Moïse and his sympathizers had no objection to hard work: "Work, yes, but not for whites."[60] Whereas Toussaint's other generals, particularly Dessalines, enforced Toussaint's draconian labor policies with a severity that recalls Ti Noel's forced labor in the new "free" Haiti, as represented in Alejo Carpentier's *El reino de este mundo*, Moïse refused to cooperate. Thus the men under Moïse's command—and Moïse had been placed in control of the whole of the colony's Northern Department by Toussaint—organized an insurrection with the aim of killing all of the whites, and when Moïse's name was chanted, his fate was sealed.

Moïse's story, and the subtle shades of his character and his political persona, are majestically evoked by James in *The Black Jacobins*, who speculates that for some of these revolutionaries the goal was to replace Toussaint with Moïse. In describing Moïse, James begins by putting forward the certainty that Moïse symbolized the revolution more than any other in the eyes of the masses, but James also admits that the historian attempting to recover Moïse has "very little to go on." Nevertheless, James suggests that on the available evidence he appears to "have been a singularly attractive and possibly profound person."[61] Thus a part of the subtlety of James's portrait of Moïse hinges on its necessary incompleteness. In contrast, Bell's version of Moïse offers a portrait that is misleadingly certain; whereas James errs on the side of sympathetic representation, Bell sees an altogether more dogmatic and unreasonable personality. For James, Moïse clearly "had a strong sympathy for the laborers and hated the old slave-owners. But he was not anti-white."[62] Bell, on the other hand, writes that Moïse "hated whites even more bitterly than Dessalines [and] had a still more intransigent attitude."[63] Representing Moïse as a man racked with hatred may serve to make a good contrast with the saintly (but adulterous) Toussaint, but it does little to help the reader understand the background to one of the revolution's crucial episodes, and the overall effect is a subtle misrepresentation of both Touissant and Moïse.

Conclusion

If we have become accustomed to different narratives, ones that place colonial events on the margins of European history, we have been seriously misled.

—Susan Buck-Morss, *Hegel, Haiti, and Universal History*

I HAVE ARGUED OVER THE COURSE OF THIS BOOK that a pantheon of twentieth- and twenty-first-century aesthetic treatments of the Haitian Revolution should be divided along a single axis of distinction: the radical and conservative. My general aim has been to demonstrate how the Haitian Revolution has profoundly influenced an important international constituency of writers and artists, and to promote the view that it should be understood in all its multiple dimensions, and honored for its aspirations and achievement. More specifically, in pursuing this line of argument, I have set out to make the case that the politics of those aesthetic works that I designate as "radical" should not be underestimated, since their recuperations of "the historical facts about freedom" in Haiti urge us to return to the "project of universal freedom" with renewed sympathy for and understanding of the agonizing difficulties that efforts at true liberation entail, but also with renewed determination for the necessity of that project, "redeemed and reconstituted."[1] Thus, it has been my intention to demonstrate that in retrieving the Haitian Revolution as a transformative moment in world history, a corpus of radical literary texts and artworks offers perspectives that might yet revitalize the moral vision and political hopes of those committed to the autonomy of peoples.

A further aim of this project has been to reveal the ideological weaknesses of a range of texts that I classify as conservative. I have argued that though their presentations of the revolution might ostensibly valorize liberation and appear to challenge traditions of imperial denigration, this corpus of texts in fact undermines the unprecedented historic actuality of the transformational actions taken by enslaved blacks in Saint Domingue between 1791 and 1804. Such disparagement is effected by discounting or even discarding the project of universal freedom to which the revolution aspired, and presenting it as outmoded in the context of a postnational political age, naïve in the face of fatalistic models of historical pessimism, or saturated in violence and prurience.

Thus, thinking through recuperations of the Haitian Revolution as either radical or conservative has not been a critical endeavor of aesthetic taxonomy, but the product of mounting a materialist critique that has been concerned to pay proper regard to the texts' and artworks' internal logics. This has enabled us to perceive the discourses in which Haiti's revolutionary tradition has commonly been filtered. I have claimed that these competing discourses have manifested themselves in a cultural and political war that has for long been raging in the archives generated by the Haitian Revolution, and I now draw these reflections to a close by turning to a speech given in 2003 by Thabo Mbeki, the former president of South Africa. I do so in order to demonstrate that conservative ways of apprehending the Haitian Revolution produce a blindness that has become normalized and permeates virtually every forum in which Haiti is discussed.

On the eve of the 2004 bicentenary of Haitian independence, Thabo Mbeki gave a speech about the African diaspora in the twenty-first century at the University of the West Indies in Kingston, Jamaica. His address reveals the extent to which the implications of the Haitian Revolution's radicalism are, on the whole, off-limits within today's mainstream political discourse. Mbeki identified the Haitian Revolution as an inspirational, but ultimately flawed example of black liberation with only limited transferable value for modern-day Africa. For Mbeki, the shortcomings of the revolution were the key lessons from which contemporary Africa would do well to learn, and he sought to justify this proposition by arguing that the material legacies of the Haitian Revolution serve to highlight an inescapable problem: "We have to contend with the fact that whereas the American and French Revolutions succeeded to [*sic*] create the conditions for the development of the American and French people, Haiti has not experienced similar development. Indeed, she has been subject to the very opposite of development."[2] Mbeki went on to insist that the "divergence of experience in the aftermath of revolutions as interconnected as were the American, French and Haitian" requires us to ask the question, "what went wrong in Haiti [?]," since its answer, Mbeki speculates, would enable us to understand the worsening "African condition" and "what went wrong" in the aftermath of decolonization everywhere. While it must be admitted that Mbeki draws attention to what he calls "the structural fault in global society and the global economy" that disadvantages the global South, Mbeki does not lay the blame for Haiti's underdevelopment at the door of a capitalist world-system, preferring instead to call on Africans throughout the diaspora to employ the virtues of "self-reliance, hard work and confidence" in order to navigate today's globalized world which he likens to "a vast, cold and turbulent ocean."[3]

Mbeki's speech, symptomatic of its political and ideological environment, highlights the paramount importance of pulling away the invisible cloak of conservatism that has had the effect of normalizing narrative falsehoods and making radical alternatives appear untenable. It is within this situation of ascendant conservatism that I maintain that the consideration of radical recuperations of the Haitian Revolution, and their emphatic intentions, is as relevant and necessary as ever.

Mbeki's rhetorical discourse in which the Haitian Revolution comes off in distant third place to the American and French Revolutions, is a common yet flawed conservative perspective. To unfavorably compare the Haitian Revolution with the American and French Revolutions requires the glossing over of the fact that of those three great revolutions that began in the final decades of the eighteenth century, only the Haitian "forced the unconditional application of the principle that inspired each one: affirmation of the natural, inalienable rights of all human beings"; as Peter Hallward explains: "Only in Haiti was the declaration of human freedom universally consistent. Only in Haiti was this declaration sustained *at all costs*, in direct opposition to the social order and economic logic of the day. Only in Haiti were the consequences of this declaration—the end of slavery, of colonialism, of racial inequality—upheld in terms that directly embraced the world as a whole."[4]

Yet, in spite of these remarkable achievements, Mbeki's take on the revolution is the one firmly fixed in establishment thinking. We live in a world in which there are endless variations of Mbeki's pessimistic take on the Haitian Revolution, and most of the time these go unchallenged. For example, in Philippe Girard's popular history of Haiti, the revolution is lamented for doing "nothing to lay the groundwork for a lasting free-market democracy."[5] And, in the aftermath of the devastating earthquake that struck Haiti in 2010, new versions of some very familiar paternalistic criticisms proliferated. The international media evoked a desperate land of criminality and barbarism that only had itself to blame since its "progress-resistant" culture had rendered it uniquely vulnerable.[6] Amid such reports, the Haitian Revolution was commonly invoked as a prelude or catalyst to an ongoing catastrophe, an observation that recalls Alejo Carpentier's comparison of the revolution to a series of devastating natural disasters that wreaked meaningless destruction in *El reino de este mundo.*

Today Haiti lacks a legitimate government and is ravaged by grinding poverty and economic deprivation. Foreign political manipulation continues to be instrumental to the disfunctioning of Haitian civil society. Its status as a failing nation-state is portrayed as interminable because inherent in its people. It is in this context that it is imperative to restore the voices of its revolution still resounding today, as radical founders in a still unfulfilled project of dignity, justice, and liberation.

Notes

Introduction

1. For two examples that have become notorious, see Bryan Edwards, *An Historical Survey of the French Colony in the Island of St. Domingo* (1797; London: 1801); and Spencer Saint-John, *Hayti; or, the Black Republic*, 2nd ed. (London: Smith, Elder, & Co., 1889).

2. Neil Lazarus, *The Postcolonial Unconscious* (Cambridge: Cambridge University Press, 2011), 22.

3. Harriet Martineau, *The Hour and the Man* (New York: Harper Brothers, 1841); Victor Hugo, *Bug Jargal*, trans. Chris Bongie (1820 and 1833; Toronto: Broadview Press, 2004); Alphonse de Lamartine, *Toussaint Louverture* (1850; Exeter. U.K.: University of Exeter Press, 1998); Heinrich von Kleist, "The Betrothal in Santo Domingo," in *The Marquise of O—and Other Stories* (1811; London: Penguin, 2004); John Greenleaf Whittier, "Toussaint Louverture" (1837), in *The Poetry of Slavery*, ed. Marcus Wood.

4. A. James Arnold, "Recuperating the Haitian Revolution in Literature: From Victor Hugo to Derek Walcott," in *Tree of Liberty: Cultural Legacies of the Haitian Revolution in the Atlantic World*, ed. Doris L. Garraway (Charlottesville: University of Virginia Press, 2008), 179, 180.

5. A note on the implications of the various spellings of "voodoo," "vodou," and "vodûn" is necessary. "Vodou" is the commonly accepted orthography in English and contrasts with the stereotypical and negative depiction of "voodoo." "Vodun" (sometimes "vodûn" or "voudoun") also refers to Haitan vodou but denotes the religion of that name in West Africa from which Haitian vodou originated.

6. Thomas Carlyle, *Occasional Discourse on the Nigger Question* [1849], in *Critical and Miscellaenous Essays. Vol. VII*, by Carlyle (London: Chapman and Hall, 1888), 104.

7. Saint John, *Hayti; or, the Black Republic*, xi.

8. Ibid., 123, 135.

9. Arthur Gobineau, *The Inequality of Human Races*, trans. Adrian Collins (1853–55; New York: Fertig, 1998).

10. Anténor Firmin, *The Equality of the Human Races: Positivist Anthropology*, trans. Asselin Charles (1885; New York: Garland, 2000).

11. Graham Greene, *The Comedians* (1965; London: Vintage, 1999).

12. Arnold, "Recuperating the Haitian Revolution in Literature," 191.

13. The most comprehensive account of the impact of the Haitian Revolution on African American culture is Maurice Jackson and Jacqueline Bacon, eds., *African Americans and the Haitian Revolution: Selected Essays and Historical Documents* (London and New York: Routledge, 2010).

14. William Faulkner, *Absalom, Absalom!* (1936; London: Vintage, 1991). Chris Bongie has persuasively argued that Faulkner's Haiti in *Absalom, Absalom!* and Conrad's Africa in *Heart of Darkness* are ripe for comparison (see Chris Bongie, *Islands and Exiles: The Creole Identities of Post/Colonial Literature* [Stanford, Calif.: Stanford University Press, 1998], 195). See also Richard King, "From Haiti to Mississippi: Faulkner and the Making of the Southern Master-Class," *International Journal of Francophone Studies* 14, nos. 1 &2 (May 2011): 93–106.

15. See also the heroic depiction of Toussaint on the cover of Wyclef Jean's 2004 album *Sak Pasé Presents: Welcome to Haiti Creole 101.*

16. See Maurice Jackson, "No Man Could Hinder Him: Remembering Toussaint Louverture and the Haitian Revolution in the History and Culture of the African American People," in *African Americans and the Haitian Revolution: Selected Essays and Historical Documents*, ed. Jackson and Jacqueline Bacon, 141–64 (New York: Routledge, 2010), 153.

17. Courtney Pine, *Transition in Tradition (En hommage à Sidney Bechet)*, Destin-E Records, 2009.

18. *Lydia Bailey*, directed by Jean Negulesco (Los Angeles: 20th Century Fox, 1952).

19. *I Walked with a Zombie*, directed by Jacques Tourneur (New York: RKO Radio Pictures, 1943); *Live and Let Die*, directed by Guy Hamilton (London: Eon Productions, 1973); *Pirates of the Caribbean: The Curse of the Black Pearl*, directed by Gore Verbinski (Santa Monica, Calif.: Jerry Bruckheimer Films, 2003); *Pirates of the Caribbean: Dead Man's Chest*, directed by Gore Verbinski (Santa Monica, Calif.: Jerry Bruckheimer Films, 2006); *Pirates of the Caribbean: At World's End*, directed by Gore Verbinski (Santa Monica, Calif.: Jerry Bruckheimer Films, 2007).

20. See "Louverture Films," www.louverturefilms.com. The latest information concerning the film's production status can be found at The Internet Move Database, www.imdb.com/title/tt0785063/. I was given a Samizdat copy of the film script on the condition that I did not cite it in this study. This was a setback as I consider it to be a meticulous, historically aware, and aesthetically achieved work.

21. Hazel Rowley, *Richard Wright: The Life and Times* (New York: Holt, 2001), 387.

22. Ibid., 575n43.

23. Doris L. Garraway, "'Légitime Defense: Universalism and Nationalism in the Discourse of the Haitian Revolution," in *Tree of Liberty*, ed. Garraway, 63–65.

24. This study, then, seeks to propel postcolonial discourse toward the kind of materialist, historically aware inquiry long advocated by such noted critics as Benita Parry and Neil Lazarus (see Benita Parry, *Postcolonial Studies: A Materialist Critique* [London: Routledge, 2004]; Neil Lazarus, *Nationalism and Cultural Practice in the Colonial World* [Cambridge: Cambridge University Press, 1999]; and Lazarus, *The Postcolonial Unconscious*).

25. Nick Nesbitt, "The Idea of 1804," in "The Haiti Issue: 1804 and Nineteenth-Century French Studies," special issue, *Yale French Studies,* no. 107 (2005): 6.

26. Nick Nesbitt, *Universal Emancipation: The Haitian Revolution and the Radical Enlightenment* (Charlottesville: University of Virginia Press, 2008), 2.

27. David Scott, *Conscripts of Modernity: The Tragedy of Colonial Enlightnement* (Durham: Duke University Press, 2004).

28. Ibid., 1, 29.

29. Peter Hallward, "The Politics of Prescription," *South Atlantic Quarterly* 104, no. 4 (Fall 2005): 769.

30. J. Michael Dash, "*Haïti Chimère*: Revolutionary Universalism and Its Caribbean Context," in *Reinterpreting the Haitian Revolution and Its Cultural Aftershocks*, ed. Martin Munro and Elizabeth Walcott-Hackshaw (Mona, Jamaica: University of the West Indies Press, 2006), 17.

31. Ibid.

32. Michel-Rolph Trouillot, *Silencing the Past: Power and the Production of History* (Boston: Beacon Press, 1995).

33. Ibid., 73.

34. Susan Buck-Morss, *Hegel, Haiti, and Universal History* (Pittsburgh: University of Pittsburgh Press, 2009), 50.

35. Ibid.

36. See, for example, Richard Gott, "Britain's Vote to End Its Slave Trade Was a Precursor to Today's Liberal Imperialism," *Guardian*, January 17, 2007, www.guardian.co.uk/commentisfree/2007/jan/17/comment.politics2.

37. The main contributions to the recent historiography include Laurent Dubois, *Avengers of the New World: The Story of the Haitian Revolution* (Cambridge: Harvard University Press, 2004); Laurent Dubois, *A Colony of Citizens: Revolution and Slave Emancipation in the French Caribbean, 1787–1804* (Chapel Hill: University of North Carolina Press, 2004); David Geggus, *Haitian Revolutionary Studies* (Bloomington: Indiana University Press, 2002); David Geggus and Norman Fiering, eds., *The World of the Haitian Revolution*

(Bloomington: Indiana University Press, 2009); Jeremy Popkin, ed., *Facing Racial Revolution: Eyewitness Accounts of the Haitian Revolution* (Chicago: University of Chicago Press, 2008); and Jeremy Popkin, *You Are All Free: The Haitian Revolution and the Abolition of Slavery* (Cambridge: Cambridge University Press: 2010). Also, David Brion Davis devotes a chapter to the French and Haitian Revolutions in David Brion Davis, *Inhuman Bondage: The Rise and Fall of Slavery in the New World* (Oxford: Oxford University Press, 2006); and Robin Blackburn devotes significant attention to the Haitian Revolution in Robin Blackburn, *The American Crucible: Slavery, Emancipation and Human Rights* (London and New York: Verso, 2011).

38. Dubois, *Avengers of the New World*, 3.

39. Nesbitt, *Universal Emancipation*, 10.

40. Ibid., 2.

41. Ulrich Bonnell Phillips, *Life and Labor in the Old South* (1929; Columbia: University of South Carolina Press, 2007); Margaret Mitchell, *Gone with the Wind* (London: Macmillan, 1936); *Gone with the Wind*, directed by Victor Fleming (Culver City, Calif., and Beverly Hills, Calif. : Selznick International Pictures/MGM, 1939).

42. Laurent Dubois has noted that it is probably impossible "to separate reality from legend in the story of Toussaint, including how he took on the name Louverture—'the opening.'" Louverture has been spelled as "L'Ouverture" or as "L'ouverture." However, shortly after adopting the name, Toussaint dropped the apostrophe, and the established orthography is to use "Louverture" (Dubois, *Avengers of the New World*, 172).

43. Mumia Abu-Jamal, "The Power of History: Haiti," radio broadcast, http://mumiapodcast.libsyn.com/the_power_of_history_haiti#.UWUkZL8ydhM.

44. Toussaint Louverture and Jean-Bertrand Aristide quoted in Martin Munro and Elizabeth Walcott-Hackshaw, "Introduction: Reinterpreting the Haitian Revolution and Its Cultural Aftershocks," *Small Axe* 9, no. 2 (2005): viii.

45. Peter Hallward, "An Interview with Jean-Bertrand Aristide," *London Review of Books*," February 22, 2007, 9.

46. Graham Gendall Norton, "France Finally Recognises a Hero after 200 Years," *Times* (London), April 5, 2003, 47.

47. Paul Breslin, "'The First Epic of the New World': But How Shall It Be Written?," in *Tree of Liberty*, ed. Garraway, 223.

48. Percy Waxman, *The Black Napoleon* (New York: Harcourt, 1931), 5.

1. Radical Universalism

1. C. L. R. James, "How I Wrote *The Black Jacobins*," lecture at the Institute of the Black World, Atlanta, Georgia, June 14, 1971, reprinted in *Small Axe* 4, no. 2 (2000): 72.

2. I therefore agree with Nick Nesbitt, who has argued that Césaire and

James considered the world-historical importance of the Haitian Revolution to reside in its politicization "of the idea of the universal human right to be free from enslavement" (Nesbitt, "The Incandescent I, Destroyer of Worlds," *Research in African Literatures* 41, no. 1 [Spring 2010]: 124).

3. See David Scott, *Conscripts of Modernity.*

4. C. L. R. James, *The Black Jacobins* (1938; rev. ed 1963; London: Penguin, 2001), xv.

5. Parry, *Postcolonial Studies*, 45.

6. Though it is commonplace to distinguish between Césaire's and Senghor's versions of négritude on these grounds, the critic A. James Arnold suggests that their views only latterly diverged (see A. James Arnold, *Modernism & Negritude: The Poetry and Poetics of Aimé Césaire* [Cambridge: Harvard University Press, 1981], 36–40, 186).

7. Aimé Césaire, *Notebook of a Return to My Native Land / Cahier d'un retour au pays natal*, trans. Mireille Rosello with Annie Pritchard (1939; Newcastle upon Tyne: Bloodaxe Books, 1995), 90–91. All quotations in the chapter text are taken from the Rosello and Pritchard translation, bilingual edition. However, I am aware of the many difficulties of translation presented by Césaire's complex and idiosyncratic poetic voice and his use of nonstandard French. In the course of preparing this chapter, I have therefore also familiarized myself with the following other translations of the *Cahier*: Aimé Césaire, *Return to My Native Land*, trans. John Berger and Anna Bostock (Harmondsworth: Penguin, 1969); Aimé Césaire, *Return to My Native Land*, trans. Emile Snyder (Paris: Présence Africaine, 1968); Aimé Césaire, "Return to the Native Land," in Aimé Césaire, *The Collected Poetry*, trans. Clayton Eshleman and Annette Smith (Berkeley, Los Angeles, and London: University of California Press, 1983): 32–85.

8. C. L. R. James, "Appendix: From Toussaint L'Ouverture to Fidel Castro," *The Black Jacobins*, 311.

9. Ibid., 314.

10. Aimé Césaire, *La tragédie du roi Christophe* (Paris: Présence Africaine, 1963). An English translation of a considerably shortened version of play has been published: Aimé Césaire, *The Tragedy of King Christophe*, trans. Ralph Manheim (New York: Grove Press, 1969). This chapter will refer to the later edition of James's play: C. L. R. James, *The Black Jacobins [Play]*, in *The C. L. R. James Reader*, ed. Anna Grimshaw (1936; Oxford, U.K., and Cambridge, Mass.: Blackwell, 1992).

11. J. Michael Dash, "Marvellous Realism: The Way out of Négritude," *Caribbean Studies* 13, no. 4 (1974): 65.

12. Ibid.

13. Ibid.

14. See Richard D. E. Burton, "Two Views of Césaire: *Négritude* and *Créolité*," *Dalhousie French Studies* 35 (1996): 135.

15. The reception and debate over négritude has produced an extensive bibliography. For an overview, see Nick Nesbitt, "Négritude," in *Africana: The Encyclopedia of the African American Experience*, 2nd ed., ed. Kwame Anthony Appiah and Henry Louis Gates Jr. (Oxford: Oxford University Press: 2005), 4: 193–99. Key texts and critiques of the movement include Léopold Sédar Senghor, *Négritude et humanisme* (Paris: Éditions de Seuil, 1964); Stanislas Spero Adotevi, *Négritude et négrologues* (1972; Paris: Le Castor Astral, 1998); René Depestre, *Bonjour et adieu à la négritude* (Paris: Seghers, 1980); Wole Soyinka, *Myth, Literature and the African World* (Cambridge: Cambridge University Press, 1976); Arnold, *Modernism and Negritude*; Nick Nesbitt, *Voicing Memory: History and Subjectivity in French Caribbean Literature* (Charlottesville: University of Virginia Press, 2003); Gary Wilder, *The French Imperial Nation-State: Negritude and Colonial Humanism between the Two World Wars* (Chicago: University of Chicago Press, 2005); and Brent Edwards, *The Practice of Diaspora: Literature, Translation, and the Rise of Black Internationalism* (Cambridge: Harvard University Press, 2003).

16. See Edward Said, "The Politics of Knowledge," *Raritan* 11, no. 1 (Summer 1991): 24.

17. Césaire, *Notebook of a Return to My Native Land / Cahier d'un retour au pays natal*, 134–35.

18. See, for example, Arnold, *Modernism and Negritude*, 133–68; André Breton, "Un grand poète noir," preface to *Cahier d'un retour au pays natal* (1944; Paris: Présence Africaine, 1971); Dominique Combé, *Aimé Césaire: Cahier d'un retour au pays natal* (Paris: Presses Universitaires de France, 1993); Maryse Condé, *Cahier d'un retour au pays natal: Analyse critique* (Paris: Hatier, 1978); Thomas Hale, "Structural Dynamics in a Third World Classic: Aimé Césaire's *Cahier d'un retour au pays natal*," *Yale French Studies,* no. 53 (1976): 163–74; Abiola Irele, *Aimé Césaire: Cahier d'un retour au pays natal* (Ibadan, Nigeria: New Horn Press, 1994); and Lilyan Kestloot, *Comprendre le "Cahier d'un Retour au Pays Natal" d'Aimé Césaire* (Issy les Molineaux: Editions Saint Paul, 1982).

19. Christopher L. Miller, *The French Atlantic Triangle: Literature and Culture of the Slave Trade* (Durham: Duke University Press, 2008), 325.

20. See, for example, Gregson Davis, *Aimé Césaire* (Cambridge: Cambridge University Press, 1997), 20–61.

21. See Nesbitt, *Voicing Memory*, 77.

22. Edouard Glissant, "Aimé Césaire: The Poet's Passion," trans. Christopher Winks, *Small Axe* 12, no. 3 (October 2008): 120.

23. Miller, *The French Atlantic Triangle*, 328.

24. Nick Nesbitt, "Négritude," in *Africana: The Encyclopedia of the African American Experience*, 193.

25. "An Interview with Aimé Césaire Conducted by René Depestre," in *Discourse on Colonialism*, by Césaire, 90.

26. William Wordsworth, "To Toussaint L'Ouverture" [1802], in *The Poetry of Slavery*, ed. Wood, 233.

27. Césaire, *Notebook of a Return to My Native Land / Cahier D'un Retour Au Pays Natal*, 90–91.

28. Ibid.

29. Aimé Césaire, *Et les chiens se taisaient* (Paris: Présence Africaine, 1962). An English translation is collected in *Aimé Césaire: Lyric and Dramatic Poetry, 1946–82*, ed. and trans. Clayton Eshleman and Annette Smith, 1–74 (Charlottesville: University of Virginia Press, 1990). The critic Keith L. Walker maintains that *Et les chiens se taisaient* was directly inspired in its dramaturgy by Nietzsche's argument for the role of the chorus in *The Birth of Tragedy* (Keith L. Walker, "Art for Life's Sake: Rituals and Rights of Self and Other in the Theatre of Aimé Césaire," in *Black Theater: Ritual Performance in the African Diaspora*, ed. Paul Carter Harrison, Victor Leo Walker, and Gus Edwards [Philadelphia: Temple University Press, 2002], 199).

30. Césaire, *Notebook of a Return to My Native Land / Cahier d'un retour au pays natal*, 90–91.

31. Ibid., 90–93.

32. See Jacqueline Leiner's interview with Aimé Césaire: Jacqueline Leiner, "Entretien avec A.C.," *Tropiques*, ed. Aimé Césaire (Paris: Éditions Jean-Michel Place, 1978), 1: xix.

33. Wole Soyinka quoted in Walker, "Art for Life's Sake," 200.

34. Wole Soyinka quoted ibid.

35. For an overview of the paradigm of the fertility myth, see Laurence Coupe, *Myth* (London: Routledge, 1997), 20–42.

36. Césaire, *La tragédie du Roi Christophe*; Aimé Césaire, *Une saison au Congo* (1967; Paris: Seuil, 1973).

37. René Depestre would also link the Haitian revolutionaries to Patrice Lumumba in his poem *Un Arc-en-ciel pour l'occident chrétien.* See my later chapter on René Depestre.

38. Césaire, *Notebook of a Return to My Native Land / Cahier d'un retour au pays natal*, 92–93.

39. Edouard Glissant, *Caribbean Discourse: Selected Essays*, trans. J. Michael Dash (Charlottesville: University of Virginia Press, 1989), 71; emphasis in original.

40. Aimé Césaire quoted in Jacqueline Leiner, *Aimé Césaire, Le terreau primordial* (Tübingen: Narr, 1993), 140; my translation; my emphasis.

41. T. S. Eliot, "Ulysses, Order and Myth," in *Selected Prose of T. S. Eliot*, ed. Frank Kermode (London: Faber, 1975).

42. Ibid., 175–78.

43. The presence of Brechtian techniques in Césaire's political theater has also been noted by A. James Arnold (Arnold, *Modernism and Negritude* [Cambridge: Harvard University Press, 1981], 306n14). Wole Soyinka has also noted

that négritude and Brechtian theater share common characteristics (Soyinka, *Myth, Literature and the African World* [Cambridge: Cambridge University Press, 1976], 66).

44. Aimé Césaire quoted in Walker, "Art for Life's Sake," 181.

45. Martin Munro, *Shaping and Reshaping the Caribbean: The Work of Aimé Césaire and René Depestre* (Leeds: Maney, 2000), 33.

46. James, *The Black Jacobins*, xvii.

47. There is no published edition of the original version titled *Toussaint Louverture*. The version referred to here is the revised and retitled version *The Black Jacobins* included in C. L. R. James and Anna Grimshaw, *The C. L. R. James Reader* (Oxford: Blackwell, 1992).

48. Robert A Hill, "C. L. R. James: The Myth of Western Civilisation," in *Enterprise of the Indies*, ed. George Lamming (Trinidad and Tobago: Institute of the West Indies, 1999), 255.

49. Cedric J. Robinson, *Black Marxism: The Making of the Black Radical Tradition* (1983; Chapel Hill: University of North Carolina Press, 2000), 314.

50. James, *The Black Jacobins*, 331.

51. Ibid., 235–37.

52. Ibid., xviii–xix.

53. Ibid., 236.

54. Wilson Harris and A. J. M. Bundy, *Selected Essays of Wilson Harris: The Unfinished Genesis of the Imagination* (London: Routledge, 1999), 149.

55. Karl Marx, "The Eighteenth Brumaire of Louis Bonaparte" (1851), in *Karl Marx: Selected Writings*, ed. David McLellan, 2nd ed. (Oxford: Oxford University Press: 2000), 329.

56. James, *The Black Jacobins*, xix.

57. Ibid., 195.

58. Ibid., 230–31.

59. Ibid., 130.

60. Ibid., 202.

61. Kara M. Rabbitt, "C. L. R. James's Figuring of Toussaint Louverture: *The Black Jacobins* and the Literary Hero," in *C. L. R. James: His Intellectual Legacies*, ed. Selwyn Reginald Cudjoe and William E. Cain (Amherst: University of Massachusetts Press, 1995).

62. Chris Bongie, *Friends and Enemies: The Scribal Politics of Post/Colonial Literature* (Liverpool, U.K.: Liverpool University Press: 2008), 262.

63. Scott, *Conscripts of Modernity*, 185.

64. James, *The Black Jacobins*, 305.

65. Ibid.

66. Ibid., 321.

67. Ibid., 326.

68. Ibid., 313.

69. C. L. R. James, "The Intelligence of the Negro: A Few Words with Dr.

Harland," *Beacon*, August 1931, 6–10. For analysis, see David Scott, *Conscripts of Modernity*, 79–81.

70. C. L. R. James, *Beyond a Boundary* (1963; London: Serpent's Tail, 2000), 119.

71. Fionnghuala Sweeney's article is the most up-to-date work on James's play, including consideration of its textual and performance history (Fionnghuala Sweeney, "The Haitian Play: C. L. R. James' *Toussaint Louverture* [1936]," *International Journal of Francophone Studies* 14, nos. 1 & 2 [May 2011]: 143–63).

72. James, *The Black Jacobins [Play]*, 68.

73. Anna Grimshaw has claimed that the play's dramatic structure collapses due to the disappearance of the masses (Anna Grimshaw, "C. L. R. James: A Revolutionary Vision for the 20th Century," www.marxists.org/archive/james-clr/biograph.htm#copyright).

74. James, *The Black Jacobins [Play]*, 69.

75. Ibid.

76. For a defense of patriarchal position taking in Aimé Césaire's anticolonial discourse, see Benita Parry, "Resistance Theory/Theorizing Resistance" in Parry, *Postcolonial Studies*, 42–43.

77. James, *The Black Jacobins [Play]*, 71.

78. Ibid.

79. Ibid., 72.

2. Langston Hughes

1. Arnold, *Modernism and Negritude*, 27.

2. Helen Pyne-Timothy, "Identity, Society and Meaning: A Study of the Early Stories of C. L. R. James," in *C.L.R. James: His Intellectual Legacies* , 58. In an interview with René Depestre, Césaire acknowledged that the Harlem Renaissance was "indispensable for a very clear coming to consciousness" (Césaire quoted in Gary Wilder, *The French Imperial Nation-State*, 345n146).

3. Pyne-Timothy, "Identity, Society and Meaning," 58.

4. *Looking for Langston*, directed by Isaac Julien (London: BFI, 1987).

5. The limited use of Hughes's poetry in the film, however, was largely due to matters of copyright emerging from conflicts with Hughes's estate about the film in general, rather than for artistic reasons (see Molly Shinhat, "Black History and Desire: An Interview with Isaac Julien," *FUSE*, June/July 1990, 37).

6. Langston Hughes, *I Wonder as I Wander: An Autobiographical Journey* (1956; New York: Hill and Wang, 1935).

7. Arnold Rampersad, introduction to *I Wonder as I Wander*, xviii–xix.

8. Henry Louis Gates and Nellie Y. McKay, eds., *The Norton Anthology of African American Literature* (New York and London: Norton, 1997), 960.

9. Arnold Rampersad, *The Life of Langston Hughes*, Vol. 1: *1902–1941: I, Too, Sing America* (New York and Oxford: Oxford University Press, 1986), 19.

10. Hughes, *I Wonder as I Wander*, 5.

11. Faith Berry, *Langston Hughes: Before and Beyond Harlem* (Westport, Conn.: Lawrence Hill, 1983), 121.

12. Ibid., 121–22.

13. Rampersad, *The Life of Langston Hughes*, 207.

14. Hughes, *I Wonder as I Wander*, 15.

15. Ibid.

16. Langston Hughes, "People without Shoes," in *I Wonder as I Wander*, by Hughes, 28.

17. James Weldon Johnson quoted in Mary A. Renda, *Taking Haiti: Military Occupation and the Culture of U.S. Imperialism, 1915–1940* (Chapel Hill: University of North Carolina Press, 2001), 276.

18. Ibid., 276–78.

19. Hughes, *I Wonder as I Wander*, 16.

20. Langston Hughes and Arna Bontemps, *Popo and Fifina* (1932; New York: Oxford University Press, 1993), 77.

21. Hughes, *I Wonder as I Wander*, 26.

22. Ibid., 157.

23. Ibid.

24. Joseph McLaren, *Langston Hughes, Folk Dramatist in the Protest Tradition, 1921–1943* (Westport, Conn.: Greenwood, 1997), 103–4.

25. Langston Hughes, *Emperor of Haiti* [1936], in *Collected Works of Langston Hughes: Gospel Plays, Operas, and Later Dramatic Works*, ed. Leslie Catherine Sanders (Columbia: University of Missouri Press, 2001), 282.

26. Ibid., 283.

27. Ibid., 310.

28. Ibid., 307.

29. Errol Hill, ed., *Black Heroes: Seven Plays* (New York: Applause Theatre, 1989), 5.

30. Hughes, *Emperor of Haiti*, 311.

31. Ibid.

32. Ibid., 313.

33. Ibid., 317.

34. Ibid., 318.

35. See Léon. D. Pamphile, *Haitians and African Americans: A Heritage of Tragedy and Hope* (Gainesville: University of Florida Press, 2002), 133–34, 147.

36. Deborah Jenson, *Beyond the Slave Narrative: Politics, Sex, and Manuscripts in the Haitian Revolution* (Liverpool, U.K.: Liverpool University Press: 2011), 82.

37. Dayan, *Haiti, History, and the Gods*, 33–36; Michael D. Largey, *Vodou Nation: Haitian Art Music and Cultural Nationalism* (Chicago: University of Chicago Press, 2006), 61–62.

38. Largey, *Vodou Nation*, 62.

39. Ibid.

40. James, *The Black Jacobins*, 299.

41. Ibid.

42. Ibid., 300, 299–300.

43. Ibid., 300–301.

44. Largey, *Vodou Nation*, 150.

45. Hughes, *Emperor of Haiti*, 284–85.

46. Ibid., 285; emphasis in original.

47. Ibid., 284–85.

48. Irving Kolodin, review of *Troubled Island*, *New York Sun*, April 1, 1949, 157–58.

49. Tammy L. Kernodle, "Arias, Communists, and Conspiracies: The History of Still's *Troubled Island*," *Musical Quarterly* 83, no. 4 (Winter 1999): 493.

50. Largey, *Vodou Nation*, 180.

51. An original recording of a live performance of the opera is available in the British Library's Sound Archive: William Grant Still, *Troubled Island: An Opera in Three Acts*, libretto by Langston Hughes (New York City Center Opera Company), (Southern Music & the Voice of America, 1949), British Library: T12097WR, 3 × 40cm vinyl discs.

52. Largey, *Vodou Nation*, 181.

53. Langston Hughes, *Troubled Island*, in *Collected Works of Langston Hughes: Gospel Plays, Operas, and Later Dramatic Works*, ed. Sanders, 17, 19.

54. Ibid., 22.

55. Ibid., 25–26.

56. Largey, *Vodou Nation*, 148.

3. Return to Négritude

1. René Depestre, *Bonjour et adieu à la négritude* (Paris: Seghers, 1980).

2. Joan Dayan, "France Reads Haiti: An Interview with René Depestre," *Yale French Studies*, no. 83 (1993): 143.

3. René Depestre, *A Rainbow for the Christian West*, trans. and introd. Joan Dayan (Amherst: University of Massachussetts Press, 1977). All the quotations in the chapter text (both original French and English translations) are taken from this bilingual edition of the poem and are hereafter cited parenthetically.

4. Césaire, *The Collected Poetry*, 370–71. This poem and historical moment has been analyzed in Nesbitt, *Voicing Memory*, 108–9; and Arnold, *Modernism and Negritude*, 180–84.

5. Dayan, "France Reads Haiti: An Interview with René Depestre," 137.

6. James, *The Black Jacobins*, 305.

7. Dayan, "France Reads Haiti: An Interview with René Depestre," 141.

8. Depestre's departure from Cuba in 1978 signalled his disillusionment

with the revolution in Cuba. Depestre claims that he could not have continued working as a writer and poet in Cuba due to censorship and other bureaucratic restrictions. See Dayan, "France Reads Haiti: An Interview with René Depestre," 138–39.

9. Frantz Fanon, *The Wretched of the Earth*, trans. Constance Farrington (1961; London: Penguin, 2001), 75–84.

10. Depestre's initial exposure to the ideas of surrealism and négritude can be traced to the visits to Haiti of Aimé Césaire and Suzanne Césaire in 1944, and André Breton in 1945. Also, in 1945, there was an exhibition in Haiti of the Cuban painter Wilfredo Lam that left a deep impression on Depestre (see Martin Munro, *Exile and Post-1946 Haitian Literature: Alexis, Depestre, Ollivier, Laferrière, Danticat* [Liverpool, U.K.: Liverpool University Press: 2007], 23–26).

11. There is an extensive body of research on surrealism's relationship with its "others" (see "Surrealism and Its Others," special issue, *Yale French Studies*, no. 109 [2006]; Michael Richardson, ed., *Refusal of the Shadow: Surrealism and the Caribbean*, trans. Michael Richardson and Krzysztof Fijałkowski [London: Verso, 1996]; and J. Michael Dash, *Literature and Ideology in Haiti, 1915–1961* [London: Macmillan, 1981], 156–79).

12. Jacques Stephen Alexis, "Of the Marvellous Realism of the Haitians," *Présence Africaine* (1956): 8–10, reprinted in *The Post-Colonial Studies Reader*, ed. Bill Ashcroft, Gareth Griffiths, and Helen Tiffin (London and New York: Routledge, 1995), 194–98.

13. Joan Dayan, introduction to *A Rainbow for the Christian West*, vii.

14. Of course, ten or so years after the publication of *Arc-en-ciel*, the symbol of the rainbow would become commonly associated with gay rights and LGBT (lesbian, gay, bisexual, and transgender) movements.

15. Joan Dayan, introduction to *A Rainbow for the Christian West*, 40.

16. Aimé Césaire, *Discourse on Colonialism*, trans. Joan Pinkham (1955; New York: Monthly Review Press, 2000), 37.

17. "Conillons" is the imperative form of the archaic verb "coniller," conjugations of which are repeatedly rhythmically fourteen times in rapid succession in this section of the poem. "Conillons" translates as "let's fuck." Joan Dayan writes that "coniller" alludes to both the expression "fuck like rabbits" (a "conillière garene" is a wild rabbit) and the verb "cogner" (to knock, bang, or drive in) (see Depestre, *A Rainbow for the Christian West*, 249n23).

18. See Dubois, *Avengers of the New World*, 70–71.

19. Jacob Lawrence, *The Life of Toussaint L'Ouverture* (1938), forty-one tempera paintings, Aaron Douglas Collection, Amistad Research Center, Tulane University, New Orleans (see numbers 16, 17, 21, 29, and 34 in the series). Digital reproductions of the paintings are available in the image archive at the Jacob Lawrence and Gwen Knight Virtual Resource Center, www.jacobandgwenlawrence.org.

20. Michel S. Laguerre, *Voodoo and Politics in Haiti* (London: Macmillan, 1989), 72.

21. Dash, *Literature and Ideology in Haiti*, 177.

22. Dayan, *Haiti, History, and the Gods*, 23.

23. René Depestre, *Cantata de Octubre a la vida y a la muerte del Comandante Ernesto Che Guevara*, trans. Max Figueroa Esteva (Havana: Instituto del Libro, 1968).

24. Connecting the Haitian revolutionaries to Patrice Lumumba and Malcolm X was something that Césaire had also attempted in his trilogy of plays *La tragédie du roi Christophe*, *Une saison au Congo*, and *Une tempête*. In *Une tempête*, Caliban states, "*Appelle-moi X*." (Call me X), recalling the defiant voice of Malcolm X.

25. William Cowper, "Epigram (Printed in the *Northampton Mercury*) (1815)," in *The Poetry of Slavery*, ed. Wood, 93.

26. See Laguerre, *Voodoo and Politics in Haiti*, 66–67, 101–20.

27. Charles Forsdick, "Late Glissant: History, 'World Literature,' and the Persistence of the Political," *Small Axe* 14, no. 3 (November 2010): 123.

28. Dayan, "France Reads Haiti: An Interview with René Depestre," 136, 150.

29. Depestre quoted in Chris Bongie, *Islands and Exiles*, 355.

30. Silvio Torres-Saillant, *Caribbean Poetics: Toward an Aesthetic of West Indian Literature* (Cambridge: Cambridge University Press, 1997), 211.

31. Jasmina Sopova, "Between Utopia and Reality: An Interview with René Depestre," *UNESCO Courier* 50, no. 12 (1997).

32. Ibid., 48

33. Ibid.

34. Ibid.

35. Nick Nesbitt, "Négritude," in *Africana: The Encyclopedia of the African American Experience*, 199.

36. Edward Said, *Culture and Imperialism* (1993; London: Vintage, 1994), 278–79.

37. Jean-Paul Sartre, "Black Orpheus," in *Race*, ed. Robert Bernasconi (Malden, Mass., and Oxford: Blackwell, 2001), 117; my emphasis.

38. Ibid., 118.

39. Ibid.

40. For an analysis of the *Debray Report* and Depestre's reaction to it, see Bongie, *Friends and Enemies*, 44–53, 67, 141–80.

41. René Depestre, "What Can Toussaint Louverture Do for the Haitians of 2004?," trans. Martin Munro, in *Reinterpreting the Haitian Revolution and Its Cultural Aftershocks*, ed.Munro and Walcott-Hackshaw, 172.

4. The Haitian Revolution and Radical Visual Politics

1. For a more complete guide to the iconography of Toussaint, see Fritz

Daguillard, *Mystérieux dans la Gloire: Toussaint Louverture (1743–1803)* (Port-au-Prince: MIPANAH, 2003).

2. Marcus Wood, *The Horrible Gift of Freedom: Atlantic Slavery and the Representation of Emancipation* (Athens: University of Georgia Press, 2010), 182.

3. Buck-Morss, *Hegel, Haiti, and Universal History*, 50.

4. Jacques de Cauna, *Haïti, l'éternelle révolution* (Port-au-Prince: Deschamps, 1997), 164–65.

5. Madison Smartt Bell, "The Image of Toussaint," http://faculty.goucher.edu/mbell/Toussaint%20Bio/Toussaint%20Biograph.htm.

6. The complete series is in the holdings of Aaron Douglas Collection, Amistad Research Center, Tulane University, New Orleans.

7. Peter T. Nesbett and Michell DuBois, eds., *Over the Line: The Art of Jacob Lawrence* (Seattle: University of Washington Press, 2000), 29.

8. Alain Locke, "Advance on the Art Front," *Opportunity*, May 1939, reprinted in *The Critical Temper of Alain Locke: A Selection of His Essays on Art and Culture*, ed. Jeffrey C. Stewart (New York: Garland, 1983), 186.

9. The serigraphs are in the holdings of the Aaron Douglas Collection, Amistad Research Center, Tulane University, New Orleans.

10. Patricia Hills, "Jacob Lawrence's Expressive Cubism," preface to *Jacob Lawrence, American Painter*, by Ellen Harkins Wheat (Seattle: University of Washington Press: 1986), 16.

11. Wheat, *Jacob Lawrence American Painter*, 38.

12. Lawrence quoted ibid., 24.

13. Leslie King-Hammond, "Inside Outside, Uptown Downtown. Jacob Lawrence and the Aesthetic Ethos of the Harlem Working-Class Community," in *Over the Line*, ed. Nesbett and DuBois, 67.

14. Ibid., 69. See also Carolyn Williams, "The Haitian Revolution and a North American Griot: The Life of Toussaint L'Ouverture by Jacob Lawrence," in *Echoes of the Haitian Revolution*, ed. Martin Munro and Elizabeth Walcott-Hackshaw (Mona, Jamaica: University of the West Indies Press: 2008), 629.

15. King-Hammond, "Inside Outside, Uptown Downtown," 77–78.

16. Maurice Jackson, "No Man Could Hinder Him: Remembering Toussaint Louverture and the Haitian Revolution in the History and Culture of the African American People," in *African Americans and the Haitian Revolution: Selected Essays and Historical Documents*, ed. Jackson and Jacqueline Bacon (London and New York: Routledge, 2010), 151. Lawrence saw the William DuBois play in 1938 at the Lafeyette Theater in Harlem while he was in the midst of his Toussaint Louverture project. Maurice Jackson has speculated that Lawrence assumed the play to have been by W. E. B. Du Bois.

17. Williams, "The Haitian Revolution and a North American Griot," 70.

18. For an explanation of Petrus Camper's "facial angle" theory, see Wood, *Blind Memory*, 176–77.

19. Bell, "The Image of Toussaint."

20. Philippe Girard, "Black Talleyrand: Toussaint Louverture's Dipomacy, 1789–1802," *William and Mary Quarterly* 66, no.1 (January 2009): 89.

21. De Cauna, *Haïti, l'éternelle révolution*, 164–65. See also Jacques de Cauna, "1802—Le véritable portrait de Toussaint Louverture: Documents sur les abolitions et le rétablissement napoléonien," http://abolitions.free.fr/IMG/article_PDF/article_129.pdf.

22. The "BLK Art Group" (also referred to as the "Black Art Movement") was founded in 1982 by four British Afro-Caribbean artists: Keith Piper, Marlene Smith, Eddie Chambers, and Donald Rodney. Their work offers a critique of institutional racism, and meditations on race, community, class, and gender relations in contemporary Britain. Their influence on a later generation of black British artists is particularly apparent in the works of the Turner Prize winners Chris Ofili and Steve McQueen (see David A Bailey, Ian Baucom, and Sonia Boyce, eds., *Shades of Black: Assembling Black Arts in 1980s Britain* [Durham: Duke University Press, 2005]).

23. Kimathi Donkor to author, e-mail message, April 10, 2013.

24. See Lawrence quoted in Jackson, "No Man Could Hinder Him," 151.

25. *Burn!*, aka *Queimada!* directed by Gillo Pontecorvo (Italy/France: Alberto Grimaldi, Europee Associate SAS Produzioni Europee Associati, 1969).

26. Donkor has drawn on the heritage of European iconographical traditions elsewhere in his work: in his 2005 *Madonna Metropolitan*, the "Madonna" is a black woman being threatened by a Metropolitan police officer.

27. For example, see Madison Smartt Bell's characterization of Claudine Arnoud and her relationship with her husband's slave girls and women (Bell, *All Souls' Rising* [New York: Vintage, 1995]).

28. Wood, *Blind Memory*, 269.

29. Toni Morrison, *Beloved* (1987; London: Vintage, 1997), 21.

30. Wood, *The Horrible Gift of Freedom*, 182–262.

31. Nesbitt, *Voicing Memory*, 9–14.

32. Donald M. Reid, "The Symbolism of Postage Stamps," *Journal of Contemporary History* 19, no. 2 (1984): 226–27.

33. For a more detailed analysis of the 25-centimes 1954 stamp, see Wood, *The Horrible Gift of Freedom*, 239–40.

34. Ibid., 240.

35. Ibid.

36. Scott, "National Icons: The Semiotics of the French Stamp," *French Cultural Studies*, 3, no. 9 (1992): 216.

37. Ibid., 232–33.

38. Wood, *The Horrible Gift of Freedom*, 241.

39. Philippe R. Girard, "Black Talleyrand: Toussaint Louverture's Diplomacy, 1789–1802," *William and Mary Quarterly* 66, no. 1 (January 2009): 88.

40. See David Geggus, "Haiti and the Abolitionists: Opinion, Propaganda,

and International Politics in Britain and France, 1804–1838," in *Abolition and Its Aftermath: The Historical Context, 1790–1916*, ed. David Richardson (Abingdon, Oxon: Frank Cass, 1985), 113–40.

41. Marcus Wood's chapter "The Horrible Gift of Freedom and the 1807/2007 Bicentennial," in *The Horrible Gift of Freedom*, 296–353, provides a detailed analysis of the 2007 bicentennial in Britain.

42. Charles Forsdick, "Interpreting 2004: Politics, Memory, Scholarship," *Small Axe* 12, no. 3 (October 2008): 3.

43. Ibid., 6.

44. Ibid., 7.

45. Ibid., 5–6. The film, although generally a critical success, provoked angry respsonses, particularly from black voices. For a detailed critique of the film that he dubs "Amazing Disgrace," see Wood, *Horrible Gift of Freedom*, 344–53.

46. This is not to discount the very real admiration for Wilberforce among early-nineteenth-century abolitionists, black and white, including Germaine de Staël (see Doris Y. Kadish, "Patriarchy and Abolition: Staël and Fathers," in *Germaine de Staël: Forging a Politics of Mediation*, ed. Karyna Szmurlo [Oxford: Voltaire Foundation, 2011], 63–78).

47. Although only six commemorative stamps were produced, a great variety of envelope designs, postmarks, and related collectible memorabilia were created that are beyond the parameters of discussion here (see Wood, *Horrible Gift of Freedom*, 199–214).

48. Ibid., 195.

49. See "Sancho, (Charles) Ignatius" entry, *The Oxford Dictionary of National Biography*, www.oxfordnb.com/view/article/24609?docPos=1; and "Sancho, Ignatius" entry, *The Oxford Companion to Black British History*, ed. David Dabydeen, John Gilmore and Cecily Jones (Oxford University Press: 2007), 428–29.

5. Edouard Glissant's *Monsieur Toussaint*

1. Edouard Glissant, *Monsieur Toussaint*, trans. J. Michael Dash and Edouard Glissant (Boulder, Colo.: Rienner, 2005). The first version of the play was written in 1959 and first published in 1961. An English translation was first published in 1981: Edouard Glissant, *Monsieur Toussaint*, trans. Joseph G. Foster and Barbara A. Franklin (Washington, D.C.: Three Continents Press, 1961). A shortened *version scénique* of the play was written in 1977: Edouard Glissant, *Monsieur Toussaint: Version Scénique* (Paris: Seuil, 1986). This chapter refers to the Dash and Glissant 2005 edition.

2. Glissant, *Monsieur Toussaint*, 15; emphasis in original.

3. Peter Hallward, *Absolutely Postcolonial: Writing between the Singular and the Specific* (Manchester and New York: Manchester University Press, 2001), 119.

4. Ibid., 68, 81. Edouard Glissant, *La Lézarde* (1958; Paris: Gallimard, 1997); Edouard Glissant, *Le quatrième siècle* (1964; Paris: Gallimard, 1997).

5. Hallward, *Absolutely Postcolonial*, 119.

6. Ibid., 131.

7. Ibid., 132.

8. Ibid., 126.

9. Bongie, *Friends and Enemies*, 329.

10. This distillation of Bongie's reading of Glissant is indebted to the analysis in Nesbitt, "The Incandescent I," 125–26.

11. Bongie, *Friends and Enemies*, 336.

12. See Charles Forsdick, "*Une vision prophétique du passé*: Edouard Glissant's Refiguring of Toussaint Louverture," *International Journal of Francophone Studies* 2, no. 1 (1999): 29.

13. Celia M. Britton, "Globalization and Political Action in the Work of Edouard Glissant," *Small Axe* 13, no. 3 (November 2009): 1–11.

14. Charles Forsdick, "Late Glissant: History, 'World Literature,' and the Persistence of the Political," *Small Axe* 14, no. 3 (November 2010): 123.

15. Ibid., 124.

16. Celia Britton, *Edouard Glissant and Postcolonial Theory: Strategies of Language and Resistance* (Charlottesville: University of Virginia Press, 1999), 11.

17. Ibid., 12.

18. See Hallward, *Absolutely Postcolonial*, 122.

19. Britton, "Globalization and Political Action," 2.

20. Edouard Glissant, *Introduction à une poétique du divers* (Paris: Gallimard, 1996), 137; my translation.

21. Forsdick, "Une vision prophétique du passé," 35.

22. Glissant, *Monsieur Toussaint*, 15; emphasis in original.

23. Ibid., 21.

24. Forsdick, "Une vision prophétique du passé," 21.

25. Césaire, *Notebook of a Return to My Native Land / Cahier d'un retour au pays natal*, 90–91.

26. J. Michael Dash, *Edouard Glissant* (Cambridge: Cambridge University Press, 1995), 102.

27. There is an extensive body of historiography on the May 1802 revolt led by Louis Delgrès (see Nesbitt, *Voicing Memory*, 49–75).

28. J. Michael Dash, "The Theater of the Haitian Revolution / The Haitian Revolution as Theater," *Small Axe* 9, no. 2 (2005): 23.

29. Glissant, *Monsieur Toussaint*, 51–52.

30. Edouard Glissant, *The Indies*, trans. Dominique O'Neill (Toronto: Éditions du Gref, 1992), 75.

31. "Mémorial de Louis Delgrès / Memorial for Louis Delgres," in Césaire, *The Collected Poetry*, 330–37.

32. Glissant, *Monsieur Toussaint*, 35.
33. Ibid., 30–31.
34. Ibid., 40–41.
35. Ibid., 41.
36. Ibid., 51.
37. James, *The Black Jacobins,* xix.
38. Glissant, *The Indies*, 83.
39. Forsdick, "Une vision prophétique du passé," 32.
40. Glissant, *Caribbean Discourse: Selected Essays*, 198.

6. Ideological Frailty and the Marvelous in Alejo Carpentier's *El reino de este mundo*

1. Timothy Brennan notes that Carpentier was "the first in Latin America to articulate the array of styles and themes later used by the 'boom' novelists" (Timothy Brennan, introduction to *Explosion in the Cathedral*, by Alejo Carpentier [1962], trans. John Sturrock [Minneapolis: University of Minnesota Press, 2001], 6; see also Edwin Williamson, "The Quixotic Roots of Magic Realism: History and Fiction in Alejo Carpentier and García Márquez," in *Cervantes and the Modernists: The Question of Influence*, ed. Edwin Williamson [London: Tamesis, 1994]).

2. Alejo Carpentier, *El reino de este mundo* (1949; Barcelona: Seix Barral, 2008). All quotations from *El reino* in this chapter are taken from Harriet de Onis's translation: Alejo Carpentier, *The Kingdom of This World*. trans. Harriet de Onis (1949; New York: Noonday Press, 1989). Alejo Carpentier, "On the Marvelous Real in America" and "The Baroque and the Marvelous Real," both in *Magical Realism: Theory, History, Community*, ed. Lois Parkinson Zamora and Wendy B. Farris (1967; Durham: Duke University Press, 1995).

3. Carpentier, "On the Marvelous Real in America," 84.

4. Carpentier, "The Baroque and the Marvelous Real," 103–4; emphasis in original.

5. Ibid., 104

6. Carpentier, "On the Marvelous Real in America," 78.

7. Ibid., 79.

8. Ibid., 83; emphases in original.

9. Fick, *The Making of Haiti*, 61.

10. Ibid., 60.

11. Carpentier, *Kingdom*, 13.

12. Ibid., 14.

13. Ibid., 19.

14. Ibid., 20.

15. Barbara Webb, *Myth and History in Caribbean Fiction: Alejo Carpentier,*

Wilson Harris, and Edouard Glissant (Amherst: University of Massachusetts Press, 1992), 29.

16. Carpentier, *Kingdom*, 108.
17. Ibid., 51.
18. Ibid., 51–52.
19. Ibid., 52.
20. There are similarities here with the colonized peasantry in twentieth-century Algeria observed by Frantz Fanon who were able to translate news received via radio of further oppression into heroic stories of resistance (see Nigel Gibson, "Jammin' the Airwaves and Tuning into Revolution: The Dialectics of the Radio In "L'an V De La Révolution Algeriénne," in *Fanon: A Critical Reader*, eds. Lewis R. Gordon, T. Denean Sharpley-Whiting, and Renée T. White [Oxford: Blackwell, 1996]).
21. Carpentier, *Kingdom*, 7.
22. Ibid., 10, 11.
23. Ibid., 11.
24. Ibid., 15.
25. Ibid.
26. A vast range of sources all point to what Doris Garraway has called "the generalized libertinage of colonial life" (Doris Garraway, *The Libertine Colony: Creoloization in the Early French Caribbean.* [Durham: Duke University Press, 2005], 228).
27. Carpentier, *Kingdom*, 60.
28. Ibid.
29. Ibid., 74.
30. James, *The Black Jacobins*, 71.
31. Carpentier, *Kingdom*, 94.
32. Ibid., 91.
33. Ibid.
34. Ibid., 93.
35. Ibid.
36. Ibid., 101.
37. Ibid. See also Timothy J. Cox, *Postmodern Tales of Slavery in the Americas: From Alejo Carpentier to Charles Johnson, Literary Criticism and Cultural Theory* (New York and London: Garland, 2001), 65.
38. Carpentier, *Kingdom*, 102.
39. Ibid., 102.
40. Ibid., 107–8.
41. Ibid., 109.
42. Ibid., 122.
43. Ibid., 123.
44. Bongie, *Islands and Exiles*, 220.

45. Robin Blackburn, *The American Crucible: Slavery, Emancipation and Human Rights* (London and New York: Verso, 2011), 272.

46. Carpentier, *Kingdom*, 184–85.

47. Ibid., 185.

7. The Aesthetics of Cyclical Pessimism

1. Derek Walcott, *The Haitian Trilogy: Plays: "Henri Christophe," " Drums and Colours," and "The Haitian Earth"* (New York: Farrar, Straus and Giroux, 2002). Hereafter the plays in this volume are cited parenthetically.

2. Chris Bongie, "'Monotonies of History': Baron De Vastey and the Mulatto Legend of Derek Walcott's *Haitian Trilogy*," *Yale French Studies*, no. 107 (2005): 70–107. According to the mulatto legend, Dessalines is characterized as despotic, barbarous, and ignorant, and Christophe as despotic and prejudiced. Pétion's characterization, on the other hand, is as liberal, civilized, and democratic (see David Nicholls, *From Dessalines to Duvalier*, 88–90).

3. See, for example, Bruce King, *Derek Walcott and West Indian Drama* (Oxford: Clarendon, 1995), 138.

4. King, *Derek Walcott: A Caribbean Life*, 76–77.

5. Ibid., 76–77, 136–37, 434–35. It is worth noting here that none of the plays are chronological, nor do they depend on each other for coherence; each play stands alone.

6. Edward Baugh, "Of Men and the Haitian Revolution," *Callaloo* 28, no. 1 (2005): 45.

7. Derek Walcott, *What the Twilight Say*, (London: Faber and Faber, 1998), 10.

8. Ibid., 11; my emphases.

9. James, *The Black Jacobins*, 299.

10. Ibid.

11. King, *Derek Walcott*, 77.

12. Ibid., 434.

8. Fantasizing the Haitian Revolution with Madison Smartt Bell

1. Madison Smartt Bell, *All Souls' Rising* (New York: Random House, Vintage, 1995); Madison Smartt Bell, *Master of the Crossroads* (New York: Vintage, 2000); Madison Smartt Bell, *The Stone That the Builder Refused* (New York: Pantheon, 2004).

2. A. James Arnold has observed that from Victor Hugo's *Bug Jargal* in 1826 through the nineteenth and twentieth centuries, mulattoes have been commonly represented as traitors and that this racial bias has alternated with its variant, "the attraction of the beautiful but doomed 'tragic mulatto' woman" (Arnold, "Recuperating the Haitian Revolution in Literature: From Victor Hugo to Derek Walcott," in *Tree of Liberty*, ed. Garraway, 181).

3. Georg Lukács, *The Historical Novel*, trans. Hannah Mitchell and Stanley Mitchell (1937; London: Merlin Press, 1962), 189.

4. Perry Anderson, "From Progress to Catastrophe," *London Review of Books* 33, no. 15 (2011), www.lrb.co.uk/v33/n15/perry-anderson/from-progress-to-catastrophe.

5. Ibid.

6. Nesbittt, *Voicing Memory*, 205.

7. Lukács, *The Historical Novel*, 174.

8. Ibid., 192.

9. Ibid., 193.

10. Ibid.

11. Morrison, *Beloved*; Edouard Glisssant, *Le quatrième siècle* (*The Fourth Century*), trans. Betsy Wing (1964; Lincoln: University of Nebraska Press 2001).

12. Nesbitt, *Voicing Memory*, 207.

13. Miller, *The French Atlantic Triangle*, 347.

14. Glisssant, *The Fourth Century*, 27.

15. Miller, *The French Atlantic Triangle*, 348.

16. The major works of academic critique the trilogy has generated thus far are Laurent Dubois, "Capturing Louverture," Charles Forsdick, "Madison Smartt Bell's Toussaint at the Crossroads: The Haitian Revolutionary between History and Fiction," Martin Munro, "Haitian Novels and Novels of Haiti: History, Haitian Writing, and Madison Smartt Bell's Trilogy," Marie-José Nzengou-Tayo, "Haitian Gothic and History: Madison Smartt Bell's Trilogy on Toussaint Louverture and the Haitian Revolution," all in *Small Axe* 11 no. 2 (2007); see also Michel-Rolph Trouillot, "Bodies and Souls: The Haitian Revolution and Madison Smartt Bell's *All Souls' Rising*," in *Novel History: Historians and Novelists Confront America's Past (and Each Other)*, ed. Mark C. Carnes (New York: Simon and Schuster, 2001).

17. From the book jacket of the first Vintage edition, November 2004.

18. See Barry S. Sapolsky, Fred Moliter, and Sarah Luque, "Sex and Violence in Slasher Films: Re-Examining the Assumptions," *Journalism and Mass Communication Quarterly* 80, no. 1 (Spring 2003): 28–38.

19. Haiti has long held an erotic fascination for Western writers (see, for example, William Seabrook, *The Magic Island* [1929; London: George G. Harrap, 1931]; and Richard A. Loederer, *Voodoo Fire in Haiti,* trans. Desmond Ivo Vesy [1935; Gretna, La.: Pelican Press, 2005]).

20. Zachary Leader, "A Popular Uprising," *Times Literary Supplement*, February 9, 1996, 23.

21. Bell, *All Souls' Rising*, 105.

22. Garraway, *The Libertine Colony*, 28–29, 230–32.

23. Ibid., 105–6.

24. Bell, *All Souls' Rising*, 65.

25. Leader, "A Popular Uprising," 23.

26. Firmin, *The Equality of the Human Race*, 301.

27. Leader, "A Popular Uprising," 23.

28. Wood, *Blind Memory*, 280.

29. Bell, *All Souls' Rising*, 88.

30. Ibid.

31. Ibid., 88–89.

32. Ibid., 91.

33. Jack Stephens, "Madison Smartt Bell," *Bomb*, no. 73 (Fall 2000), http://bombsite.com/issues/73/articles/2346.

34. Bell, *All Souls' Rising*, 233.

35. Bell, *Master of the Crossroads*, 106, 107.

36. Ibid., 180.

37. Ibid.

38. Ibid., 359.

39. Ibid., 360.

40. Ibid., 361.

41. Ibid.

42. Ibid., 362.

43. Morrison, *Beloved*, 35.

44. Forsdick, "Madison Smartt Bell's Toussaint at the Crossroads," 202.

45. Stephens, "Madison Smartt Bell."

46. Morrison, "The Site of Memory," in *Inventing the Truth: The Art and Craft of Memoir*, ed. William Knowlton Zinsser (Boston: Houghton Mifflin, 1987), 196.

47. Madison Smartt Bell, *Toussaint Louverture: A Biography* (New York: Pantheon, 2007), 299.

48. James, *The Black Jacobins*, xviii–xix.

49. Ibid., 87.

50. Bell, *Toussaint Louverture: A Biography*, 3.

51. Ibid., 56.

52. Ibid., 78.

53. Ibid., 79.

54. Ibid. Early proponents of the conspiracy theory in the historiography include Thomas Madiou, *Histoire d'Haïti*, 3 vols. (Port-au-Prince, 1847); and Céligny Ardouin, *Études surl'histoire d'Haïti*, 11 vols. (Paris: 1853–65). Jacques de Cauna sides with Madison Smartt Bell in the debate and has recently defended the conspiracy theory (Jacques de Cauna, *Haïti: l'éternelle revolution*). However, the argument for the idea of a royalist plot having incited the original slave insurrection remains a minority view (see David Brion Davis, "He Changed the New World. Toussaint Louverture: A Biography by Madison Smartt Bell [Review]," *New York Review of Books*, May 31, 2007, 56; Forsdick, "Madison Smartt Bell's Toussaint at the Crossroads," 194–208; and Marie-José Nzengou-Tayo, "Haitian Gothic and History: Madison Smartt Bell's trilogy on

Toussaint Louverture and the Haitian Revolution," *Small Axe* 11, no. 2 [June 2007]: 184–93). Bell also argues for the conspiracy theory in "Sa Nou Pa We Yo (the Invisible Ones): A Reply to Four Readers," *Small Axe* 11, no. 2 (June 2007).

55. Bell, *Toussaint Louverture: A Biography*, 16.

56. Ibid., 199.

57. Ibid., 77.

58. Ibid., 71.

59. James, *The Black Jacobins*, 224.

60. Ibid., 224.

61. Ibid., 225, 225.

62. Ibid., 225.

63. Bell, *Toussaint Louverture: A Biography*, 205.

Conclusion

1. Buck-Morss, *Hegel, Haiti, and Universal History*, 74–75.

2. Thabo Mbeki, "Address at the University of West Indies," Kingston, Jamaica, June 30, 2003, www.dfa.gov.za/docs/speeches/2003/mbek0630.htm.

3. Ibid.

4. Peter Hallward, *Damming the Flood: Haiti, Aristide, and the Politics of Containment* (London: Verso, 2008), 11; emphasis in original.

5. Philippe Girard, *Haiti: The Tumultous History—From Pearl of the Caribbean to Broken Nation*, 2nd ed. (New York: Palgrave, 2010), 58.

6. David Brooks, "The Underlying Tragedy,"editorial, *New York Times*, January 14, 2010, www.nytimes.com/2010/01/15/opinion/15brooks.html?_r=0.

Bibliography

Abu-Jamal, Mumia. "The Power of History: Haiti." Radio broadcast. http://mumiapodcast.libsyn.com/the_power_of_history_haiti#.UWUkZL8ydhM.

Accilien, Cécile, Jessica Adams, and Elmide Méléance, eds. *Revolutionary Freedoms: A History of Survival, Imagination and Strength in Haiti.* Coconut Creek, Fla.: Caribbean Studies Press, 2006.

Adorno, Theodor. "The Actuality of Philosophy." In *The Adorno Reader*, edited by Brian O'Connor, 23–39. London: Blackwell, 2000.

Adotevi, Stanislas Spero. *Négritude et négrologues.* 1972. Paris: LeCastor Astral, 1998.

Agbetu, Toyin. "My Protest Was Born of Anger, Not Madness." *Guardian*, April 3, 2007. www.guardian.co.uk/theguardian/2007/apr/03/features11g2.

Alexis, Jacques Stephen. "Of the Marvellous Realism of the Haitians." *Présence Africaine* (1956): 8–10. Reprinted in *The Post-Colonial Studies Reader*, edited by Bill Ashcroft, Gareth Griffiths, and Helen Tiffin, 194–98. London and New York: Routledge, 1995,

Altman, D. *Paper Ambassadors: The Politics of Stamps.* North Ryde, NSW, Australia: Angus and Robertson, 1991.

Anderson, Benedict. *Imagined Communities.* London: Verso, 1991.

Anderson, Paul Allen. *Deep River: Music and Memory in Harlem Renaissance Thought.* Durham: Duke University Press, 2001.

Anderson, Perry. "From Progress to Catastrophe." *London Review of Books* 33, no. 15 (2011). www.lrb.co.uk/v33/n15/perry-anderson/from-progress-to-catastrophe.

Annesley, James. *Fictions of Globalization: Consumption, the Market and the Contemporary American Novel.* London: Continuum, 2006.

Ardouin, Céligny. *Études sur l'histoire d'Haïti.* 11 vols. Paris, 1853–65.

Arnold, A. J. *Modernism and Negritude: The Poetry and Poetics of Aimé Césaire.* Cambridge: Harvard University Press, 1981.

———. "Recuperating the Haitian Revolution in Literature: From Victor Hugo to Derek Walcott." In *Tree of Liberty: Cultural Legacies of the Haitian*

Revolution in the Atlantic World, edited by Doris L. Garraway, 179–99. Charlottesville: University of Virginia Press, 2008.

Ashcroft, Bill, Gareth Grifiths, and Helen Tiffin, eds. *The Postcolonial Studies Reader.* London: Routledge, 1994.

Auerbach, Erich, and Willard R. Trask. *Mimesis: The Representation of Reality in Western Literature.* Princeton: Princeton University Press, 2003.

Austin, David. "The Black Jacobin: C.L.R. James." Radio broadcast. *Ideas.* CBC Radio One. Canada. May 3, 10, and 17, 2005.

Bailey, David A., Ian Baucom, and Sonia Boyce, eds. *Shades of Black, Assembling Black Arts in 1980s Britain.* Durham: Duke University Press, 2005.

Bailey, Marianne Wichmann. *The Ritual Theater of Aimé Césaire: Mythic Structures of the Dramatic Imagination.* Tübingen: Narr, 1992.

Baker, Russell, and William Knowlton Zinsser. *Inventing the Truth: The Art and Craft of Memoir.* Boston: Houghton Mifflin, 1987.

Banfield, Chris. "Derek Walcott and a Caribbean Theatre of Revelation." With Brian Crow. In Banfield with Crow, *An Introduction to Post-Colonial Theatre*, 18–40. Cambridge: Cambridge University Press, 1996.

Baugh, Edward. *Derek Walcott.* Cambridge: Cambridge University Press, 2006.

———. "Of Men and the Haitian Revolution." *Callaloo* 28, no. 1 (2005): 45–54.

Beard, J. R. *The Life of Toussaint L'Ouverture.* London: Ingram and Cooke, 1853.

Bell, Bernard W. *The Contemporary African American Novel: Its Folk Roots and Modern Literary Branches.* Amherst: University of Massachusetts Press, 2004.

Bell, Madison Smartt. *All Souls' Rising.* New York: Vintage 1995.

———. "Engaging the Past." In *Novel History: Historians and Novelists Confront America's Past, and Each Other*, edited by Mark C. Carnes, 197–208. New York: Simon and Schuster, 2001.

———. "The Image of Toussaint." http://faculty.goucher.edu/mbell/Toussaint%20Bio/Toussaint%20Biograph.htm.

———. *Master of the Crossroads.* New York: Vintage, 2000.

———. "Mine of Stones: With and without the Sprits along the Cordon De L'Ouest." *Harper's*, January 2004.

———. "Sa Nou Pa We Yo (the Invisible Ones): A Reply to Four Readers." *Small Axe* 11, no. 2 (2007): 209–16.

———. *The Stone That the Builder Refused.* New York: Pantheon, 2004.

———. "Toussaint between Two Worlds." *Journal of Haitian Studies* 11, no. 2 (2005): 30–44.

———. *Toussaint Louverture: A Biography.* New York: Pantheon, 2007.

Bell, Michael. *Literature, Modernism and Myth: Belief and Responsibility in the Twentieth Century.* Cambridge: Cambridge University Press, 1997.

Benjamin, Walter. *The Arcades Project.* Edited by Rolf Tiedemann. Translated by Howard Eiland and Kevin McLaughlin. Cambridge: Belknapp Press of Harvard University Press, 1999.

———. *Illuminations: Essays and Reflections*. Translated by Harry Zohn. Edited by Hannah Arendt. New York: Schocken: 1969.

———. "Theses on the Philosophy of History." 1940. In *Illuminations*, translated by Harry Zohn; edited by Hannah Arendt, 253–64. New York: Schocken, 1969.

———. *The Origin of German Tragic Drama*. Translated by John Osborne. London: Verso, 2003.

Bernabé, Jean, Patrick Chamoisseau, and Raphäel Confiant. "In Praise of 'Creoleness.'" *Callaloo* 13, no. 4 (Autumn 1990): 886–909.

Bernasconi, Robert, ed. *Race*. Oxford: Blackwell, 2001.

Berry, Faith. *Langston Hughes: Before and Beyond Harlem*. Westport: Lawrence Hill, 1983.

Bethel, Elizabeth Rauh. "Images of Hayti: The Construction of an Afro-American *Lieu De Mémoire*." *Callaloo* 15, no. 3 (1992): 827–41.

Blackburn, Robin. *The American Crucible: Slavery, Emancipation and Human Rights*. London: Verso, 2011.

———. "Haiti, Slavery, and the Age of the Democratic Revolution." *William and Mary Quarterly* 63, no. 4 (October 2006): 643–74.

———. *The Making of New World Slavery: From the Baroque to the Modern 1492–1800*. London: Verso, 1997.

———. "Of Human Bondage." *Nation*, October 4, 2004. www.thenation.com/article/human-bondage.

———. *The Overthrow of Colonial Slavery 1776–1848*. London: Verso, 1988.

Blake, David. *Toussaint, Or the Aristocracy of the Skin. An Opera in Three Acts*. Libretto by Anthony Ward. Borough Green, Kent: Novello, 1977.

Blassingame, John W., John R. McKivigan, Gerald W. Fulkerson, eds. *The Frederick Douglass Papers*. Volume 5, *1891–95*. *Series 1: Speeches, Debates and Interviews*. New Haven and London: Yale University Press, 1992.

Blight, David W. "The Birth of a Genre: Slavery on Film." *Common-Place* 1, no. 4 (July 2001). www.common-place.org/vol-01/no-04/slavery/blight.shtml.

Boland, Roy C., and Sally Harvey, eds. *Magical Realism and Beyond: The Contemporary Spanish and Latin American Novel*. Madrid: Vox/AHS, 1991.

Bongie, Chris. *Friends and Enemies: The Scribal Politics of Post/Colonial Literature*. Liverpool, U.K.: Liverpool University Press, 2008.

———. *Islands and Exiles: The Creole Identities of Post/Colonial Literature*. Stanford, Calif.: Stanford University Press, 1998.

———. "'Monotonies of History': Baron De Vastey and the Mulatto Legend of Derek Walcott's *Haitian Trilogy*." *Yale French Studies* 107 (2005): 70–107.

Bontemps, Arna. *Black Thunder*. 1936. Boston: Beacon Press, 1968.

———. *Drums at Dusk*. New York: Macmillan, 1939.

Boseley, Sarah. "Our Moral Superiority about Sex Is Proving Deadly."

Guardian, November 24, 2006. www.guardian.co.uk/commentisfree/2006/nov/24/comment.health.

Boylan, Charles, and Kevin Pina. "Rolling Haiti Back to Colonialism" [Charles Boylan interviews Kevin Pina]. September 21, 2004. www.africaspeaks.com/haiti2004/2309.html.

Brathwaite, Kamau. *Contradictory Omens: Cultural Diversity and Integration in the Caribbean*. Mona, Jamaica: Savacou, 1974.

Brecht, Bertolt. *Brecht on Theatre: The Devlopment of an Aesthetic*. Edited and translated by John Willett. London: Methuen, 1964.

Brennann, Timothy. Introduction to *Explosion in the Cathedral*, by Alejo Carpentier. Minneapolis: University of Minnesota Press, 2001.

Brereton, Bridget, and Kevin A. Yelvington. *The Colonial Caribbean in Transition: Essays on Postemancipation Social and Cultural History*. Gainesville: University Press of Florida, 1999.

Breslin, Paul. "The Cultural Address of Derek Walcott." *Modernism / Modernity* 9, no. 2 (2002): 319–25.

———. "Derek Walcott's "'Reversible World' Centers, Peripheries, and the Scale of Nature." *Callaloo* 28, no. 1 (2005): 8–24.

———. "'The First Epic of the New World': But How Shall It Be Written?" In *Tree of Liberty: Cultural Legacies of the Haitian Revolution in the Atlantic World*, edited by Doris Garraway, 223–47. Charlottesville: University of Virginia Press, 2008.

Breton, André. *Manifestoes of Surrealism*. Translated by Richard Seaver and Helen R. Lane. 1924. Ann Arbor: University of Michigan Press, 1969.

———. "Un grand poète noir." 1944. Preface to *Cahier d'un retour aupays natal*, by Aimé Césaire. Paris: Présence Africaine, 1971.

Brière, Jean-François. "Abbé Grégoire and Haitian Independence." *Research in African Literatures* 35, no. 2 (2004): 34–43.

Britton, Celia. *Edouard Glissant and Postcolonial Theory: Strategies of Language and Resistance*. Charlottesville: University Press of Virginia, 1999.

———. "Globalization and Political Action in the Work of Edouard Glissant." *Small Axe* 13, no. 3, (November 2009): 1–11.

Brooks, David. "The Underlying Tragedy." Editoral. *New York Times*, January 14, 2010. www.nytimes.com/2010/01/15/opinion/15brooks.html?_r=0.

Buck-Morss, Susan. "Hegel and Haiti." *Critical Inquiry* 26, no. 4 (2000): 821–65.

———. *Hegel, Haiti and Universal History*. Pittsburgh: University of Pittsburgh Press, 2009.

———. *The Origin of Negative Dialectics*. New York: Free Press, 1977.

Bundy, Andrew, ed. *Selected Essays of Wilson Harris: The Unfinished Genesis of the Imagination*. London: Routledge, 1999.

Burnett, Paula. *Derek Walcott: Politics and Poetics*. Gainesville: University Press of Florida 2000.

Burton, Richard D. E. "Two Views of Césaire: *Négritude* and Créolité." *Dalhousie French Studies* 35 (1996): 135–52.

Cailler, Bernadette. Review of *Poetics of Relation*, by Edouard Glissant, translated by Betsy Wing. Ann Arbor: University of Michigan Press, 1997. *Research in African Literatures* 30, no. 1 (1999): 235–37.

Carby, Hazel V. "Ideologies of Black Folk: The Historical Novel of Slavery." In *Slavery and the Literary Imagination*, edited by Deborah E. McDowell and Arnold Rampersad. Baltimore: Johns Hopkins University Press, 1989.

Carlyle, Thomas. "Occasional Discourse on the Nigger Question." 1849. In *Critical and Miscellaneous Essays. Volume VII.* (London: Chapman and Hall, 1888).

Carpentier, Alejo. "The Baroque and the Marvelous Real." 1975. In *Magical Realism: Theory, History, Community*, edited by Lois Parkinson Zamora and Wendy B. Farris, 89–108. Durham: Duke University Press, 1995:

———. "De lo real maravilloso Americano." In *Tientos y Diferencias*, 96–112. Montevideo: Arca, 1967.

———. *El reino de este mundo*. 1949. Barcelona: Seix Barral, 2008.

———. *Explosion in a Cathedral*. 1962. Translated by John Sturrock. Minneapolis: University of Minnesota Press, 2001.

———. *The Kingdom of This World*. 1949. Translated by Harriet de Onís. New York: Noonday Press; Farrar, Straus and Giroux, 1989.

———. *The Lost Steps*. Translated by Harriet de Onís. Harmondsworth, U.K.: Penguin, 1956.

———. *Music in Cuba*. Translated by Alan West-Durán. 1946. Minneapolis: University of Minnesota Press, 2002.

———. "On the Marvelous Real in America." In *Magical Realism: Theory, History, Community*, edited by Lois Parkinson Zamora and Wendy B. Farris, 75–88. Durham: Duke University Press, 1995.

Carroll, Rory. "Venezuela Giving Danny Glover $18m to Direct Film on Epic Slave Revolt." *Guardian*, 21 May 2007. www.guardian.co.uk/world/2007/may21/film/Venezuela.

Casas, Bartolomé de las. *A Short Account of the Destruction of the Indies*. 1552. London: Penguin, 2004.

Césaire, Aimé. *Aimé Césaire: Lyric and Dramatic Poetry, 1946–82*. Translated by Clayton Eshleman and Annette Smith. Charlottesville: University of Virginia Press, 1990.

———. *The Collected Poetry*. Translated by Clayton Eshleman and Annette Smith. Berkeley and Los Angeles: University of California Press, 1983.

———. *Discourse on Colonialism*. 1955. Translated by Joan Pinkham. New York: Monthly Review Press, 2000.

———. *Et les chiens se taisaient*. Paris: Présence Africaine, 1962.

———. "An Interview with Aimé Césaire Conducted by René Depestre." 1967. In Aimé Césaire, *Discourse on Colonialism*.

———. *La tragédie du roi Christophe*. Paris: Présence Africaine, 1963.

———. *Notebook of a Return to My Native Land / Cahier d'un retour au pays natal*. 1939. Translated by Mireille Rosello with Annie Pritchard. Newcastle upon Tyne: Bloodaxe, 1995.

———. *Return to My Native Land*. 1939. Translated by Emile Snyder. Paris: Présence Africaine, 1968.

———. *Return to My Native Land*. 1939. Translated by John Berger and Anna Bostock. Harmondsworth: Penguin, 1969.

———. *Toussaint Louverture*. Paris: Présence Africaine, 1981.

———. *The Tragedy of King Christophe*. Translated by Ralph Manheim. New York: Grove Press, 1969.

———. *Une saison au Congo*. 1967. Paris: Seuil, 1973.

———. *Une tempête*. Paris: Seuil, 1969.

Chatterjee, Partha. *The Nation and Its Fragments: Colonial and Postcolonial Histories*. Princeton: Princeton University Press, 1993.

Chomsky, Noam. "The Tragedy of Haiti." In *Year 501: The Conquest Continues*, by Noam Chomsky, 197–220. Cambridge: South End Press, 1993.

Clark, Vèvè A. "Haiti's Tragic Overture: (Mis)Representations of the Haitian Revolution in World Drama (1796–1975)." In *Representing the French Revolution: Literature, Historiography, and Art*, edited by James A. W. Heffernan. Hanover: University Press of New England, 1992.

Cobb, Martha. *Harlem, Haiti, and Havana: A Comparative Critical Study of Langston Hughes, Jacques Roumain, Nicolás Guillén*. Washington, D.C: Three Continents Press, 1979.

Collier, Gordon. "The "Noble Ruins" of Art and the Haitian Revolution: Carpentier, Césaire, Glissant, James, O'Neill, Walcott and Others." In *Fusion of Cultures?*, edited by Peter O'Stummer and Christopher Balme. Amsterdam and Atlanta: Rodopi, 1996.

Columbus, Christopher. *The Four Voyages of Christopher Columbus*. Translated by J. M. Cohen. London: Penguin, 1969.

Combé, Dominique. *Aimé Césaire: Cahier d'un retour au pays natal*. Paris: Presses Universitaires de France, 1993.

Concannon, Brian, and Mario Joseph. "Chávez—a Hero in Haiti," April 9, 2007. www.africaspeaks.com/haits2004/1042007.html.

Condé, Maryse. *"Cahier d'un retour au pays natal": Analyse critique*. Paris: Hatier, 1978.

———. "Négritude césairienne, négritudesenghorienne." *Revue de literature comparée* 48 (1974): 409–19.

Conley, Katharine, and Pierre Taminiaux. Editors' Preface. "Surrealism and Its Others." Special issue, *Yale French Studies*, no. 109 (2006): 1–3.

Conner, Marc C. "From the Sublime to the Beautiful: The Aesthetic Progression of Toni Morrison." In *The Aesthetics of Toni Morrison*, edited by Marc C. Conner. Jackson: University Press of Mississippi, 2000.

Connerton, Paul. *How Societies Remember.* Cambridge: Cambridge University Press, 1989.

Corbett, Bob. "Bibliography on the Haitian Revolution." June 25, 1995. http://hartford-hwp.com/archives/43a/099.html.

Coupe, Laurence. *Myth.* London: Routledge, 1997.

Cowart, David. *History and the Contemporary Novel: Crosscurrents / Modern Critiques.* Carbondale: Southern Illinois University Press, 1989.

Cowper, William. "Epigram (Printed in the *Northampton Mercury*)." 1815. In *The Poetry of Slavery: An Anglo-American Anthology 1764–1865*, edited by Marcus Wood, 93. Oxford: Oxford University Press, 2003.

Cox, Timothy J. *Postmodern Tales of Slavery in the Americas: From Alejo Carpentier to Charles Johnson.* New York: Garland, 2001.

Cripps, Thomas. *Slow Fade to Black: The Negro in American Film, 1900–1942.* New York: Oxford University Press, 1977.

Cudjoe, Selwyn Reginald, and William E. Cain, eds. *C. L. R. James: His Intellectual Legacies.* Amherst: University of Massachusetts Press, 1995.

Dabydeen, David, John Gilmore, and Cecily Jones, eds. *The Oxford Companion to Black British History.* Oxford: Oxford University Press, 2007.

Dace, Letitia. *Langston Hughes: The Contemporary Reviews.* Cambridge: Cambridge University Press, 1997.

Daguillard, Fritz. *Mystérieux dans la Gloire: Toussaint Louverture (1743–1803).* Port-au-Prince: MIPANAH, 2003.

Dasenbrock, Reed Way. "Imitation versus Contestation: Walcott's Postcolonial Shakespeare." *Callaloo* 28, no.1 (2005): 104–13.

Dash, J. Michael. *Edouard Glissant.* Cambridge: Cambridge University Press, 1995.

———. "Haïti Chimère: Revolutionary Universalism and Its Caribbean Context." In *Reinterpreting the Haitian Revolution and Its Cultural Aftershocks*, edited by Martin Munro and Elizabeth Walcott-Hackshaw. Mona, Jamaica: University of the West Indies Press, 2006.

———.Marvellous Realism: The Way out of Négritude." *Caribbean Studies* 13, no. 4 (1974): 57–70.

———. *Literature and Ideology in Haiti, 1915–1961.* London: Macmillan, 1981.

———. "Nineteenth-Century Haiti and the Archipelago of the Americas: Anténor Firmin's Letters from St. Thomas." *Research in African Literatures* 35, no. 2 (2004): 44–53.

———. *The Other America: Caribbean Literature in a New World Context.* Charlottesville: University of Virginia Press, 1998.

———. "The Theater of the Haitian Revolution / the Haitian Revolution as Theater." *Small Axe* 9, no. 2 (2005): 16–23.

Dash, J. Michael, and Charles Arthur, eds. *A Haiti Anthology: Libète.* London: Latin American Bureau, 1999.

Dash, J. Michael, Dany Laferrière, Louis-Philippe Dalembert, Edwidge

Danticat, and Evelyne Trouillot. "Roundtable: Writing, History, and Revolution." *Small Axe*, 9 no. 2 (2005): 189–99.

Davis, David Brion. "He Changed the New World." *New York Review of Books*, May 31 2007, 54–58.

———. *Inhuman Bondage: The Rise and Fall of Slavery in the New World.* Oxford: Oxford University Press, 2006.

———. *The Problem of Slavery in the Age of Revolution, 1770–1823.* 1975. New York: Oxford University Press, 1999.

———. *The Problem of Slavery in Western Culture.* Ithaca, N.Y.: Cornell University Press, 1966.

Davis, Gregson. *Aimé Césaire.* Cambridge: Cambridge University Press, 1997.

Davis, Natalie Zemon. *Slaves on Screen: Film and Historical Vision.* Cambridge: Harvard University Press, 2000.

Dayan, Joan. "A Few Stories about Haiti, or, Stigma Revisited." *Research in African Literatures* 35, no. 2 (2004): 157–72.

———."France Reads Haiti: An Interview with René Depestre." In "Post/Colonial Conditions: Exiles, Migrations, and Nomadisms." Special issue, *Yale French Studies* 2, no. 83: (1993): 136–53.

———. *Haiti, History, and the Gods.* Berkeley and London: University of California Press, 1995.

———. Introduction to *A Rainbow for the Christian West*, translated by Dayan. Amherst: University of Massachussetts Press, 1977.

de Cauna, Jacques. "1802—Le véritable portrait de Toussaint Louverture. Documents sur les abolitions et le rétablissement napoléonien." http://abolitions.free.fr/IMG/article_PDF/article_129pdf.

———. *Haïti, l'éternelle révolution*, Port-au-Prince: Deschamps, 1997.

Deans, Phil, and Hugo Dobson. "Introduction: East Asian Postage Stamps as Socio-Political Artefacts." *East Asia* 22, no. 2 (2005): 3–7.

Denning, Michael. *Culture in the Age of Three Worlds.* London: Verso, 2004.

Depestre, René. *Bonjour et adieu à la négritude.* Paris: Seghers, 1980.

———. *Cantata de Octubre a la vida y a la muerte del Comandante Ernesto Che Guevara.* Translated by Max Figueroa Esteva. Havana: Instituto del Libro, 1968.

———. *Encore une mer à traverser.* Paris: La Table Ronde, 2005.

———. "Les métamorphoses de la négritude en Amerique." *Présence Africaine* 75 (1970).

———. *A Rainbow for the Christian West.* 1967. Translated with an introduction by Joan Dayan. Amherst: University of Massachussetts Press, 1977.

———. *Un arc-en-ciel pour l'occident Chrétien.* Paris: Présence Africaine, 1967.

———. "What Can Toussaint Louverture Do for the Haitians of 2004?" Translated by Martin Munro. In *Re-Interpreting the Haitian Revolution and Its Cultural Aftershocks*, edited by Martin Munro and Elizabeth

Walcott-Hackshaw, 168–72. Mona, Jamaica: University of the West Indies Press, 2006.

Doneday, Anne, and H. Adlai Murdoch, eds. *Postcolonial Studies in a Francophone Frame: Intersections and Re-Visions.* Gainsville: University Press of Florida, 2004.

Donkor, Kimathi. *Toussaint L'Ouverture at Bedourete.* 2004. Oil painting on linen, 136 × 183cm. Collection of the artist.

———. *The Small Axe.* 2004. Oil painting on linen, 70 × 100 cm. Private collection.

Douglass, Frederick. "Lecture on Haiti." 1893. In *The Frederick Douglass Papers.* Vol. 5, *1891–95. Series 1, Speeches, Debates and Interviews.* Edited by John R. McKivigan, John W. Blassingame, and Gerald W. Fulkerson. New Haven: Yale University Press, 1992.

Driskell, David C. *Two Centuries of Black American Art.* New York: Knopf, 1976.

Dubois, Laurent. *Avengers of the New World: The Story of the Haitian Revolution.* Cambridge: Harvard University Press, 2004.

———. "Capturing Louverture." *Small Axe* 11, no. 2 (2007): 177–83.

———. *A Colony of Citizens: Revolution and Slave Emancipation in the French Caribbean, 1787–1804.* Chapel Hill: University of North Carolina Press, 2004.

———. *Haiti: The Aftershocks of History.* New York: Metropolitan Books; Henry Holt, 2012.

———. "A Free Man." *Nation*, April 16, 2007. www.thenation.com/article/free-man.

Dubois, Laurent, and Julius S. Scott, eds. *Origins of the Black Atlantic.* New York and London: Routledge, 2010.

Du Bois, W. E. B. "Haiti." *Crisis*, October 1915, 291.

———. "Krigwa Players Little Negro Theatre." *Crisis*, August 1926, 134–36.

———. *The Souls of Black Folk.* 1903. New York: Vintage, 1990.

———. *The Suppression of the African Slave Trade to the United States of America.* 1896. In *W. E. B. Du Bois: Writings*, 1–356. New York: Library of America, 1986.

DuBois, William. *Haiti.* In *The Federal Theatre Project*, edited by Pierre de Rohan. New York: Random House, ca. 1938.

Dunkel, G. "Haitian President-Elect Turns to Cuba, Venezuela." April 27, 2006. www.africaspeaks.com/haiti2004/270406.html.

Dupuy, Alex. *Haiti in the World Economy: Class, Race, and Underdevelopment since 1700.* Boulder, Colo.: Westview Press, 1989.

Eagleton, Terry. *The English Novel.* Oxford: Blackwell, 2005.

Edwards, Brent. *The Practice of Diaspora: Literature, Translation, and the Rise of Black Internationalism.* Cambridge: Harvard University Press, 2003.

Edwards, Bryan. *An Historical Survey of the French Colony in the Island of St. Domingo.* 1797. London, 1801.

Eliot, T. S. "Ulysses, Order and Myth." In *Selected Prose of T. S. Eliot*, edited by Frank Kermode. London: Faber, 1975.

Ellison, Ralph. "Mister Toussan.'" 1941. In *Flying Home and Other Stories*. London: Penguin, 1998.

———. *Shadow and Act*. 1953. New York: Vintage, 1995.

Endore, Guy. *Babouk*. 1934. New York: Monthly Review Press, 1991.

Fanning, Sara C. "The Roots of Early Black Nationalism: Northern African Americans' Invocations of Haiti in the Early Nineteenth Century." *Slavery and Abolition* 28, no. 1 (2007): 61–85.

Fanon, Frantz. "Address to the First Congress of Negro Writers and Artists, Paris," 1956. Reprinted as "Racism and Culture" in *Toward the African Revolution*, by Fanon, translated by Haakon Chevalier. New York: Grove Press, 1967.

———. *Black Skin, White Masks*. 1952. Translated by Charles Mann Markmann. London: Pluto, 1986.

———. *The Wretched of the Earth*. 1961. Translated by Constance Farrington. London: Penguin, 2001.

Fared, Grant. "'Victorian with the Rebel Seed': C. L. R. James, Postcolonial Intellectual." *Social Text*, no. 38 (1994): 21–38.

Farmer, Paul. *The Uses of Haiti*. Monroe, Me.: Common Courage Press, 1994.

———. "Who Removed Aristide?" *London Review of Books* 26, no. 8 (2004).

Farred, Grant. "First Stop, Port-Au-Prince: Mapping Postcolonial Africa through Toussaint L'ouverture and His Black Jacobins." In *The Politics of Culture in the Shadow of Capital*, edited by Lisa Lowe and David Lloyd. Durham: Duke University Press, 1997.

———. *Rethinking C. L. R.James: A Critical Reader*. Oxford: Blackwell, 1996.

Faulkner, William. *Absalom, Absalom!* 1936. London: Vintage, 1991.

Fick, Carolyn E. *The Making of Haiti: The Saint Domingue Revolution from Below*. Knoxville: University of Tennessee Press, 1990.

Finn, Julio. *Voices of Négritude*. London: Quartet, 1988.

Firmin, Anténor. *The Equality of the Human Races: Positivist Anthropology*. 1885. Translated by Charles Asselin. New York: Garland, 2000.

Fleming, Victor. Director. *Gone with the Wind*. Culver City, Calif., and Beverly Hills, Calif.: Selznick International Pictures / MGM, 1939.

Forsdick, Charles. "Between French and Francophone: French Studies and the Postcolonial Turn." *French Studies* 59, no. 4 (2005): 523–30.

———. "The Black Jacobin in Paris." *Journal of Romance Studies* 5, no. 3 (2005): 9–24.

———. "Interpreting 2004: Politics, Memory, Scholarship." *Small Axe* 12 no. 3 (2008): 1–13.

———. "Late Glissant: History, 'World Literature,' and the Persistence of the Political." *Small Axe* 14, no. 3 (2010): 121–34.

———. "Madison Smartt Bell's Toussaint at the Crossroads: The Haitian

Revolutionary between History and Fiction." *Small Axe* 11, no. 2 (2007): 194–208.

———. "Refiguring Revolution: The Myth of Toussaint Louverture in C. L. R. James and Edouard Glissant." *New Comparison*, nos. 27–28 (1999): 259–72.

———. "Situating Haiti in Francophone Studies: Early Nineteenth-Century Representations of Toussaint Louverture." *International Journal of Francophone Studies* 10, no. 1 (2007): 17–34.

———. "The Spectral Presence of Toussaint Louverture." *International Journal of Francophone Studies* 11, no. 3 (2008): 327–44.

———. "The Travelling Revolutionary: Translations of Toussaint Louverture." In *Re-Interpreting the Haitian Revolution and Its Cultural Aftershocks*, edited by Martin Munro and Elizabeth Walcott-Hackshaw. Mona, Jamaica: University of the West Indies Press, 2006.

———. "Une vision prophétique du passé: Edouard Glissant's Refiguring of Toussaint Louverture." *International Journal of Francophone Studies* 2, no. 1 (1999): 28–35.

Forsdick, Charles, and David Murphy, eds. *Francophone Postcolonial Studies: A Critical Introduction*. London: Arnold, 2003.

Frank, Alan G. *Horror Movies: Tales of Terror in the Cinema*. New Port: Cathay, 1974.

Fraser, R. *West African Poetry: A Critical History*. Cambridge: Cambridge University Press, 1986.

Gair, Christopher, ed. *Beyond Boundaries: C. L. R. James and Postnational Studies*. London: Pluto Press, 2006.

Garraway, Doris. "'*Légitime Défense*': Universalism and Nationalism in the Discourse of the Haitian Revolution." In *Tree of Liberty: Cultural Legacies of the Haitian Revolution in the Atlantic World*, edited by Garraway, 63–88. Charlottesville: University of Virginia Press, 2008.

———. *The Libertine Colony: Creolization in the Early French Caribbean*. Durham: Duke University Press, 2005.

———, ed. *Tree of Liberty: Cultural Legacies of the Haitian Revolution in the Atlantic World*. Charlottesville and London: University of Virginia Press, 2008.

Gaspar, David Barry, and Michel-Rolph Trouillot. "History, Fiction, and the Slave Experience." Afterword to *Babouk*, by Guy Endore. New York: Monthly Review Press, 1991.

Gates, Henry Louis, Jr. *The Signifying Monkey: A Theory of African-American Literary Criticism*. New York: Oxford University Press, 1988.

Gates, Henry Louis, Jr., and K. A. Appiah, eds. *Langston Hughes: Critical Perspectives Past and Present*. Amistad Literary Series. New York: Amistad, 1993.

Gates, Henry Louis, Jr., and Nellie Y. McKay, eds. *The Norton Anthology of African American Literature*. New York: Norton, 1997.

Geggus, David Patrick. "Haiti and the Abolitionists: Opinion, Propaganda, and International Politics in Britain and France, 1804–1838." In *Abolition and Its Aftermath: The Historical Context, 1790–1916*, edited by David Richardson, 113–40. Abingdon, Oxon: Frank Cass, 1985.

———. "The Haitian Revolution." In *The Modern Caribbean,* edited by Franklin W. Knight and Colin A. Palmer, 21–50. Chapel Hill: University of North Carolina Press, 1989.

———. *Haitian Revolutionary Studies.* Bloomington and Indianapolis: Indiana University Press, 2002.

———. "Haitian Voodoo in the Eighteenth-Century: Language, Culture, Resistance." *Jahrbuch für Geschichte von Staat, Wirtschaft und Gesellschaft Lateinamerikas* 28 (1991): 21–51.

———, ed. *The Impact of the Haitian Revolution in the Atlantic World.* Columbia: University of South Carolina Press, 2001.

———. *Slavery, War, and Revolution: The British Occupation of Saint Domingue, 1793–1798.* Oxford: Clarendon Press, 1982.

Geggus, David Patrick, and Norman Fiering, eds. *The World of the Haitian Revolution.* Bloomington: Indiana University Press, 2009.

Genovese, Eugene. *Roll, Jordan, Roll: The World the Slaves Made.* New York: Vintage, 1976.

Genovese, Eugene, and Laura Foner, eds. *Slavery in the New World.* Englewood Cliffs, N.J.: Prentice Hall, 1969.

Gibson, Nigel. "Jammin' the Airwaves and Tuning into Revolution: The Dialectics of the Radio in "L'an V de la révolution algeriénne." In *Fanon: A Critical Reader*, edited by Lewis R. Gordon, T. Denean Sharpley-Whiting, and Renée T. White, 273–82. Oxford: Blackwell, 1996.

Gigsby, Darcy Grimaldo. *Extremities: Painting Empire in Post-Revolutionary France.* New Haven: Yale University Press, 2002.

Gikandi, Simon, ed. *Encyclopedia of African Literature.* New York: Routledge, 2003.

Gilroy, Paul. *The Black Atlantic: Modernity and Double Consciousness.* London: Verso, 1993.

Gindine, Yvette. "The Magic of Black History: Images of Haiti." *Caribbean Review* 6, no. 4 (1974): 25–30.

Girard, Philippe. "Black Talleyrand: Toussaint Louverture's Diplomacy, 1789–1802." *William and Mary Quarterly* 66, no. 1 (2009): 87–124.

———. *Haiti: The Tumultous History—From Pearl of the Caribbean to Broken Nation.* 2005. New York: Palgrave Macmillan, 2010.

Glissant, Edouard. "Aimé Césaire: The Poet's Passion." Translated byChristopher Winks. *Small Axe* 27 (October 2008): 119–23.

———. *Black Salt: Poems by Édouard Glissant.* Translated by Betsy Wing. Ann Arbor: University of Michigan Press, 1998.

———. *Caribbean Discourse: Selected Essays.* Translated by J. Michael Dash. Charlottesville: University of Virginia Press, 1989.

———. *The Fourth Century / Le quatrième siècle.* 1964. Translated by Betsy Wing. Lincoln: University of Nebraska Press, 2001.

———. *The Indies.* Translated by Dominique O'Neill. Toronto: Éditions du Gref, 1992.

———. *Introduction à une poétique du divers.* Paris: Gallimard, 1996.

———. *La Lézarde.* 1958. Paris: Gallimard, 1997.

———. *Le quatrième siècle.* 1964. Paris: Gallimard, 1997.

———. *Monsieur Toussaint.* Translated by J. Michael Dash and Edouard Glissant. Boulder, Colo.: Rienner, 2005.

———. *Monsieur Toussaint.* Translated by Joseph G. Foster and Barbara A. Franklin. Washington, D.C.: Three Continents Press, 1981.

———. *Monsieur Toussaint. Version scénique.* Paris: Seuil, 1986.

———. *Poetics of Relation.* Translated by Betsy Wing. Ann Arbor: University of Michigan Press, 1997.

Gobineau, Arthur. *The Inequality of Human Races.* 1853–55. Translated by Adrian Collins. New York: Fertig, 1998.

González Echevarría, Roberto. *Alejo Carpentier: The Pilgrim at Home.* 1977. Austin: University of Texas Press, 1990.

Gordon, Lewis R., T. Denean Sharpley-Whiting, and René T. White. eds. *Fanon: A Critical Reader.* Blackwell Critical Readers. Oxford: Blackwell, 1996.

Gott, Richard. "Britain's Vote to End Its Slave Trade Was a Precursor to Today's Liberal Imperialism." *Guardian*, January 17, 2007. www.guardian.co.uk/commentisfree/2007/jan/17/comment.politics2.

———. *Cuba: A New History.* New Haven and London: Yale University Press, 2004.

Greaney, Michael. *Contemporary Fiction and the Uses of Theory: The Novel from Structuralism to Postmodernism.* Basingstoke: Palgrave Macmillan, 2006.

Greenblatt, Stephen. *Marvelous Possessions: The Wonder of the New World.* Chicago: University of Chicago Press, 1991.

Greene, Graham. *The Comedians.* 1965. London: Vintage, 1999.

Gigsby, Darcy Grimaldo, *Extremities: Painting Empire in Post-Revolutionary France.* New Haven: Yale University Press, 2002.

Grimshaw, Anna. "C. L. R. James: A Revolutionary Vision for the 20th Century." www.marxists.org/archive/james-clr/biograh.htm#copyright.

Guha, Ranajit, and Gayatri Chakravorty Spivak, eds. *Selected Subaltern Studies.* Oxford: Oxford University Press, 1988.

Hale, Thomas. "Structural Dynamics in a Third World Classic: Aimé Césaire's *Cahier d'un retour au pays natal.*" *Yale French Studies* 53 (1976): 163–74.

Hall, Stuart. "C. L. R. James: A Portrait." In *C. L. R. James's Caribbean*, edited by Paget Henry and Paul Buhle, 3–16. Durham: Duke University Press, 1992.

Hallward, Peter. *Absolutely Postcolonial.* Manchester: Manchester University Press, 2001.

———. *Damming the Flood: Haiti, Aristide, and the Politics of Containment.* London: Verso, 2008.

———. "Edouard Glissant between the Singular and the Specific." *Yale Journal of Criticism* 11, no. 2 (1998): 441–64.

———. "An Interview with Jean-Bertrand Aristide," *London Review of Books*, February 22, 2007, 9–13.

———. "Option Zero in Haiti." *New Left Review*, no. 27 (2004): 23–47.

———. "The Politics of Prescription." *South Atlantic Quarterly* 104, no. 4 (Fall 2005): 769–89.

Hamilton, Guy, dir. *Live and Let Die.* London: Eon Productions, 1973.

Hamner, Robert D., ed. *Critical Perspectives on Derek Walcott.* Boulder, Colo., and London: Three Continents Press, 1993.

———. *Derek Walcott.* Boston: Twayne; Hall, 1981.

———. "Dramatizing the New World's African King: O'Neill, Walcott and Césaire on Christophe." *Journal of West Indian Literature* 5, nos. 1–2 (1992): 30–47.

———. "Introduction: Out of the Ordinary, Derek Walcott." *Callaloo* 28, no.1 (2005): 1–6.

Harland, Sidney C. "Race Admixture." *Beacon* 1, no. 4 (July 1931): 25–29.

Harris, Wilson. *Selected Essays of Wilson Harris: The Unfinished Genesis of the Imagination.* Edited by Andrew Bundy. London: Routledge, 1999.

Harrison, Paul Carter, Victor Leo Walker, and Gus Edwards. *Black Theatre: Ritual Performance in the African Diaspora.* Philadelphia: Temple University Press, 2002.

Harvey, Sally. *Carpentier's Proustian Fiction: The Influence of Marcel Proust on Alejo Carpentier.* London: Tamesis, 1994.

Hayley, Alex. 1976. *Roots.* London: Vintage, 1991.

Henderson, Mae G. "Toni Morrison's *Beloved.* Remembering the Body as Historical Text." In *Toni Morrison's "Beloved": A Casebook*, edited by William L. Andrews and Nellie Y. McKay. New York: Oxford University Press, 1999.

Hill, Errol, ed. *Black Heroes: Seven Plays.* New York: Applause Theatre, 1989.

Hill, Errol G., and James V. Hatch. *A History of African American Theatre.* Cambridge Studies in American Theatre and Drama. Cambridge: Cambridge University Press, 2006.

Hill, Robert A. "C. L. R. James: The Myth of Western Civilisation." In *Enterprise of the Indies*, edited by George Lamming. Trinidad and Tobago: Institute of the West Indies, 1999.

Hills, Patricia. "Jacob Lawrence's Expressive Cubism." Preface to *Jacob Lawrence American Painter*, by Ellen Harkins Wheat. Seattle: University of Washington Press, 1986.

Hobsbawm, Eric. *The Age of Capital, 1848–1875.* 1975. London: Abacus, 1988.

Hoffman, Léon-François. *Essays on Haitian Literature.* Washington, D.C., 1983.

———. *Haitian Fiction Revisted.* Pueblo, Colo.: Passeggiata Press, 1999.

Horner, Lance, and Kyle Onstott. *The Black Sun.* London: Allen, 1968.

Huggins, Nathan Irvin. *Harlem Renaissance.* New York: Oxford University Press, 1971.

———, ed. *W. E. B. Du Bois: Writings.* New York: Penguin, 1986.

Hughes, Langston. *The Big Sea.* New York and London: Knopf, 1940.

———. *The Collected Works of Langston Hughes.* Edited by Arnold Rampersad, Dolan Hubbard, Leslie Catherine Sanders, Christopher C. De Santis, Dianne Johnson-Feelings, and Joseph McLaren. 16 vols. Columbia: University of Missouri Press, 2001.

———. *Emperor of Haiti.* 1936. In *Collected Works of Langston Hughes: Gospel Plays, Operas, and Later Dramatic Works*, edited by Leslie Catherine Sanders. Columbia: University of Missouri Press, 2001.

———. *I Wonder as I Wander: An Autobiographical Journey.* 1956. New York: Hill and Wang, 1993.

———. "People without Shoes." *New Masses*, October 1931, 12.

———. *Troubled Island: An Opera in Three Acts.* 1936. Libretto by Langston Hughes. In *Collected Works of Langston Hughes: Gospel Plays, Operas, and Later Dramatic Works*, edited by Leslie Catherine Sanders. Columbia: University of Missouri Press, 2001.

———. "White Shadows in a Black Land." *Crisis,* May 1932, 157.

Hughes, Langston, and Arna Bontemps. 1932. *Popo and Fifina.* New York: Oxford University Press, 1993.

Hugo, Victor. *Bug Jargal.* 1820. Translated by Chris Bongie. Toronto: Broadview Press, 2004.

Hunt, Alfred N. *Haiti's Influence on Antebellum America: Slumbering Volcano in the Caribbean.* Baton Rouge: Louisiana State University Press, 1988.

Hutcheon, Linda. "Historiographic Metafiction: Parody and the Intertextuality of History." In *Intertextuality and Contemporary American Fiction*, edited by Patrick O'Donnell and Robert Con Davis, 3–32. Baltimore: Johns Hopkins University Press, 1989.

Irele, Abiola. *Aimé Césaire: "Cahier d'un retour au pays natal."* Ibadan, Nigeria: New Horn Press, 1994.

Jack, Belinda Elizabeth. *Negritude and Literary Criticism: The History and Theory of "Negro-African" Literature in French.* Westport, Conn., and London: Greenwood Press, 1996.

Jackson, Maurice, and Jacqueline Bacon, eds. *African Americans and the Haitian Revolution: Selected Essays and Historical Documents.* New York and London: Routledge, 2010.

Jackson, Maurice. "No Man Could Hinder Him: Remembering Toussaint Louverture and the Haitian Revolution in the History and Culture of the African American People." In *African Americans and the Haitian Revolution:*

Selected Essays and Historical Documents, edited by Maurice Jackson and Jacqueline Bacon, 141–64. New York: Routledge, 2010.

James, C. L. R. *Beyond a Boundary*. 1963. London: Serpent's Tail, 2000.

———. *The Black Jacobins*. 1938. Rev. ed. 1963. London: Penguin, 2001.

———. *The Black Jacobins" [Play]*. 1936. In *The C. L. R. James Reader*, edited by Anna Grimshaw. Oxford, U.K., and Cambridge, Mass.: Blackwell, 1992.

———. *The C. L. R. James Reader*. Edited by Anna Grimshaw. Oxford: Blackwell, 1992.

———. "Lectures on "The Black Jacobins." 1971. *Small Axe* 4, no. 2 (2000): 65–112.

———. "The Intelligence of the Negro: A Few Words with Dr. Harland." *Beacon* 1, no. 5 (August 1931): 6–10.

Jameson, Frederic. "On Magical Realism in Film." *Critical Inquiry* 12 no. 2 (1986): 301–25.

———. *The Political Unconscious: Narrative as a Socially Symbolic Act*. London: Methuen, 1981.

Jean, Wyclef. *Toussaint St. Jean—From the Hut, to the Projects, to the Mansion*. Carnival House Records, 2009.

Jenson, Deborah. *Beyond the Slave Narrative: Politics, Sex, and Manuscripts in the Haitian Revolution*. Liverpool, U.K.: Liverpool University Press, 2011.

Johnson, James Weldon. "Self-Determining Haiti." *Nation*, August 28, 1920.

Jones, Robert A. "Heroes of the Nation? The Celebration of Scientists on the Postage Stamps of Great Britain, France and West Germany." *Journal of Contemporary History* 36, no. 3 (2001): 403–22.

Julien, Isaac, dir. *Looking for Langston*. London: British Film Institute, 1988.

Kachun, Mitch. "Antebellum African Americans, Public Commemoration, and the Haitian Revolution." *Journal of the Early Republic* 26, no. 2 (2006): 249–73.

Kadish, Doris Y. "Haiti and Abolitionism in 1825: The Example of Sophie Doin." In "The Haiti Issue: 1804 and Nineteenth-Century French Studies." Special issue, *Yale French Studies,* no. 107 (2005): 108–30.

———. "Patriarchy and Abolition: Staël and Fathers." In *Germaine de Staël: Forging a Politics of Mediation*, edited by Karyna Szmurlo, 63–78. Oxford: Voltaire Foundation, 2011.

Keenan, Catherine Ann. "Memory, History and the Contemporary Novel." D.Phil Thesis, University of Oxford, Faculty of English Language and Literature and Christ Church, 2002.

Kelley, Robin D. G. Introduction to *A History of Negro Revolt*, edited by C. L. R. James. Chicago: Kerr, 1995.

Kemedjio, Cilas. "Postcolonial Mythologies: Jean Métellus and the Writing of Charismatic Memory." *Research in African Literatures* 35, no. 2 (Summer 2004): 91–113.

Kermode, Frank, ed. *Selected Prose of T. S. Eliot*. London: Faber and Faber, 1975.

Kernodle, Tammy L. "Arias, Communists, and Conspiracies: The History of Still's *Troubled Island*." *Musical Quarterly* 83, no. 4 (Winter1999): 487–508.

Kershaw, Ian. *Hitler, 1889–1936*. London: Hubris, 1998.

———. *Hitler, 1936–1945*. London: Nemesis, 2000.

Kesteloot, Lilyan. *Anthologie Négro-Africaine: Panorama critique des prosateurs, poétes et dramaturges noirs du XXes Siècle*. Verviers: Gérard, 1967.

———. *Comprendre le "Cahier d'un retour au pays natal" d'Aimé Césaire*. Issy les Molineaux: Éditions Saint Paul, 1982.

Killam, D., and R. Rowe, eds. *The Companion to African Literatures*. Oxford: James Cury, 2000.

King, Bruce. *Derek Walcott: A Caribbean Life*. Oxford: Oxford University Press, 2000.

———. *Derek Walcott and West Indian Drama*. Oxford: Clarendon, 1995.

King, John, ed. *Modern Latin American Fiction: A Survey*. London: Faber and Faber, 1987.

King, Richard. "From Haiti to Mississippi: Faulkner and the Making of the Southern Master-Class." *International Journal of Francophone Studies* 14, nos. 1 & 2 (2011): 93–106.

King-Hammond, Leslie. "Inside Outside, Uptown Downtown: Jacob Lawrence and the Aesthetic Ethos of the Harlem Working-Class Community." In *Over the Line: The Art and Life of Jacob Lawrence*, edited by Peter T. Nesbett and Michelle DuBois. Seattle: University of Washinton Press, 2000.

Kleist, Henrich Von. *The Betrothal in Santo Domingo*. 1811. In *The Marquise of O—and Other Stories*. London: Penguin, 2004.

Kolodin, Irving. Review of *Troubled Island*. *New York Sun*, April 1 1949, 157–58.

Korngold, Ralph. *Citizen Toussaint*. London: Victor Gollancz, 1945.

Krasner, David. "What Have We Learned?" *Theatre Journal* 57, no. 4 (2005): 585–87.

Kraus, Joe. "Through Loins and Coins: Derek Walcott's Weaving of the West Indian Federation." *Callaloo* 28, no. 1 (2005): 60–74.

Kulin, Katalin. *Modern Latin American Fiction: A Return to Didacticism*. Budapest: Akadâemiai Kiadâo, 1988.

Laguerre, Michel S. *Voodoo and Politics in Haiti*. London: Macmillan, 1989.

Lamartine, Alphonse de. *Toussaint Louverture*. 1850. Exeter: University of Exeter Press, 1998.

Lamming, George. *Season of Adventure*. London: Allison and Busby, 1979.

———. *Water with Berries*. Port of Spain, Trinidad: Longman, 1971.

Largey, Michael D. "How to Watch a Voodoo Movie: Rules for a Postmodern Age." *Ryder*, October 1998, 28–31.

———. *Vodou Nation: Haitian Art Music and Cultural Nationalism*. Chicago and London: University of Chicago Press, 2006.

Laroche, Maximilien. "The Founding Myths of the Haitian Nation." Translated by Martin Munro. *Small Axe* 9 no. 2 (2005): 1–15.

Lawrence, Jacob. *The Life of John Brown.* 1941. Twenty-two paitings, gouache on paper. Detroit Institute of Arts, Detroit, Mich.

———. *The Life of Frederick Douglass.* 1938–39. Thirty-two paintings, casein tempera on hardboard. Hampton University Museum, Hampton, Va.

———. *The Life of Toussaint L'Ouverture.* 1938. Forty-one paintings, tempera on paper. Aaron Douglas Collection, Amistad Research Center, Tulane University, New Orleans.

———. *The Life of Toussaint L'Ouverture.* 1986–97. Fifteen serigraphs. Aaron Douglas Collection, Amistad Research Center, Tulane University, New Orleans.

———. *The Life of Harriet Tubman.* 1939–40. Thirty-one paintings, casein tempera on hardboard. Hampton University Museum, Hampton, Va.

Lazarus, Neil, ed. *The Cambridge Companion to Postcolonial Literary Studies.* Cambridge: Cambridge University Press, 2004.

———. *Nationalism and Cultural Practice in the Postcolonial World.* Cambridge: Cambridge University Press, 1999.

———. *The Postcolonial Unconscious.* Cambridge: Cambridge University Press, 2011.

Leader, Zachary. "A Popular Uprising." *Times Literary Supplement*, February 9, 1996, 23.

LeFalle-Collins, Lizzetta. "The Critical Context of Jacob Lawrence's Early Works, 1938–1952." In *Over the Line: The Art and Life of Jacob Lawrence*, edited by Peter T. Nesbett and Michelle DuBois. Seattle: University of Washinton Press, 2000.

Leiner, Jacqueline. *Aimé Césaire, Le terreau primordial.* Tübingen: Narr, 1993.

———. "Entretien avec A.C." In *Tropiques*, vol. 1, edited by Aimé Césaire, v–xxiv. Paris: Éditions Jean-Michel Place, 1978.

Leyburn, James. *The Haitian People.* New Haven: Yale University Press, 1941.

Library of Congress. American Memory. "The New Deal Stage: Selections from the Federal Theatre Project, 1935–1939." http//memory.loc.gov/ammem/fedtp/fthome.html.

Locke, Alain. "Advance on the Art Front." *Opportunity*, May 1939. Reprinted in *The Critical Temper of Alain Locke: A Selection of His Essays on Art and Culture*, edited by Jeffrey C. Stewart, 185–89. New York: Garland, 1983.

Loederer, Richard A. *Voodoo Fire in Haiti.* 1935. Translated by Desmond Ivo Vesy. Gretna, La.: Pelican Press, 2005.

Luis, William. *Voices from Under: Black Narrative in Latin America and the Caribbean.* Westport, Conn.: Greenwood, 1984.

Lukács, Georg. *The Historical Novel.* 1937. Translated by Hannah and Stanley Mitchell. London: Merlin Press, 1962.

"'Lydia Bailey,' Fox Movie Based on Kenneth Roberts Novel, Opens at Roxy Theatre; 'Girl in White,' Starring June Allyson, at Loew's State—'Fighter' at the Mayfair." *New York Times*, May 31, 1952, 12.

Macey, David. *Frantz Fanon: A Life*. London: Granta, 2000.

Madiou, Thomas. *Histoire d'Haïti*. 3 vols. Port-au-Prince, 1847.

Maja-Pearce, A., ed. *The Heinemann Book of African Poetry in English*. Oxford: Heinemann, 1990.

Mardorossian, Carine. "From Fanon to Glissant: A Martinican Genealogy." *Small Axe* 13 no. 3 (2009): 12–24.

Marley, Bob. "Small Axe." Produced by Lee Scratch Perry. Upsetter Records, 1971. Vinyl 7" single.

Márquez, Roberto. "Nationalism, Nation, and Ideology: Trends in the Emergence of a Caribbean Literature." In *The Modern Caribbean*, edited by Franklin W. Knight and Colin A. Palmer, 293–340. Chapel Hill: University of North Carolina Press, 1989.

Marshall, Bill. *France and the Americas: Culture, Politics, and History*. 3 vols. New York: ABC-Clio, 2005.

Martineau, Harriet. *The Hour and the Man*. New York: Harper Brothers, 1841.

Marx, Karl. *Capital: A Critique of Political Economy*. 1867. Harmondsworth: Penguin, 1991.

Matheus, John, and Clarence Cameron White. *Ouanga! Opera in a Prologue and Three Acts Based on the Haitian Drama by John F. Matheus*. Clarence Cameron White Collection. Schomburg Center for Research in Black Culture. New York Public Library. 1932.

Mbeki, Thabo. "Address at the University of West Indies." Kingston, Jamaica. June 30, 2003. www.dfa.gov.za/docs/speeches/2003/mbek0630.htm.

McKay, Claude. *Home to Harlem*. New York: Harper and Row, 1928.

McLaren, Joseph. *Langston Hughes, Folk Dramatist in the Protest Tradition, 1921–1943*. Westport, Conn.: Greenwood, 1997.

Métraux, Alfred. *Voodoo in Haiti*. 1959. Translated by Hugo Charteris. London: Schocken, 1972.

Miller, Christopher L. "Forget Haiti: Baron Roger and the New Africa." In "The Haiti Issue: 1804 and Nineteenth-Century French Studies." Special issue, *Yale French Studies*, no. 107 (2005): 39–69.

———. *The French Atlantic Triangle: Literature and Culture of the Slave Trade*. Durham: Duke University Press, 2008.

Mingus, Charles. *The Clown*. New York: Atlantic Records, 1957. Reissued by Rhino, 2000. CD.

Mitchell, Margaret. *Gone with the Wind*. London: Macmillan, 1936.

Mittelholzer, Edgar. *Children of Kaywana*. London: Grafton, 1986.

———. *Kaywana Blood*. London: Grafton, 1986.

———. *Kaywana Stock*. London: Grafton, 1986.

———. *Kaywana Heritage*. London: Grafton, 1986.

Moore, G., and U. Beier, eds. *The Penguin Book of Modern African Poetry*. Harmondsworth, U.K.: Penguin, 1984.

Moretti, Franco. *Atlas of the European Novel, 1800–1900*. London: Verso, 1998.

———. *Modern Epic: The World-System from Goethe to García Márquez.* London: Verso, 1996.

Moretti, Franco, and Susan Fischer. *Signs Taken for Wonders: Essays in the Sociology of Literary Forms.* Rev. ed. London: Verso, 1988.

Morrison, Toni. *Beloved.* 1987. London: Vintage, 1997.

———. *The Bluest Eye.* 1970. London: Chatto and Windus, 1993.

———. "The Site of Memory." In *Inventing the Truth: The Art and Craft of Memoir*, edited by William Knowlton Zinsser, 183–200. Boston: Houghton Mifflin, 1987.

Moya Pons, Frank. "The Land Question in Haiti and Santo Domingo: The Sociopolitical Context of the Transition from Slavery to Free Labour, 1801–1843." In *Between Slavery and Free Labour*, edited by Frank Moya Pons, Manuel Moreno Fraginals, and Stanley Engerman, 181–214. Baltimore: Johns Hopkins University Press, 1985.

Mullen, Edward J., ed. *Langston Hughes in the Hispanic World and Haiti.* Hamden, Conn.: Archon, 1977.

Munro, Martin. "Can't Stand up for Falling Down: Haiti, Its Revolutions, and Twentieth-Century Negritudes." *Research in African Literatures* 35, no. 2 (2004): 1–17.

———. *Echoes of the Haitian Revolution 1804–2004.* Mona, Jamaica: University of the West Indies Press, 2008.

———. *Exile and Post-1946 Haitian Literature: Alexis, Despetre, Ollivier, Laferrière, Danticat.* Liverpool, U.K.: Liverpool University Press, 2007.

———. "Haitian Novels and Novels of Haiti: History, Haitian Writing, and Madison Smartt Bell's Trilogy." *Small Axe* 11 no. 2 (Summer 2007): 163–76.

———. "Petrifying Myths: Lack and Excess in Caribbean and Haitian Histories." In *Reinterpretting the Haitian Revolution and Its Cultural Aftershocks*, edited by Munro and Elizabeth Walcott-Hackshaw, 20–37. Mona, Jamaica: University of the West Indies Press, 2006.

———. *Shaping and Reshaping the Caribbean: The Work of Aimé Césaire and René Depestre.* Leeds, U.K.: Maney, 2000.

Munro, Martin, and Elizabeth Walcott-Hackshaw, eds. *Reinterpreting the Haitian Revolution and Its Cultural Aftershocks.* Mona, Jamaica: University of the West Indies Press, 2006.

Naipaul, V. S. *The Middle Passage: Impressions of Five Societies.* London: Picador, 2001.

Negulesco, Jean, director. *Lydia Bailey.* Los Angeles: 20th Century Fox, 1952.

Nesbett, Peter T. & Michelle DuBois. *Jacob Lawrence: Paintings, Drawings, and Murals (1935–1999): A catalogue raisonné.* Seattle: University of Washington Press, 2000.

———, eds. *Over the Line: The Art of Jacob Lawrence.* Seattle: University of Washington Press, 2000.

Nesbitt, Nick. "The Idea of 1804." In "The Haiti Issue: 1804 and Nineteenth-Century French Studies." Special issue, *Yale French Studies,* no. 107 (2005): 6–38.

———. "The Incandescent I, Destroyer of Worlds." *Research in African Literatures* 41, no. 1 (2010): 121–41.

———. "Négritude." In *Africana: The Encyclopedia of the African American Experience*, 2nd ed., vol. 4, edited by Kwame Anthony Appiah and Henry Louis Gates Jr., 193–199. Oxford: Oxford University Press: 2005.

———. "Troping Toussaint, Reading Revolution." *Research in African Literatures* 35, no. 2 (2004): 18–33.

———."Turning the Tide: The Problem of Popular Insurgency in Haitian Revolutionary Historiography." *Small Axe* 12, no. 3 (October 2008): 14–31.

———. *Universal Emancipation: The Haitian Revolution and the Radical Enlightnment*. Charlottesville and London: University of Virginia Press, 2008.

———. *Voicing Memory: History and Subjectivity in French Caribbean Literature*. Charlottesville and London: University of Virginia Press, 2003.

Nicholls, David. 1979. *From Dessalines to Duvalier: Race, Colour and National Independence in Haiti*. London: Macmillan, 1996.

Nicol, Bran. *Postmodernism and the Contemporary Novel: A Reader*. Edinburgh: Edinburgh University Press, 2002.

Nietzsche, Friedrich. *The Birth of Tragedy*. 1872. Translated by Shaun Whiteside. London: Penguin, 1993.

Norton, Graham Gendall. "France Finally Recognises a Hero after 200 Years." *Times* (London), April 5, 2003, 47.

Nwoga, D. I., ed. *West African Verse*. Harlow: Longman, 1967.

Nyong'o, Tavia. "Black Theatre's Closest Drama." *Theatre Journal* 57, no. 4 (2005): 590–92.

Nzengou-Tayo, Marie-José. "Haitian Gothic and History: Madison Smartt Bell's Trilogy on Toussaint Louverture and the Haitian Revolution." *Small Axe* 11, no. 2 (Summer 2007): 184–93.

Ormerod, Beverley. "Beyond *Négritude*: Some Aspects of the Work of Édouard Glissant." *Contemporary Literature* 15, no. 3 (1974): 360–69.

Ostrom, Hans. *A Langston Hughes Encyclopedia*. Wesport, Conn. and London: Greenwood Press, 2002.

Ott, Thomas O. *The Haitian Revolution, 1789–1804*. Knoxville: University of Tennessee Press, 1973.

Pachonski, Jan. *Poland's Caribbean Tragedy: A Study of Polish Legions in the Haitian War of Independence, 1802–03*. New York: Columbia University Press, 1986.

Pamphile, Léon D. *Haitians and African Americans: A Heritage of Tragedy and Hope*. Gainesville: University of Florida Press, 2002.

Paravisini-Gebert, Lizebeth. "The Haitian Revolution in Interstices and Shadows: A Re-Reading of Alejo Carpentier's *The Kingdom of This World*." *Research in African Literatures* 35, no. 2 (2004): 114–27.

Parkinson, Wenda. *"This Gilded African": Toussaint L'ouverture*. London and New York: Quartet, 1978.

Parry, Benita. "Is There a Third World Aesthetic?" Inaugural talk to the Warwick Research Collective (WReC): Materialist Studies in World Literature. 2007.

———. *Postcolonial Studies: A Materialist Critique.* London: Routledge, 2004.

———. "Resistance Theory / Theorizing Resistance or Two Cheers for Nativism." In *Postcolonial Studies: A Materialist Critique*, 37–54. London: Routledge, 2004.

Peach, Linden. *Toni Morrison.* London: Macmillan, 1995.

Phillips, Caryl. *The Atlantic Sound.* London: Vintage, 2001.

———. "C. L. R. James: The Most Noteworthy Mind of the Twentieth Century." *Journal of Blacks in Higher Education*, no. 33 (Autumn 2001): 118–20.

Phillips, Ulrich Bonnell. *Life and Labor in the Old South.* 1929. Columbia: University of South Carolina Press, 2007.

Pine, Courtney. *Transition in Tradition (En hommage à Sidney Bechet).* Destin-E Records, 2009. CD.

Plummer, Brenda Gayle. "The African-American Response to the Ocupation of Haiti, 1915–1934." *Phylon* 43, no. 2 (1982): 125–43.

Pontecorvo, Gillo, dir. *Burn!* aka *Queimada!* Italy/France: Alberto Grimaldi, Europee Associate SAS Produzioni Europee Associati, 1969.

Popel, Dora Reynolds. "Review: *The Black Consul*, Anatoli Vinogradov." *Journal of Negro History* 22, no. 3 (1937): 356–58.

Popkin, Jeremy, ed. *Facing Racial Revolution: Eyewitness Accounts of the Haitian Revolution.* Chicago: University of Chicago Press, 2008.

———. *You Are All Free: The Haitian Revolution and the Abolition of Slavery.* Cambridge: Cambridge University Press, 2010.

Prakash, Gyan. *After Colonialism: Imperial Histories and Postcolonial Displacements.* Princeton: Princeton University Press, 1995.

Prasad, Pratima. *Colonialism, Race, and the French Romantic Imagination.* New York: Routledge, 2009.

Price-Mars, Jean. *So Spoke the Uncle.* Washington, D.C.: Three Continents Press, 1983.

Public Enemy. "Fight the Power." Motown Records, 1989. Vinyl 7" single.

Rampersad, Arnold. *The Life of Langston Hughes.* Vol. 1. New York Oxford: Oxford University Press, 1986.

———. *The Life of Langston Hughes.* Vol. 2. New York and Oxford: Oxford University Press, 1988.

Rampersad, Arnold, and Deborah E. McDowell, eds. *Slavery and the Literary Imagination.* Selected Papers from the English Institute, 1987; New Series, no.13. Baltimore and London: Johns Hopkins University Press, 1989.

Reid, Donald M. "The Symbolism of Postage Stamps." *Journal of Contemporary History* 19, no. 2 (1984): 223–49.

Reinhardt, Catherine A. *Claims to Memory: Beyond Slavery and Emancipation in the French Caribbean.* New York: Berghahn, 2006.

Reiss, Timothy J. *Sisyphus and Eldorado: Magic and Realism in Caribbean Literature.* Trenton, N.J.: Africa World Press, 2003.

Renda, Mary A. *Taking Haiti: Military Occupation and the Culture of U.S. Imperialism, 1915–1940.* Chapel Hill: University of North Carolina Press, 2001.

Richardson, Michael, ed. *Refusal of the Shadow: Surrealism and the Caribbean.* Translated by Michael Richardson and Krzysztof Fijałkowski. London: Verso, 1996.

Roberts, Kenneth. *Lydia Bailey.* 1947. New York: Down East Books, 2001.

Robinson, Cedric. *Black Marxism: The Making of the Black Radical Tradition.* 1983. Chapel Hill: University of North Carolina Press, 2000.

Rowley, Hazel. *Richard Wright: The Life and Times.* New York: Holt, 2001.

Rushdy, Ashraf H. A. *Neo-Slave Narratives: Studies in the Social Logic of a Literary Form.* New York and Oxford: Oxford University Press, 1999.

Said, Edward. *Culture and Imperialism.* London: Vintage, 1994.

———. *On Late Style: Music and Literature Against the Grain.* New York: Pantheon, 2006.

———. *Orientalism.* 1979. London: Penguin, 2003.

———. "The Politics of Knowledge." *Raritan: A Quarterly Review* 11, no. 1 (1991): 17–31.

Saint-John, Spencer. *Hayti; or, the Black Republic.* 2nd ed. London: Smith, Elder, and Co., 1889.

Saint-Méry, Moreau de. *Dance.* 1796. Translated by Lily Hastings and Baird Hastings. Brooklyn: Dance Horizons, 1975.

———. *Description topographique, physique, civile, politique, et historique de la partie française de l'isle Saint-Domnigue.* 1797. 3 vols. Paris: Société de l'histoire des colonies françaises, 1958.

Saint-Pierre, Bernardin de. *Paul and Virginia.* 1787. Philadelphia: Hogan and Thompson, 1849.

Sale, Kirkpatrick. *The Conquest of Paradise: Christopher Columbus and the Columbian Legacy.* London: Hodder and Stoughton, 1991.

"Sancho, (Charles) Ignatius." *The Oxford Dictionary of National Biography.* www.oxforddnb.com/view/article/24609?docPos=1.

Santana. *Santana III.* Columbia Studios, 1971. Reissued by Sony, 2008. CD.

Sapolsky, Barry S., Fred Molitor, and Sarah Luque. "Sex and Violence in Slasher Films: Re-Examining the Assumptions." *Journalism and Mass Communication Quarterly* 80, no. 1 (Spring 2003): 28–38.

Sartre, Jean-Paul. *Black Orpheus.* Translated by S. W. Allen. Paris: Présence Africaine, 1976.

———. *Black Orpheus.* In *Race*, edited by Robert Bernasconi, 115–65. Malden, Mass., and Oxford, U.K.: Blackwell, 2001.

———. *Colonialism and Neo Colonialism.* 1964. Translated by Steve Brewer, Terry McWilliams, and Azzedine Haddour. London and New York: Routledge, 2001.

———. *"What Is Literature?" and Other Essays*. Cambridge: Harvard University Press, 1988.

Sauerberg, Lars Ole. *Fact into Fiction: Documentary Realism in the Contemporary Novel*. London: Macmillan, 1991.

Schmidt, Hans. *The United States Occupation of Haiti, 1915–1934*. 1971. Piscataway, N.J..: Rutgers University Press, 2006.

Schwarz, Bill. "Breaking Bread with History: Stuart Hall Interviewed by Bill Schwarz." *History Workshop Journal*, no. 46 (1998): 17–31.

Scott, David. (a) *Conscripts of Modernity: The Tragedy of Colonial Enlightenment*. Durham: Duke University Press, 2004.

———. *Refashioning Futures: Criticism after Postcoloniality*. Princeton, N.J.: Princeton University Press, 1999.

Scott, David. (b) "National Icons: The Semiotics of the French Stamp." *French Cultural Studies* 3, no. 9 (1992): 215–34.

———. "Semiotics and Ideology in Mixed Messages: The Postage Stamp." In *The Pictured Word: Word and Image Interactions II*, edited by Martin Heusser, Claus Clüver, Lauren Weingarden, and Leo Hoek, 301–14. Amsterdam: Rodpoi, 1998.

Scott, Jonathan. *Socialist Joy in the Writing of Langston Hughes*. Columbia: University of Missouri Press, 2006.

Seabrook, W. B. *The Magic Island*. 1929. London: Harrap, 1931.

Senanu, K. E., and T. Vincent, eds. *A Selection of African Poetry*. Harlow: Longman, 1988.

Senghor, Léopold Sédar. *Négritude et humanisme*. Paris: Éditions de Seuil, 1964.

Shakespeare, William. *King Lear*, ca. 1604–5. London: Arden, 1997.

Shange, Ntozake. *for colored girls who have considered suicide when the rainbow is enuf*. New York: Scribner Poetry, 1997.

Sheller, Mimi. *Democracy after Slavery: Black Publics and Peasant Radicalism in Haiti and Jamaica*. Gainesville: University of Florida Press, 2000.

Shinhat, Molly. "Black History and Desire: An Interview with Isaac Julien." *FUSE* 13, no. 5 (June/July 1990): 33–37.

Silenieks, Juris. "The Maroon Figure in Caribbean Francophone Prose." In *Voices from Under: Black Narrative in Latin America and the Caribbean*, edited by William Luis, 115–25. Westport, Conn.: Greenwood Press, 1984.

Sopova, Jasmina. "Between Utopia and Reality. An Interview with René Depestre." *UNESCO Courier* 50, no. 12 (1997): 47.

Sourieau, Marie-Agnès. "Dessalines in Historic Drama and Haitian Contemporary Reality." *Small Axe* 9, no. 2 (September 2005): 24–38.

Soyinka, Wole. *Myth, Literature and the African World*. Cambridge: Cambridge University Press, 1976.

———, ed. *Poems of Black Africa*. London: Secker and Warburg, 1975.

Spector, Jack J. *Surrealist Art and Writing 1919–1939*. Cambridge: Cambridge University Press, 1997.

Spengler, Oswald. *The Decline of the West*. 1926. New York: Oxford University Press, 1991.

Spivak, Gayatri Chakravorty, and Michael Ryan. "Anarchism Revisted: A New Philosophy." *Diacritics* 8, no. 2 (June 1978): 66–79.

Stannard, Richard E. *American Holocaust: Columbus and the Conquest of the New World*. New York: Oxford University Press, 1992.

Stephens, Jack. "Madison Smartt Bell." *Bomb*, no. 73 (Fall 2000). http://bombsite.com/issues/73/articles/2346.

Still, William Grant. *Troubled Island: An Opera in Three Acts*. Libretto by Langston Hughes. Sound recording. Performed by the New York City Center Opera Company. Southern Music & the Voice of America, 1949. British Library: T12097WR, 3 × 40 cm vinyl discs.

Stoler, Ann Laura. *Race and the Education of Desire: Foucault's History of Sexuality and the Colonial Order of Things*. Durham: Duke University Press, 1995.

Strachan, Ian Gregory. *Paradise and Plantation: Tourism and Culture in the Anglophone Caribbean*. Charlottesville: University of Virginia Press, 2002.

Su, John J. *Ethics and Nostalgia in the Contemporary Novel*. Cambridge: Cambridge University Press, 2005.

Suk, Jeannie C. Y. *Postcolonial Paradoxes in French Caribbean Writing: Césaire, Glissant, Condé*. Oxford Modern Languages and Literature Monographs. Oxford: Clarendon Press, 2001.

Susman, Warren I. *Culture as History*. New York: Pantheon, 1984.

Sweeney, Fionnghuala. "The Haitian Play: C. L. R. James' *Toussaint Louverture* (1936)." *International Journal of Francophone Studies* 14, nos. 1 & 2 (2011): 143–63.

Tebbel, John William. *Fact and Fiction: Problems of the Historical Novelist*. Lansing: Historical Society of Michigan, 1962.

"Theatre: New Plays in Manhattan: Mar. 14, 1938." *Time*, March 14, 1938. www.time.com/time/magazine/article/09171,759300,00.

Thieme, John. "Beyond Manicheism: Derek Walcott's Henri Christophe and Dream on Monkey Mountain." In *Comparing Postcolonial Literatures: Dislocations*, edited by Ashok Bery and Patricia Murray. New York: Macmillan, 2000.

———. *Derek Walcott*. Manchester: Manchester University Press, 1999.

Torres-Saillant, Silvio. *Caribbean Poetics: Toward an Aesthetic of West Indian Literature*. Cambridge: Cambridge University Press, 1997.

Tourneur, Jacques, dir. *I Walked with a Zombie*. New York: RKO Radio Pictures, 1943.

Tracy, Steven C., ed. *A Historical Guide to Langston Hughes*. New York: Oxford University Press, 2004.

Trouillot, Michel-Rolph. "Bodies and Souls: The Haitian Revolution and Madison Smartt Bell's *All Souls' Rising*." In *Novel History: Historians and*

Novelists Confront America's Past, and Each Other, edited by Mark C. Carnes, 184–96. New York: Simon and Schuster, 2001.

———. *Silencing the Past: Power and the Production of History*. Boston: Beacon Press, 1995.

Tyson, George F., Jr., ed. *Toussaint Louverture: Great Lives Observed*. Englewood Cliffs, N.J.: Prentice Hall, 1973.

Vastey, Baron de. *An Essay on the Causes of the Revolution and Civil Wars of Hayti, Being a Sequel to the Political Remarks upon Certain French Publications and Journals Concerning Hayti*. Exeter, 1812.

Verbinski, Gore, dir. *Pirates of the Caribbean: The Curse of the Black Pearl*. Santa Monica, Calif.: Jerry Bruckheimer Films, 2003.

———, dir. *Pirates of the Caribbean: Dead Man's Chest*. Santa Monica, Calif.: Jerry Bruckheimer Films, 2006.

———, dir. *Pirates of the Caribbean: At World's End*. Santa Monica, Calif.: Jerry Bruckheimer Films, 2007.

Vinogradov, Anatoli. *The Black Consul*. 1935. Translated by Emile Burns. New York: Viking Press, 1937.

Wakefield, Steve. *Carpentier's Baroque Fiction: Returning Medusa's Gaze*. Woodbridge: Tamesis, 2004.

Walcott, Derek. "Another Life." 1973. In *Collected Poems, 1948–1984*. London: Faber, 1992.

———. *Collected Poems, 1948–1984*. London: Faber and Faber, 1992.

———. *The Haitian Trilogy: Plays: "Henri Christophe," "Drums and Colours," and "The Haitian Earth."* New York: Farrar, Straus and Giroux, 2002.

———. "Omeros." In *Collected Poems*. New York: Farrar, 1986.

———. *What the Twilight Says*. London: Faber and Faber, 1998.

Walcott-Hackshaw, Elizabeth. "My Love Is Like a Rose: Terror, Territoire, and the Poetics of Marie Chauvet." *Small Axe* 9, no. 2 (2005): 40–51.

Walcott-Hackshaw, Elizabeth, and Martin Munro. "Introduction: Reinterpreting the Haitian Revolution and Its Cultural Aftershocks." *Small Axe* 9, no. 2 (2005): viii–ix.

———, eds. *Reinterpreting the Haitian Revolution and Its Cultural Aftershocks*. Mona, Jamaica: University of the West Indies Press, 2006.

Walker, Ethel Pitts. "Krigwa, a Theatre by, for, and About Black People." *Perspectives in Theatre History* 40, no. 3 (1988): 347–56.

Walker, Keith L. "Art for Life's Sake: Rituals and Rights of Self and Other in the Theatre of Aimé Césaire." In *Black Theatre: Ritual Performance in the African Diaspora*, edited by Paul Carter Harrison, Victor Leo Walker, and Gus Edwards, 181–208. Philadelphia: Temple University Press, 2002.

Waxman, Percy. *The Black Napoleon*. New York: Harcourt, 1931.

Webb, Barbara J. *Myth and History in Caribbean Fiction: Alejo Carpentier, Wilson Harris, and Edouard Glissant*. Amherst: University of Massachusetts Press, 1992.

West, Michael O., William G. Martin, and Fanon Che Wilkins, eds. *From Toussaint to Tupac: The Black International since the Age of Revolution.* Chapel Hill: University of North Carolina Press, 2009.

Weston, Helden D. "Representing the Right to Represent: The Portrait of Citizen Belley, ex-representative of the colonies by A.L. Girodet." *Res* 26 (Autumn 1994): 83–100.

Wheat, Ellen Harkins. *Jacob Lawrence, American Painter.* Seattle: University of Washington Press, 1986.

White, Hayden. *Metahistory: The Historical Imagination in Nineteenth-Century Europe.* Baltimore: Johns Hopkins University Press, 1975.

———. *Tropics of Discourse.* Baltimore: Johns Hopkins University Press, 1978.

Wilder, Gary. *The French Imperial Nation-State: Negritude and Colonial Humanism between the Two World Wars.* Chicago: University of Chicago Press, 2005.

———. "Untimely Vision: Aimé Césaire, Decolonization, Utopia." *Public Culture* 21, no. 1 (Winter 2009): 101–40.

Williams, Carolyn. "The Haitian Revolution and a North American Giot: *The Life of Toussaint L'Ouverture* by Jacob Lawrence." In *Echoes of the Haitian Revolution 1804–2004*, edited by Martin Munro and Elizabeth Walcott-Hackshaw, 61–85. Mona, Jamaica: University of the West Indies Press: 2008.

Williams, Eric. *Capitalism and Slavery.* 1944. Chapel Hill: University of North Carolina Press, 1994.

Williams, Raymond. *Marxism and Literature.* Oxford: Oxford University Press, 1978.

Williamson, Edwin, ed. *Cervantes and the Modernists: The Question of Influence.* London: Tamesis, 1994.

———. "Coming to Terms with Modernity: Magic Realism and the Historical Process in the Novels of Alejo Carpentier." In *Modern Latin American Fiction*, edited by John King, 78–100. London: Faber and Faber, 1987.

———. *The Penguin History of Latin America.* London: Penguin, 1993.

———. "The Quixotic Roots of Magic Realism: History and Fiction in Alejo Carpentier and García Márquez." Edited by Edwin Williamson, 103–20. *Cervantes and the Modernists: The Question of Influence.* London: Tamesis, 1994.

Wolin, Richard. *Walter Benjamin: An Aesthetic of Redemption.* Berkeley and Los Angeles: University of California Press, 1994.

Wood, Marcus. *Blind Memory: Visual Representations of Slavery in England and America.* Manchester: Manchester University Press, 2000.

———. *The Horrible Gift of Freedom: Atlantic Slavery and the Representation of Emancipation.* Athens and London: University of Georgia Press, 2010.

———, ed. *The Poetry of Slavery : An Anglo-American Anthology, 1764–1865.* Oxford: Oxford University Press, 2003.

———. *Slavery, Empathy, and Pornography.* Oxford: Oxford University Press, 2002.

Wordsworth, William. "To Toussaint L'ouverture." 1802. In *The Poetry of Slavery: An Anglo-American Anthology, 1764–1865*, edited by Marcus Wood. Oxford: Oxford University Press, 2003.

Wright, Richard. *Native Son*. London: Vintage, 1940.

Young, Richard A. *Carpentier, "El reino de este mundo."* London: Tamesis, 1983.

Zamora, Lois Parkinson, and Wendy B. Faris, eds. *Magical Realism: Theory, History, Community*. Durham: Duke University Press, 1995.

Zinsser, William Knowlton, ed. *Inventing the Truth: The Art and Craft of Memoir*. Boston: Houghton Mifflin, 1987.

Index

Recent Books in the New World Studies Series

Nick Nesbitt, *Universal Emancipation: The Haitian Revolution and the Radical Enlightenment*

Doris L. Garraway, editor, *Tree of Liberty: Cultural Legacies of the Haitian Revolution in the Atlantic World*

Dawn Fulton, *Signs of Dissent: Maryse Condé and Postcolonial Criticism*

Michael G. Malouf, *Transatlantic Solidarities: Irish Nationalism and Caribbean Poetics*

Maria Cristina Fumagalli, *Caribbean Perspectives on Modernity: Returning the Gaze*

Vivian Nun Halloran, *Exhibiting Slavery: The Caribbean Postmodern Novel as Museum*

Paul B. Miller, *Elusive Origins: The Enlightenment in the Modern Caribbean Historical Imagination*

Eduardo González, *Cuba and the Fall: Christian Text and Queer Narrative in the Fiction of José Lezama Lima and Reinaldo Arenas*

Jeff Karem, *The Purloined Islands: Caribbean-U.S. Crosscurrents in Literature and Culture, 1880–1959*

Faith Smith, editor, *Sex and the Citizen: Interrogating the Caribbean*

Mark D. Anderson, *Disaster Writing: The Cultural Politics of Catastrophe in Latin America*

Raphael Dalleo, *Caribbean Literature and the Public Sphere: From the Plantation to the Postcolonial*

Maite Conde, *Consuming Visions: Cinema, Writing, and Modernity in Rio de Janeiro*

Monika Kaup, *Neobaroque in the Americas: Alternative Modernities in Literature, Visual Art, and Film*

Marisel C. Moreno, *Family Matters: Puerto Rican Women Authors on the Island and the Mainland*

Supriya M. Nair, *Pathologies of Paradise: Caribbean Detours*

Colleen C. O'Brien, *Race, Romance, and Rebellion: Literatures of the Americas in the Nineteenth Century*

Kelly Baker Josephs, *Disturbers of the Peace: Representations of Madness in Anglophone Caribbean Literature*

Christina Kullberg, *The Poetics of Ethnography in Martinican Narratives: Exploring the Self and the Environment*

Maria Cristina Fumagalli, Bénédicte Ledent, and Roberto del Valle Alcalá, editors, *The Cross-Dressed Caribbean: Writing, Politics, Sexualities*

Philip Kaisary, *The Haitian Revolution in the Literary Imagination: Radical Horizons, Conservative Constraints*